Man the Footballer
HOMO PASSIENS

This book
is dedicated to Hugh Carter
whose vision and love of football were
critical to its evolution.

Man the **Footballer**
HOMO PASSIENS

The Missing Link in Human Evolution (Arguably)

Mike McInnes
With a Foreword by Irvine Welsh

Meyer & Meyer Sport

Originally published as: *Homo Passiens: Man the Footballer* by Swan & Horn, 2017

British Library Cataloguing in Publication Data
A catalogue record for this book is available from the British Library

Man the Footballer – Homo Passiens
Maidenhead: Meyer & Meyer Sport (UK) Ltd., 2018
ISBN 978-1-78255-156-0 (UK)
978-1-78255-144-7 (US)

Aachen, Auckland, Beirut, Dubai, Hägendorf, Hong Kong, Indianapolis, Cairo, Cape Town, Manila, Maidenhead, New Delhi, Singapore, Sydney, Teheran, Vienna

 Member of the World Sports Publishers' Association (WSPA), www.w-s-p-a.org

Printed by Print Consult, GmbH, Munich, Germany

MIX
Paper from responsible sources
FSC
www.fsc.org FSC® C084279

ISBN 978-1-78255-156-0 (UK)
978-1-78255-144-7 (US)
E-mail: info@m-m-sports.com
www.m-m-sports.com

Praise for

MAN THE FOOTBALLER: HOMO PASSIENS!

"This is hilarious!"—Editor of Howler Magazine, New York Review of Football Literature

"This is fantastic! I think I may have trouble *not* taking this seriously!"—Professor David Kilpatrick, historian at New York Cosmos and Professor of Language and Literature at Mercy College New York

"This appears to be totally brilliant!"—Robert Sapolsky, world-leading evolutionary biologist and author of "Junk Food Monkeys"

"Wow, what an extraordinary production! And I love the pictures."—Professor David Spieglehalter, Cambridge Centre for Mathematical Sciences

"Very clever and very funny! But I was raised to believe that humanity evolved through the development of the use of hands, which not only enabled the creation of tools, but also the ability to handle and pass an ovoid object (the egg of course being the basic building block of life). Thus, *Homo leaguiens*, I would suggest, is clearly the most advanced species of the genus *Homo*!"—Professor Tony Collins, International Centre for Sports History & Culture, De Montfort University

"Looks fascinating!"—Professor John Hughson, Professor of Sport and Cultural Studies and Director of the International Football Institute

"Very cute! But you forget to mention the Many Worlds Interpretation according to which Hibs' success in next year's Champions League is assured, at least in some alternative dimension (possibly Leicester). Unfortunately, when confronted with observers, a collapse into a more normal state is nearly certain."—Professor Graeme Ackland, School of Physics & Astronomy, University of Edinburgh and Institute for Condensed Matter and Complex Systems

Contents

Acknowledgements

I cannot thank Matt Kenyon enough for his fabulous and iconic illustrations, without which this book would simply not have been possible.

Many thanks also to Ian Dewsbery for his wonderful work in producing the Homo Passiens Taverns Map.

Words cannot express my gratitude to my publisher, Maria Hampshire-Carter, for her belief in this mad book, for her insight, for her support, and for her patient editing of such a crazy mixture of lunacy, science, nonsense and general football infanity.

Foreword (or Forward)

BY IRVINE WELSH

Now I get it! Homo sapiens is a recently arrived imposter in the evolution of the genus Homo – a mountebank, a charlatan, a confidence trickster, a fraud, a fraudster, a rogue, a villain, a scoundrel, a quack! All that academic stuff about consciousness, language, civilisation, farming, technology, science, philosophy, music, literature, poetry, art – and so on – emanating exclusively from (and created by) Homo sapiens is evolutionary hogwash!

It all came, not from *Homo sapiens* – as this recently arrived pathological lying subspecies claims endlessly and repeatedly in schools, in text books, in literature, in countless evolutionary and cultural journals, and in all institutions of higher learning – but from the original and founder species *Homo passiens* – Man the Footballer!

Standing on two legs – bipedalism – as a locomotive strategy is frankly nuts! No sentient species would voluntarily choose to adopt such a ludicrous hodgepodge of anatomical features, with a ground speed of less than half that of a lazy geriatric predator, with no effective body armour or protection, with no offensive claws worthy of the name, with lettuce-crunching teeth that would be rejected by even the most docile herbivore, and with such a narrow pelvis and hinged legs below – which ensures that bipedal locomotion is a form of translocation so shaky, so wobbly and unstable, that an anatomical engineer would consider that this form of locomotion had been perversely designed to stagger, to stumble, to collapse, to topple over or fall down in any chase to catch a prey, or escape from a predator, and in any evolutionary design school it would be rejected as the work of an indolent student of evolution who had spent their whole study time in the cafes, betting shops, bars and dancing clubs of their university town.

Bipedalism is so stupid and unstable that humans have actually invented games to take advantage of it – and to effect falls – such as in rugby league, rugby union, and National League football. If we had four, or even *three* legs, these games could not exist. Infants fall down. Toddlers fall down. Children fall down. Juveniles fall down. Adults fall down. And elderly adults frequently die from falls. No sensible architect would design a building with only two supports!

In war zones, mines are laid not to kill, but rather to disable one limb and renderthe victim immobile, and therefore impose a burden on the opposing forces. If we had chosen to sacrifice only *one* of our four legs and become tripedal, we would have significantly improved our survival chances. The people and ancients on the Isle of Man, Sicily and Japan have a long and noble association with tripedalism; if you go there you will learn exactly how much superior is that form of locomotion compared with our witless evolutionary selection of bipedalism. Since there is a long and successful industry of manufacturing sticks into extra third legs (known as walking sticks – actually stability sticks) for bipedal humans to improve locomotive efficiency, why was it that we did not select a tripedal or *quadrupedal* solution to improve survival and locomotive efficiency and safety?

Four legs are better than three. Three legs are better than two. So why have we – the *Homo* species – most bizarrely selected for locomotion on two legs only? The reason? Football!

No other explanation, no other reason for our absurd, derisory, farcical anatomical mix of primate foetal features interwoven with – bundled with – such a patchwork of semi-adult characteristics that result in a neotenous half-foetal/half-adult complex – a clownman – *Homo passiens* – but a clown so *beautifully* engineered and so *exquisitely* formed to express Bipedal Football: flat brow, domed head, opposable goalkeeping thumbs, knock-knees, a flat and levered foot with outstep and instep, and finally – and fantastically – non-opposable big toes and a big greedy brain of such absurd and poetic linguistic and sensorimotor beauty, that billions of fans will follow their dream-team, enter the lucid REM dream-game, sing their dream-songs, call their dream-chants, and neuropower their gamma-wave electrophysiology, fire their mirror forward and reverse neuro-modulations, seeking both dopamine-reward facilitation and opiate emotional homeostasis via transcendence and lucid suspension of entropy, at every available opportunity.

Now I get it about the evolutionary nonsense I was taught in biology classes, a romantic fiction about the clever intelligent species *Homo sapiens* that appeared suddenly from nowhere around 200,000 years ago, and supposedly gave rise to our big brain, and to consciousness, language, farming, civilisation, technology, science, literature, art and poetry. RUBBISH!

Homo passiens – we, the neotenous, upright, bipedal species, with narrow pelvis, opposable thumbs, knock-knees, flat cushioned and levered foot, non-opposable big toes, are the nominate superspecies that gave birth to the big intelligent and embodied bipedal brain – an evolutionary anatomical joke, but an evolutionarily poetic joke, an anatomical *franken*-freak, an anatomical *franken*-clown, and a weird evolutionary farce that made us what we are and what we do, every Saturday of every week, when the dream-game is played (and which we miss every alternate Saturday).

We opposable-thumbed, we two-legged, we two-footed, we non-opposably big-toed, and we neotenously brained evolutionary absurdity – *we* are the true source of human consciousness, intelligence and cognition.

We may be on the lower rungs of evolutionary science, but we are rapidly ascending, and with our eyes firmly on the prize of the Premier Division, and recognition as the true founder and future species of the genus *Homo*. We are happy to share our knowledge of neoteny, of the lucid REM-wake dream-game, of dream-song and dream-chant physiology, of dopamine/hopamine, opiate/ hopiate, vasopressin and hypno-oxytocin hormone metabolism, and of the consciousness of the football, expressed as pre(pro) cociousness.

If we fail to do this, *Homo sapiens* will rapidly degenerate and disappear from the evolutionary record, just as suddenly as that subordinate species appeared, and as surely as the thousands of species and subspecies that have come and gone in the many extinction events of the past.

Dear Football Fans and Football Geeks

WELCOME TO THIS SERIOUS NONSENSE!

Man the Footballer: Homo Passiens is a fun book. It is not to be taken seriously. But it does use some principles drawn from the evolutionary and cultural history of mankind such that, if it were true, it would fit in with a crazy hypothesis that humans evolved bipedalism (walking on two legs) to play football.

Two very important principles in this respect are "neoteny" and "ludeny". The theory of neoteny was around for more than a century before being developed by the real-life American biologist and author Stephen Jay Gould. The theory is that we humans keep our infant genes and anatomy throughout our lives – we do not metamorphose into an adult form like other primates, such as chimpanzees. This shows strongly in our facial features and our flat baby faces. If our jaws extended forwards and our brows angled backwards – like they "should do" – we would not be able to head a football! Neoteny also explains other oddities, such as our lifelong curiosity, inventiveness and nosiness. Simply put, we never fully grow up.

The next important real-life theory is ludeny. This was thought up by the Dutch cultural historian Johan Huizinga. You can read all about it in his original book *Homo Ludens*. It is based on the idea that all human culture – technology, science, language, literature, art, music and poetry – stems from adult "game-playing". The

Latin word *ludens* is derived from *ludus* which refers to sport, play, school, and practice.

It isn't difficult to connect the two theories. Humans (as far as we know) are the only species in which the adults still play games – which neatly brings us back to the subject of bipedal football, known to be the largest and most universal form of game-playing we know of. If football were a country, it would be the largest in the world with around 2.5 *billion* citizens (fans and players), and its annual turnover would exceed that of the world's largest economy – the United States of America. Once you accept that *Homo passiens* is the original species of the genus *Homo*, you will never be the same again. You will know that *Homo sapiens* is a derivative, an offshoot, and as your primal unconscious mind already knows, bipedal football expresses the deepest essence of what it is to be human. You will know that your children and grandchildren will grow up in a football environment, and will become *Homo passiens*, or the sibling species *Femo passions*, to become football players and/or football fans. You will learn that *Homo passiens* and *Femo passiens* predate *Homo sapiens* by about two and a half million years, and you will discover all about football anatomy, physiology and psychology, and the genes, glands and hormones that characterise this wonderful bipedal football species.

You will meet Professor Gordon P. McNeil in the pages of this book, Professor of Archaeology and Paleoanthropology at St Andrews University, Fife, Scotland, and you will admire how brilliantly and persistently he demolishes the concept proposed by Professor Yuvel Noah Harari in his twenty-first-century book *Sapiens: A Brief History of Humankind*, in which Harari makes the outrageous claim that humans express no genes for football! This is a massive own goal and the greatest *faux pass* in the history of science. This is what Harari said:

> *"Evolution did not endow humans with the ability to play football. True, it produced legs for kicking, elbows for fouling and mouths for cursing, but all that this enables us to do is perhaps practise penalty kicks by ourselves. To get into a game with strangers we find in the schoolyard on any given afternoon, we not only have to work in concert with ten teammates we may never have met before, we also need to know that the other players on the opposing team are playing by the same rules. Other animals that engage strangers in ritualised aggression do so largely by instinct – puppies throughout the world have the rules for rough-and-tumble play hard-wired into their genes. But human teenagers have no genes for football. They can nevertheless play the game with complete strangers because they have all learned an identical set of ideas about football. These ideas are entirely imaginary, but if everyone shares them, we can all play the game."*

Harari may have taken *sapiens* science to a new level of understanding, but he failed to examine the role of *passiens* as our founding species, and he missed the critical role of "neoteny" in our evolution, without which we would not have developed our juvenile, curious, innovative, endlessly creative minds that characterises our strange bipedal, foetalistic, semi-adult species. Professor McNeil couldn't ignore the comment that we have "no genes for football" and curtly elbowed the claim in the following letter.

Dear Professor Harari

Never in the history of evolutionary science, either before or after Charles Darwin, has an eminent and respected academic of evolutionary history been so erroneous in his or her analysis of the underpinning, founding seed and driving forces of the evolution of the genus Homo. With respect, Professor Harari, a penalty kick requires a goalkeeper and a goal; the species Homo exists as a socially and environmentally constrained species, or it is simply not human. A penalty kick – far from being a solitary and introverted illustration of human conduct – is actually one of the highest expressions of bipedal neotenous culture and behaviour of the genus Homo.

If an elbow is not an anatomical and physiological instrument of high-value fouling, then what may it be? A Stephen Jay Gould spandrel or exaptation? An evolutionary by-product? Or an adaptation for which there is no clear fitness or survival advantage? No! The elbow of the Homo species is not some kind orphan anatomical offshoot without significant function, rather it is an exquisitely engineered evolutionary skeletal instrument for violently inhibiting opponents during open bipedal neotenous football play.

A recent and seminal paper, published in the Journal of Passienic Sciences found, through a series of elegant studies conducted at the Sep Blatter Faculty of Forensic and Passienic Anatomy at the University at Visp, in the canton of Valais, that a set of related elbow and hip genes and gene sequences correlate with both elbow and hip hit-plasias (ELB-HIT alpha-1 and HIP-HIT beta-2), and these are expressed in the teenagers of Homo sapiens, Homo passiens and Femo passiens, most potently of all in Homo passiens professional football players, with the highest expression occurring in defenders who have secured the most yellow and red cards during highly-charged contests (particularly during Derby matches between local rivals).

So indeed, Professor Harari, since you raise the issue, evolution did produce elbows for sophisticated gain of function fouling, and now we have plenty of beautiful genetic information that confirms that.

With the greatest respect, and acknowledging your excellent work in a number of fields, it must be stated that your attempt to intervene in the field of bipedal neotenous football is indicative of a degenerate and profoundly unfruitful adherence to a "sapiens" mindset that is long out of date, and which denies bipedal neotenous football as the generative seed and driving force of human evolution.

With a view to finally establishing whether indeed Homo passiens is the original founding species of the genus Homo from 2.5 million years ago, and Homo sapiens is a recent and derivative species from 200,000 years ago, I challenge you to a debate in the town of Stenhousemuir in the Forth Valley, Stirlingshire, Scotland. A suitable time would be during the Forth Valley Festival of Passienic Culture and Arts, held annually in that town, which attracts many thousands of football fans, academics and student visitors from around the world. As a World

Archaeology Heritage Status Area, Stenhousemuir is the spiritual home of prehistoric football archaeology and artefacts, and is therefore a highly appropriate venue to hold an international forum and invite public discussion on whether bipedal neotenous football is the true seed and driving force of human evolution, so that this issue may be finally settled—for all time.

Yours sincerely
Professor Gordon P. McNeil
Departments of Anthropology and Palaeontology
St Andrews University
Scotland

The Passiens Taverns

AND WHERE TO FIND THEM

The "Passiens" taverns are the hallowed sites of colourful conversations between the Author and Professor P. McNeil in the current day, as well as the arguable more erudite discussions between scientists, philosophers, absurdists and surrealists from all walks of life over the last couple of hundred years. All the taverns have names that both recognise and pay tribute to their role in "passienic" matters over the centuries, as well as pub-names by which they are better known within the football-fan fraternity (as listed below). The link between football and the rich passienic discourse within these inns and taverns is not coincidental.

Most of the taverns are dotted around the Scottish city of Edinburgh, with others in Glasgow, Stenhousemuir and County Durham. On the following page is a map that will help you find them on your sociocultural tour of mankind's footballing past, present and future. And if you visit on any Saturday during the dream-game season, you may just find yourself drawn into conversation with our protagonists.

Albert Camus Bar, also known as the Standing Order
62–66 George Street, Edinburgh EH2 2LR

Arthur's O'on Bar, also known as the Ochilview Bar
76 Tryst Rd, Stenhousemuir, Larbert FK5 4QJ

Dreamsong Bar, also known as Bennets Bar
8 Leven St, Edinburgh EH3 9LG

The Femo Passiens Tavern, also known as The Sheepheid Inn
43-45 The Causeway, Duddingston Village, Edinburgh EH15 3QA

Fitba' Petrosphere Bar, also known as All Bar One
50 Lothian Road, Edinburgh EH3 9BY

Football Absurdity Bar, also known as the Café Royal
19 West Register Street, Edinburgh EH2 2AA

Football Infanity Bar, also known as Milnes
Rose St/35 Hanover St, Edinburgh EH2 2PJ

Homo Ludens Bar, also known as the Alexander Graham Bell
128 George St, Edinburgh EH2 4JZ

Jock Jones Legs, also known as the Eden Arms
8 Staindrop Rd, West Auckland DL14 9JX

Johan Cruyff Tavern, also known as Deacon Brodie's Tavern
435 Lawnmarket, Edinburgh EH1 2NT

Lev Yashin Arms, also known as Mathers
1 Queensferry St, Edinburgh EH2 4PA

Lionel Messi Tavern, also known as the Abbotsford Bar
3–5 Rose Street, Edinburgh EH2 2PR

Opposable Thumb Arms, also known as Clarks
142 Dundas Street, Edinburgh EH3 5DQ

Football Lucidity Bar, also known as the Horseshoe Bar
17–19 Drury Street, Glasgow G2 5AE

Robo Passiens Bar, also known as the Central Bar
7–9 Leith Walk, Edinburgh EH6 8LN

McCrae's Battalion Bar, also known as the Athletic Arms
(Diggers)
1–3 Angle Park Terrace, Edinburgh EH11 2JX

The Opposable Thumb Bar (0.2 miles)

Stockbridge

The New
Town

The Arthur O'on Bar, Stenhousemuir (30 miles)
The Football Lucidity Bar, Glasgow (50 miles)

Heriot Row
Queen Street Gardens

QUEEN STREET

GEORGE ST

GEORGE ST

The Lev Yashin Arms

Rose St
PRINCES STREET

East Princes Str

West Princes Street Gardens

West
End

JOHNSTON TERRACE

GRASSMARKET

The Archaeology of
Football Petrospheres

MORRISON STREET

by Gordon P. McNeil

The Fitba' Petrosphere Bar

BREAD ST

WEST PORT

The C
Tow

Haymarket

EAST FOUNTAINBRIDGE

LAURISTON PLACE

Fountainbridge

Tollcross

The

McCrae's Battalion Bar
(0.3 miles)

Bruntsfield Links

The Homo Ludens

Union Canal

The Dreamsong Bar

Map designed and produced by Lovell Johns Ltd. Oxford. UK
www.lovelljohns.com

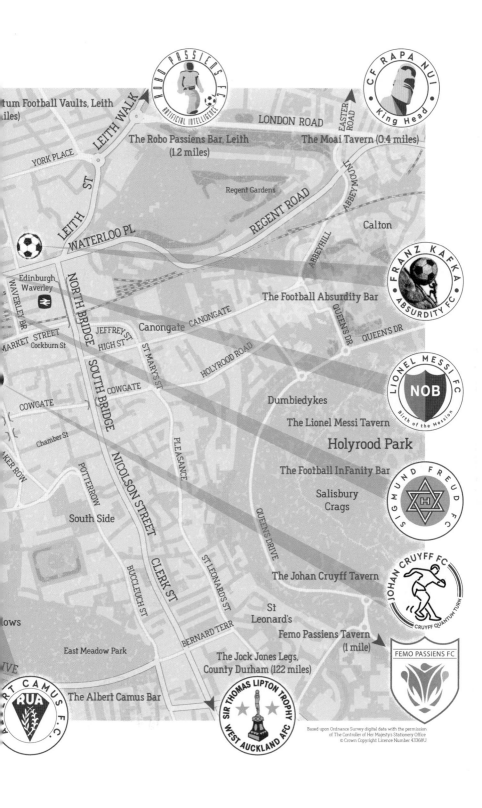

ROBO PASSIENS F.C. · ARTIFICIAL INTELLIGENCE ·

CF RAPA NUI · King Head

tum Football Vaults, Leith
iles)

The Robo Passiens Bar, Leith
(1.2 miles)

LONDON ROAD

EASTER ROAD

The Moai Tavern (0.4 miles)

LEITH WALK

YORK PLACE

Regent Gardens

ABBEY MOUNT

REGENT ROAD

Calton

LEITH ST

WATERLOO PL

ABBEYHILL

Edinburgh Waverley

NORTH BRIDGE

WAVERLEY BR

The Football Absurdity Bar

FRANZ KAFKA · ABSURDITY FC ·

QUEEN'S DR

QUEEN'S DR

MARKET STREET
Cockburn St

JEFFREY ST
HIGH ST

Canongate   CANONGATE

ST MARY'S ST

HOLYROOD ROAD

SOUTH BRIDGE

COWGATE

COWGATE

Dumbiedykes

LIONEL MESSI FC
NOB
Birth of the Messi

The Lionel Messi Tavern

Chamber St

KER ROW

PLEASANCE

Holyrood Park

The Football InFanity Bar

SIGMUND FREUD FC

Salisbury Crags

POTTERROW

NICOLSON STREET

South Side

QUEENS DRIVE

JOHAN CRUYFF FC

The Johan Cruyff Tavern

CRUYFF QUANTUM TURN

BUCCLEUCH ST

CLERK ST

ST LEONARD'S ST

St Leonard's

FEMO PASSIENS FC

Femo Passiens Tavern
(1 mile)

BERNARD TERR

lows

East Meadow Park

The Jock Jones Legs,
County Durham (122 miles)

ALBERT CAMUS F.C.
RUA

The Albert Camus Bar

SIR THOMAS LIPTON TROPHY
WEST AUCKLAND AFC

Based upon Ordnance Survey digital data with the permission
of The Controller of Her Majesty's Stationery Office
© Crown Copyright Licence Number 43368U

ANTHROPOLOGY AND THE SOCIAL KICKSHIP TIES OF FOOTBALL

Puskas F, Yashin L, Gascoigne P, Best G, Smith G, Messi L, Ronaldo C.

Department of Social and Cultural Anthropology, Passienic University of the Isles, Isle of Eriskay, Scotland

Published in the *Journal of Passienic Anthropology* on 1st April 2017

On any day, but particularly on any Saturday, of any week, of any month, of any year, stretching both far into our past and also infinitely into our future, an ancient and deeply beloved ritual takes place, in every hamlet, every village, every town, every city and every metropolis around the world; a ritual that describes and defines what it is to be a *human being* – with flat face and brow, domed head, two arms with opposable thumbs, narrow pelvis, knock-knees, and the ability to stand upright on two flat and levered feet, with non-opposable big toe, moving by forward kicking each leg in sequence, whilst standing or pivoting on the other foot, and from time to time utilising this curious locomotive facility to kick a moving object, known as a ball, usually in the direction of a region of space defined by a rectangular skeletal or wooden construct, comprising two upright posts some eight yards apart, supporting a horizontal bar eight feet from the ground, and known as a goal, and whenever the ball passes between the posts and beneath the bar, a goal is scored.

This lovely ritual usually takes place on a flat field of ground, often (although not always)

with grass underfoot, on a rectangular pitch, one hundred yards in length and fifty in breadth, marked into precise geometric patterns, and divided into two halves, which define the rules of the cultural practice.

The participants divide into two teams, based on social "kickship" ties (as opposed to kinship ties), usually comprising eleven individuals, known as players (collectively,as teams), on each side. One player from each team, known as the goalkeeper, is selected to protect the aforementioned goal. The goalkeeper is allowed to use his hands and opposable thumbs to catch or deflect the ball, to avoid a goal being scored between the posts and beneath the bar. Outfield players may kick or head the ball to propel it towards – or into – the goal. Only if the ball crosses the side-lines may outfield players throw or shy the ball into play, using their opposable thumbs; otherwise, if they handle the ball at any time, an offence or foul is committed.

The outfield players are organised into defence, midfield and forward positions, although these are flexible, and they can adopt any position to reflect the flow of play. An official known as a referee, with allegiance to neither team, regulates the play of both, according to an agreed set of rules that may also vary over time.

This ancient and beloved ritual is the *most universal expression* of two-footed, bipedal game-playing in human culture. It confirms our neotenous and curious evolutionary history, which means that we never fully become adults as a species, and we play games from birth to death – a practice not found in any other species we know of.

Both sexes play and love the Game – male and female. The sibling species are *Femo passiens* and *Homo passiens*, and the billions who follow the Game around the world, are known as football supporters or football fans. Infants, children, juveniles – and those we call adults – attend the Game, or follow it electronically on radio, television and the internet, in newspapers, magazines and other literature, and expend large sums of their income on doing so. Apart from the high cost of attendance, they choose to purchase team flags, banners, pendants and items of clothing that carry team colours and team badges. If Football was a country, it would have the largest population in the world, and its economy would exceed that of the world's current largest – the United States of America.

Science has discovered that every football fan present at, or viewing or listening to a game, enters a unique blend of physiology and psychology, known as a super-lucid wake-REM dream-state. It is characterised by the manifestation of specialised gamma-waves, along with expression of hopamine goal award-seeking, combined with hopiate-generated emotional homeostasis.

No other game-playing or artistic practice, no musical event, painting, sculpture, literature or poem, reaches or compares to the extraordinary electro-*wave* field levels as the highly charged game of football when attended by thousands of fans, where a super-lucid, pass, move, block, tackle, save or goal may reach such beauty of articulation that a fan gamma-wave electromagnetic storm crescendo is released across the stadium, that is sufficient to light a small town, and that may be viewed from, and measured by, satellites in distant space.

CHAPTER 1

Introducing Man the Footballer:
Homo passiens

A spectre is haunting the university corridors, the libraries, the classrooms and lecture theatres, the journals, the laboratories, the field stations, the professors, the academics, and students of evolutionary biology. A spectre that challenges and revises, and yet simultaneously upholds and maintains the fundamental principles of evolutionary science, originally outlined by Charles Darwin in his famous book *On the Origin of Species* published in November 1859.

Evolutionary science is having a nervous breakdown. A new evolutionary discipline has emerged in recent years, one that threatens to challenge and defeat some of the most basic notions of what it is to be *Homo* – or human – and of why the human brain is shrinking for the first time in our evolutionary history. This discipline is known as bipedal neoteny, as discovered and articulated by Professor Gordon P. McNeil at the University of St Andrews in Scotland; it states that the species known as

Homo actually consists of two species, or subspecies – not one as previously taught in all disciplines that inform evolutionary science – and that *Homo sapiens* is the subordinate and not the nominate, or founder, species. The nominate species is *Homo passiens* (perhaps better termed, Man the Footballer), which predates *sapiens* by millions of years, and falls under the category "superspecies". Our ancestor primates descended from the trees around 5 million years ago, became fully functioning bipeds from around 2.5 million years ago, and thereafter their brains grew steadily until some 200,000 to 100,000 years ago. However, *sapiens* may be dated to only around 200,000 years ago. The growth of the large human brain predates *sapiens* by more than two million years, and is directly correlated to the earlier appearance of *Homo passiens* in the record.

In early 1992, Professor Gordon P. McNeil and his team from St Andrews, working in East Africa, announced the discovery of an almost complete skeleton of a young man, dating back to 0.9 million years ago. In his statement to the press, Professor McNeil said that this young man had the physique of an athlete, that he was certainly right-sided, and that his athletic stature and the injuries he had received during life reminded him of a young professional footballer in his prime. "*Homo passiens*," he smiled. "Man the Footballer". He named him Gordon, not after himself but after his favourite footballer, Gordon Smith of Hibernian and Scotland, the famous right-winger of the great 1950s team.

The joke was quickly passed around the world's media: that humans had evolved bipedalism to play football. But it was soon forgotten. Professor McNeil did not immediately follow up his suggestion that the bipedalism expressed in football had played a significant role in evolution, or indeed that football was the initiating and driving force of language, civilisation, culture and everything that we associate with being human. In fact, it was another decade before news of this astonishing discovery and its implications for the science of evolution began to gain traction in the various fields of evolutionary science, and to attract a new generation of scholars to the hypothesis that *Homo sapiens* was merely a subspecies of the genus *Homo*, and that *H. passiens* was actually the original founder and nominate species.

Artist's impression of athletic, right-sided "Man The Footballer" based on skeletal remains from 0.9 million years ago, unearthed in East Africa.

I was introduced to the Professor by friends in the winter of 2010. They were involved with a group of radical journalists, musicians, writers, scientists, poets and ageing fanatics of Hibernian Football Club who regularly met in the Albert Camus Tavern in George

Street, Edinburgh, to talk about football brains, football genes, football hormones, football anatomy, football metabolism, football glands, football history, football philosophy, football economics, football politics … and everything else football, including Football Man – *H. passiens*. The Professor was legendary among this loquacious and bibulous crew, who told me that he was both an anthropologist and palaeontologist, who had studied the evolution and history of football at St Andrews University. Of course it was well known that the game of football began in China, although the modern version was forged in England.

Gordon P. McNeil, however, had proved beyond doubt, during his lifetime of meticulous evolutionary research, that football was far more ancient than that – indeed it had developed much earlier in our prehistoric and evolutionary past. The fact that he shared his name with the greatest right-winger in the world, Gordon Smith of the wonderful Hibernian team of the 1950s may have been coincidental, but he was happy to let many people, when the occasion allowed it, to assume that he was the other footballer. (Readers may be interested to know that the Author remembers the Hibs team as a schoolboy, and was present when they thrashed Manchester United 5–0 at Easter Road before 40,000 fans. Yes, these were the Busby Babes. Smith was unstoppable that floodlit evening and scored a brilliant goal.)

I explained to the Professor at our first meeting that I was interested in the growth and evolution of the human brain (and its recent contraction – the shrinking human brain) and that his work was not unconnected to mine, because the initial growth was from 2.5 million years ago, when humans were well established as upright and bipedal – the key to expansion of the human brain. I asked him if I could interview him about his work.

Gordon: Of course, Mike. Let's see where it may lead. The key moments or steps – or better still, kicks – are upright bipedalism and the narrow pelvis that forced our ancestors to exit the birth canal after nine months of pregnancy. This in turn resulted in the growth of the brain and, more importantly, its development for three decades after birth – a potent forcing ground for the growth of cognition, language and culture during an extended childhood. It's not found in other primates. Johan Huizinga quite brilliantly noticed this – the role of play in all human culture – not only as a function, but rather as the key generating influence. Only the genus *Homo* preserves play into adulthood, and this brings us to neoteny – the preservation of embryonic forms into the fully formed adult, which goes hand in hand with early birth, big brains, extended childhood and juvenilia, long legs, domed head, flat face. They're all aspects of development that are lost in primate adults, but retained in humans. We are essentially bipedal primate infants grown large and breeding as adults.

Mike: I know about this, Gordon. The Mexican axolotl, my favourite species, comes to mind, a beautiful example of neoteny. It is born as a fish and transmutes into a salamander. If there is no iodine in the lake, the juveniles fail to form thyroid-stimulating hormones and cannot therefore metamorphose into the adult salamander form. But they solve this brilliantly by activating sexual maturity and developing into large breeding adult versions of the embryonic form. Humans express this quite beautifully. If you look at any primate infant you can see the face of your local bank manager! Exactly like the adult *Homo sapiens*. Later the chin develops forward and the brow angles backward to form an adult. Essentially the *Homo* species is that of a foetal primate that expresses a form of arrested development, that does not metamorphose into the adult form. In our case it seems that it is bipedalism and the narrow pelvis that is decisive.

Gordon: Well said, Mike. *Homo* species is in denial of its true heritage as a large breeding bipedal primate infant. It is also in denial that its brain is an embodied bipedal organ, and that it is simply a quite recent offshoot of the founder species, *H. passiens* – and one with a questionable future. *Homo sapiens* has arrogated to itself the notion that it is the only, and full, expression of an intelligent *Homo* species, and it seeks to take credit for all the aspects that we associate with being truly human. Far from it – not only has *sapiens* denied its evolutionary origins – *Homo passiens* – but it denies its juvenility, and playfulness, as the foundation of all human culture. You only have to attend a football match to negate this ridiculous notion – the fans have no such illusions.

Mike: You mean the dream-game.

Gordon: Yes I do. Fans watching a football game enter a state of lucid dreaming. Call it a state of emotional homeostasis associated with, and 'activated by', rapid eye movements, or REM, in the passienic region of the hippocampus – a kind of lucid dream-enactment behaviour expressed by gamma-wave frequency and dopamine activation – along with motor-affective resonance, generated by the mirror neuron system. A dream-game, not dissimilar to aboriginal dream-time experiences. Emotion-specific dream-enacting behaviours correlate positively with mirror behaviour emotive expression – in particular anger or joy, the pain of losing, or the pleasure of winning. Only play, and in particular bipedal football, can demonstrate this ancient and prehistoric expression of the embodied collective unconscious, which is both bipedal and Passienic, and articulated collectively in the dream-game, by players and fans.

Mike: Is this cultural epigenetics?

Gordon: Yes indeed! Generated by and articulated in play – and profoundly influencing gene expression. Play is one of the highest expressions of emotional–cognitive regulation. It's how a child uses emotional expression as a survival strategy to learn just what works, and what does not work, in relation to obtaining the necessary social armour – like parents and other people – to survive. To get food and be nurtured. At any football game you will invariably find a much higher ratio of Jungian psychologists to Freudian psychologists. Jung himself said: "The creation of something new is not accomplished by the intellect but by the play instinct acting from inner necessity".

The Cernes Abbas Giant as it appeared in 990 A.D., created to celebrate Cernes Abbas F.C. winning the cup for the tenth time. The trophy in the giant's hand was later removed and replaced with a giant club – the version we are more familiar with today.

Mike: Is this associated with the fanabbinoid hormones, close relations of the cannabinoids? The hormones in the system are fanandamide-1 and fannandamide-2. Fanandamide-1 is for reward and pleasure, and fanandamide-2 is for anger and fear.

Gordon: That's right. They're located in the nucleus accumbens, one in each cerebral hemisphere. Only recently discovered, of course, by the brilliant team at the Passienic University of Socrates and Pele in Sao Paulo, Brazil.

Mike: That's interesting. The same region also correlates with reward and reinforcing stimuli, and to addiction? That is, to learning and dopamine pathways. May this in any sense be connected to the universal culture of drug taking in all ancient and modern societies?

Gordon: You bet. Let's follow this up later.

Mike: Thank you, Gordon. Where can we meet to continue this discussion?

Gordon: May I suggest the Homo Ludens Bar, in George Street?

Mike: Okay. Until then …

CHAPTER 2

Football Anatomy and the Coefficient of Reciprocal and Non-Reciprocal Passing Altruism

I met Gordon in the Homo Ludens Bar, at the west end of George Street, on a bright and windy day in February.

The Bar is a lovely old Edinburgh tavern that used to house discussions during the Scottish Enlightenment, with patrons including Adam Smith and David Hume among others. The atmosphere that day was quiet, intense, committed, competitive. Groups of drinkers were playing games – dominoes, chess, poker, backgammon, snakes and ladders and ludo – and Lego construction projects. The bar is also known locally as the Alexander Graham Bell Tavern, in honour of Alexander Graham Bell, who was born just a few metres from the establishment. Bell was awarded the first patent for the invention of the telephone in the USA in 1876. He was successful in many other fields of invention, such as optical telecommunications, hydrofoil and aeronautics, and regarded the telephone as something of a diversion from his more serious interests.

Educated at the Royal High School of Edinburgh and Weston House Academy in Elgin, Moray, he continued his studies at the universities of Edinburgh and London before emigrating to Canada with his family. Members of his extended family still return to drink in the lovely and ancient hostelry.

The great Scottish thinker Alexander Dunedin also drank in this tavern in the nineteenth century, with his friend Charles Darwin, who was studying in Edinburgh at that time. Dunedin was the author of a famous book that challenged the notion that the large human brain is the main influence on human cognition and intelligence; he ranked bipedalism instead as the major event separating humans from their primate ancestors. Dunedin, who was also a major figure in the Edinburgh Football Phrenology fraternity, wrote the seminal book, *The Playful and Walking History of Mankind*, which was published in Dutch, and according to Gordon P. McNeil was an influence on Johan Huizinga, the Dutch cultural historian and thinker who wrote the pioneering book Homo Ludens, which was first published in 1938 and which articulates the theory that adult play is generative of human culture (a perspective that correlates to neoteny), and to the retention of infantile physiology and psychology into adult humans, or as Gordon P. McNeil claims, after Stephen Jay Gould – humans never fully metamorphose into their fully formed adult organism, or more simply put, they never truly grow up. According to a local legend, during his visits to the UK, Stephen Jay Gould would often meet with Gordon P. McNeil in the Homo Ludens Bar to discuss the theory of *Homo passiens*. Although Professor Gould would not accept the theory of bipedal football as generative of human evolutionary advance as correct, he did agree that it provided many interesting insights into the utterly strange evolution of a neotenous upright bipedal species, with flat face, domed head, and with a narrow pelvis, knock-knees, and flat and levered foot, that has eluded evolutionary science for many decades.

This elegant tavern remains a popular haunt of neoteny and game-playing cultural academics, evolutionary biologists, passienic researchers, free market economists, materialist philosophers, cultural anthropologists, and football cultural historians. The debate about the evolution of *Homo* and *Homo passiens*, about the neotenous and ludenic physiology, psychology and psychiatry of *Homo* and of *Homo passiens*, the founder species, continues late into the night on most nights of the week.

Among the many visitors are Dutch and international cultural historians: anthropologists who study the ludenic origins of the genus *Homo*, and who are influenced by the writings of Johan Huizinga, the author of *Homo Ludens*. Johan Huizinga was born in the town of Groningen in 1872, and studied Indo-Germanic languages before turning to history. He became Professor of General and Dutch History at Groningen University, and later, in 1915, Professor of General History at Leiden University, where he remained until 1942 when he was detained, until his death in 1945, for opposition to the Nazis. The work of Johan Huizinga has been consistently underestimated by evolutionary biologists of the *Homo sapiens* mindset, due to their inability to understand the role of adult game-playing in the genus *Homo*, and its role in the cognitive, emotional homeostatic, and cultural evolution of *Homo sapiens* and *Homo passiens*. Only by correlating ludenic psychology and physiology with neoteny, as developed by

Gordon P. McNeil, may the species be more fully understood. Of course the highest expression of ludenic culture, art and behaviour is that of neotenous bipedal football.

Mike: What do you think, Gordon, are the most significant anatomical and physiological attributes that characterise *Homo passiens*, the only primate species that is upright, bipedal and plays football?

Gordon: Okay, Mike. No problem. One: the human head is the same size as a football – one and a half litres. This is not a coincidence; football technology emanates from the *Homo* brain, and I agree with the Scottish philosopher Andy Clark that all technology represents and expresses the extended mind. Two: the human head is domed, allowing for subtle and controlled heading.

Mike: Okay, that makes perfect sense. No primate could direct a ball with such precision?

Gordon: That's right. So, three is: the human face and brow is flat, allowing for power heading with direction.

Mike: The primate face is flat in infancy and then develops fully into the adult, the chin advances and the brow recedes and angles backward … this means that the *Homo* species just never grew up?

Gordon: Yes, precisely. Humans are neotenous, underdeveloped foetal primates, arrested in extended infancy.

Mike: Well, well, well … Although the benefit of early ejection from the womb, effectively as a foetus at nine months, allows for extended brain development over three decades – thirty years! Hence our big brains!

Gordon: Again, you have hit the nail on the head. Number four: the human head is fully upright, centred and hinged on the spinal column, via the unique centralised foramen magnum. This arrangement allows for lateral vision, for forward vision during motion, for spatial awareness when upright, and for motor sensibility in both lower limbs.

Mike: We're designed for spatial awareness?

Gordon nods in agreement and holds up the little finger of his left hand, then extends both arms outwards and upward with a flourish.

Gordon: Five. Human arms provide balance during jumping – handy for saving and heading – and during upright forward, backward and eccentric bipedal motion.

Gordon: Number six. Let me think. Oh yes! The human hand has opposable thumbs, like all other primate species. So this allows for grasping the ball, particularly useful for goalkeepers, but also for shying – and for holding opponents when necessary.

Mike: The opposable thumb was biologically engineered perfectly for tool making, but more significantly for bipedal football goalkeeping expression?

Gordon: Right. Our seventh feature is the human pelvis. It is structured for ease of upright motion, with the legs hinged directly below, allowing for upright bipedal forward, backward and eccentric motion – and more particularly for kicking, dribbling and shooting. Then there is number eight – bipedal motion. What we call walking or running is actually bipedal kicking. This is very easy to demonstrate, by taking a few steps, each so-called step is actually a kick.

Mike: I've tried it and it works beautifully. What of our knock-knees?

Gordon: A-hah. Our knock-knees. Number nine. Bipedal locomotion – walking, running, kicking, jumping (and heading) – would be impossible without that absolute characteristic of the *Homo* species – knock-knees. The valgus angle of the femur of the upper leg leads downward from the pelvis so that the knees are closely aligned to the centre of gravity! This enables all of the bipedal locomotive features associated with *Homo passiens* – without which football would be impossible.

Mike: Lovely! And the foot?

Gordon: This is number ten. And I think it is my favourite! That great mystery of bipedal anatomy – the flat foot. It's cushioned, long-heeled, short-toed and levered for propulsion. But it attains full evolutionary significance only in relation to the non-opposable great toe, which is aligned and parallel to the other digits. This gives not only stability during upright forward, backward and eccentric motion, but also the instep and outstep allows curling and slicing the ball, inside and outside flicking, kicking and skilful ball control. No other primate discovered to date can do this.

Mike: In a manner of speaking, the bipedal foot is the embodied father and mother of the bipedal brain.

Gordon: You know, I think that should be the very first item in any anthropological lecture series, at all levels. Now, where were we. Ten … eleven. Yes, eleven. Bipedalism. When our primate ancestors came down from the trees and stood upright for the first time, bipedalism emerged as the first step (kick) on the road to *Homo passiens*. That was around 5 million years ago. The development of the large brain – our domed head, actually, emerged some 2.5 million years ago, and this, along with our relatively long legs – that's neoteny again and the reversion to infantile form – set the new species on its final path towards *Homo passiens*, which appears fully formed in the records from some 500,000 years ago. Of course they went on to developed language, art, burial, farming, culture, religion, advanced tool making, civilisation and all the other aspects of the species we are today.

Mike: Astounding stuff. Are there any representations in ancient art?

Gordon: A search of prehistoric art forms reveals numerous examples of cave art representing balls, and a great variety of early forms of skeletal goalposts. If these clear references to our past have remained hidden from us up to now, it simply tells us that those who have looked have been looking with blinkered vision – a vision biased towards a species with a so-called "rational" mind, a mind disconnected to a body, a disembodied mind … a mind without football! An armless, legless, footless mind.

Mike: What you are saying is that it is only within the context of neotenous bipedal football that all of our special developments may be understood?

Gordon: Exactly Mike. The human brain grew relative to body size from 2.5 million years ago, and may also be viewed from this perspective. Why is the brain this size, and not another? How did thought and language arise in the way that they did, metaphorically grounded as they are in the body in motion – in a bipedal upright body, above all, a body which deals in, and with, space, time, motion, cause and effect (kick–connect), and a body which runs, kicks and scores?

Prehistoric cave art depicting early humans playing football. Note the primitive balls and skeletal goalposts.

Mike: And saves, Gordon! It seems that bipedal neoteny is the foundation of the human brain.

Gordon: Football – above all – is the metaphorical source of this armed, legged and befooted mind of humans – this embodied mind. This mind with two arms, two legs and two footballing feet. The disembodied mind – the so-called analytical and "rational" mind of western philosophy – is a mind arising somehow, in and of *itself*, without reference to its body; it's a fleshless, heartless, gutless philosophical myth, and its been foisted on generations of scholars and students by a tradition with no knowledge of football – a tradition that denies not only our evolutionary heritage, but our very footballing essence.

Mike: And language? Where does language come into this?

Gordon: When a striker shouts, yells "Cross" to his winger, he shouts a linguistic, striking, and compelling metaphor. A linguistic command in the form of a metaphor, which includes information as to his position in space, and his motion – where he is going – and his timing – when he will get there – and the cause and effect – that is, the connection, from the kick to the header.

Mike: So here we have the real origin of language and thought. Its embodied, grounded, in flesh, in heads, legs, arms and feet. A mind pregnant, messy, pulsating, sweating, shaking, bursting, convulsing with body. A mind replete, infected with body. A bloodied, boned, fleshed mind. A muscled mind. A watered, fatted, protein, skinned, earthed and corporeal mind … And yet a mind clothed in rich metaphorical thought and language, and with such potent metaphorical and orally poetic power that it unites the sensorimotor biology of the two players – the striker and the winger – one with the other though space, time, motion, causality and – as it happens – the ball.

Gordon: Well articulated, Mike.

Mike: Only football can explain this.

Gordon: We, the passienologists, are the spectre that haunt not only the anti-passienic evolutionary biologists – the football deniers – but also the philosophers of the "rational" disembodied mind: the legless, armless and footless mind.

Mike: No other species has made the leap to football?

Gordon: No. That's right. It's only within the context of football that all these and many other seemingly – for a primate – bizarre aspects of human psychology, philosophy, psychiatry, physiology, anatomy and biology may be understood. These aspects have puzzled evolutionary biologists, anthropologists, archaeologists, palaeontologists, geneticists, anatomists, physiologists, psychologists, neurologists, and embryologists, for many generations.

Mike: It's only now with the emergence of passienology – as the science explaining the true driving force of human evolution – that the true essence of man – and woman (*Femo passiens*) is appearing ... that of Man the Footballer: the kicking species, the heading species, the jumping, dribbling, passing, back-heeling, shying, goalkeeping, saving, defending, attacking, stepping over, crossing, free-kicking, penalty kicking, tripping, tackling, injuring, and diving species. And this includes refereeing man?

Gordon: Got it, Mike. Passienology does not contradict the fundamental tenets of evolutionary biology – that's heredity, variety and selection – but it refines, develops and extends them scientifically. It provides us with the *missing* link, a link that so far has eluded all other attempts to explain the how and the when and the why of this strange upright, big-brained bipedal kicking species.

Mike: That missing link is football?

Gordon: It has been said many times, Mike, that for new ideas to emerge a generation has to die. This is a call to arms – and legs, if you will – for the new generation of passienologists. We will not wait for this to happen! We announce our arrival in the field of human evolution with scientific confidence ... with energy, with dynamism, with industry, with optimism, with pride, self-belief and enthusiasm. With motivation. And with professionalism. If at present we languish in the lower divisions of the evolutionary scientific leagues, make no mistake – we are on our way up.

Mike: *Homo passiens* has arrived?

Gordon: *Homo passiens* has most certainly arrived! And evolutionary science must finally grasp this most fundamental and beautiful truth.

Mike: And your book on the subject?

Gordon: Yes, there is one. It's called *The Evolution of Neotenous Bipedal Football Anatomy*. It's going to be published by the *Journal of Passienology* at the University of Dublin in the next couple of years.

Mike: Great!

The drinkers, who had been listening to our discussion with studied interest, were discussing their own ideas about Homo passiens. The conversation on that particular morning in the Homo Ludens Bar, was around the question of brilliant and skilful football players, especially strikers, and whether willingness to drive for an individual goal, or release of the ball to a better positioned teammate, was a learned or a genetic trait. I relayed the question to Gordon.

Mike: Do you think, Gordon, that the key to team survival and success is to be found in selflessness and altruism? That is, in suppressing individual talent and skill if that's required in any given game – if you like, a "reciprocal passing altruism"?

Gordon: The key to all great football teams, Mike, is the coefficient of *non*-reciprocal passing altruism. Every pass – every given ball – is an example of passing reciprocal altruism, a pass that may benefit the team but not necessarily the passer – the assist. Of course the *gifted* pass may be returned later – or in another game. If the giver expects or demands the ball in return – or refuses to return the pass – he expresses non-reciprocal passing altruism. He wants, *demands* the ball – even if the outcome may not benefit the whole team. And having been given the pass, he is not likely to return it, regardless of the outcome. Cristiano Ronaldo in his early years was such a football player. He would reluctantly part with the ball only on the condition that it would be returned, and score – or not score – on his own initiative. He was generally incapable of reciprocal passing altruism!

Mike: An attacking forward in a difficult situation around the penalty box always has the advantage of surprise, because the defenders would expect him to pass in such a situation. By not passing, he opens up space to allow him to shoot?

Gordon: This is true, Mike. Non-reciprocal passing altruism is not usually learned or adaptive. It's always more genetic. Because, by doing the unexpected, space usually opens up and a potentially unfruitful situation becomes a situation in which a goal is a distinct possibility.

Mike: This selfish non-reciprocal passing altruism may result in a positive outcome, then?

Gordon: Yes, yes. This is where the "selfish" team gene benefits both the individual team player and the team as a whole. For example, in a two-on-one situation, where two forwards are approaching the goalkeeper, where one's been given the ball by the other in the approach, the keeper would usually expect a reciprocal pass. If the striker carrying the ball rounds the keeper instead of passing, the outcome is likely to be a goal – especially if there is little room for the holder to make an angle to score. The greater the odds against scoring, the greater and more beautiful and lucidic the goal! So you see, selfishness pays off for both for the ball carrier and for his marginalised teammate. It's a striking example of the selfish team gene in action.

Mike: Or an example of successful non-reciprocal passing altruism. It may even be termed "reverse-reciprocal passing altruism"?

Gordon: Yes. Reverse-reciprocal passing altruism is okay.

There was much nodding interest among the drinkers, and satellite discussions were flowering all around the crowded bar. Gordon continued.

Gordon: We all love individual ball skill, but, in general, players with the greatest individual skills are a questionable asset in the team. In any football team, team genes are shared equally by each player. A team is composed of eleven individuals who carry and contribute to one eleventh of the team "genome", for want of a better word. If we include substitutes who are called on to play, they contribute a proportional amount to the team genome depending on how much time they spend on the pitch. For example, a substitute who comes on at half-time would contribute a one twenty-second portion of the team genome of the total to that game, and the substituted player, one twenty-second portion less. And so on. Pro rata for other substitutes. Each player's relationship with his teammates is genomically identical, and therefore – theoretically – we should have a completely altruistic genomic environment. In this situation, reciprocal passing altruism should be a given. However, a 'give and go' need not necessarily be reciprocated if the dynamic favours the first receiver. The altruistic gene does not need to be expressed at this moment. Here, reciprocal passing altruism should be *suppressed*. A pass should – or should not – be delivered according to the state of play, the nature of the opposition, the period in the game, and any particular dynamic circumstances. The key parameter for expressing or suppressing reciprocal passing altruism depends entirely on the outcome and benefit for the team.

Mike: Where is the faculty in which this has been studied?

Gordon: Of course, the George Best Faculty of Reciprocal and Non-Reciprocal Passing Altruism, at Cregagh, East Belfast, Northern Ireland.

Mike: Have you written about this Gordon?

Gordon: I have, Mike, in my book, *The Decline of Non-Reciprocal Passing Altruism*, to be published by Reciprocal Passing Altruism Publications in Lisbon next autumn. Modern and bureaucratic coaching is destroying the free-rider non-reciprocal passing altruism genetic expression.

He pulled a battered manuscript out from under his seat, briefly waved it around, and returned it. Around the pub, the drinkers were furiously discussing, arguing, describing and displaying the relative benefits of reciprocal and non-reciprocal passing altruism, using pints as the players and glasses of whisky for the balls.

Mike: Are team genes derived from, or adaptations of, kin genes, and if so what if a player moves from one club to another, and how does this affect his original team genes?

Gordon: Mike, genes are not absolute entities. If this were so why bother to train? Moulding, sculpting and modulating team genes takes place during training, and are profoundly influenced by the coach, himself a carrier. If team genes were fixed absolutes it would be impossible to change club. Think of young adolescent primates. They leave their mother troop and join another. Their genes have to adapt to the new situation, via gene enhancement expression or suppression, a move that improves gene diversity. There are powerful pressures on the young primate to move troop, to increase his reproductive opportunities, to spread his genes. Football is similar.

Mike: Modern coaches have adapted this genetic manipulation and environmental exposure via the loan system?

Gordon: Yes. There is certainly overriding selfish gene pressure, but in the new environment the primate youngster is going to have to find comrades and friends, and here he will have to mobilise his cooperative or altruistic genes, or he will not survive. A new terrain opens for him, no need here for some random mutation to appear, simply switching team gene sequences becomes the survival mechanism. How often have we seen great individual footballers, with the finest passienic genes, move club and fail to succeed? Any good team, any great team, may be ruined by a player with a poorly adaptive football team genome. Human and passienic team genomes are adaptable, they are not fixed entities.

Mike: Does this also apply to fans?

Gordon: My team is Hibs. If I watch Hearts do you think my genes are indifferent to that? No disrespect, Hearts is a very great club with a wonderful history. However it is not my club, and therefore do you think watching Hearts would express the same metabolic, physiological, psychological, psychiatric, cognitive, and emotional outcome as would be the case if I were watching Hibs?

Mike: No. Never. The passienic, the football environment, is now hostile – not so much physically but psychologically. Dawkins is right to suggest that genes are inherently selfish, but is any team genome that lacks empathic cooperative genes heading for trouble, or for relegation, and are fans likewise deeply affected?

Gordon: Yes, however, we have to admit that football teams with these rogue free-rider selfish genes provide us with excellent spectator sport, wonderful individual skills, unexpected changes of pace and direction, and occasional bursts of explosive and lucidic brilliance. They are prime examples of non-reciprocal passing altruists, or as some players would have it – passing free-riders. When you give the ball to such a player, you do not wait for the return pass. Also they tend to be greedy, impulsive and inconsistent, and often may represent a burden that other teammates may not wish to carry.

Mike: May this be calibrated mathematically?

Gordon: Of course, Mike. Team success can evolve where the benefit of the ratio of non-reciprocal passing altruism over reciprocal passing altruism is higher than the cost of the ratio of reciprocal passing altruism over non-reciprocal passing altruism, and that is where the benefit of not passing, exceeds the cost of passing.

Mike: How did you derive this formula – an algorithm?

Gordon: No – an algolithim, Mike. I have to thank the great evolutionary biologist William Hamilton, from whom I developed a mathematical algolithim, for his analysis of reciprocal and non-reciprocal altruism in kin selection, for pointing out these relationships, and providing me with a mathematical model for passienology. Team genomes and their expression do offer us an excellent model for the operation of, may I say, kick and kin selective forces, both in evolutionary biology and passienology. I have further elaborated these questions in my seminal book *A Brief Introduction to Passienic Team Genomes* – available soon from the Passienic University of the Isles at Barra.

Mike: What, Gordon, are the correlations between *Homo passiens'* success and *Homo* evolutionary advance – are there parallel genes, gene sequences and consequent hormone and enzyme expressions?

Gordon: There are, Mike, certainly so. We can refer again to the fabulous work of William Hamilton many decades ago, who based his ideas on social insect genetic evolution, and suggested that altruistic genes may be related to the altruistic loss of reproductive ability, whereby some insects are infertile but facilitate fertility, and reproduction in close kin.

Mike: A bit like a brother or sister, who does not reproduce, but consciously helps siblings to do so in some way, such as via shelter, food, or economically?

Gordon: Yes, we can correlate passienic gene expression for bipedal football fitness in a similar way.

Mike: Okay. The direct correlation would be the creative football artist who facilitates and assists teammates, but never personally scores a goal?

Gordon: Yes, great creative players may rarely, if ever, score a goal, but they altruistically serve as facilitators for their team genome.

Mike: It may be said that they are non-reproductive in goal-driven football terminology, but are profoundly productive as team genome facilitators?

Gordon: Exactly – they may carry …

Mike: But not express the football gene for goal-driven reward expression, expressed by dopamine reward-seeking facilitation?

Gordon: Of course.

Mike: And also facilitate the use of the goal-driven gene in teammates who may carry the gene but have difficulty in expression?

Gordon: This is key – it matters not so much what genes a passienic bipedal footballer may carry. It matters significantly more which of these genes are activated and not suppressed.

Mike: Are there any specific studies in this field?

Gordon: You may not be surprised that we have a wonderful study from the Alex Ferguson Passienic Faculty of Genomic Studies in Broomloan, Govan, Glasgow.

Mike: No, I am not surprised. Did they reference any *Homo sapiens* work?

Gordon: Yes they did. A brilliant 2013 Canadian paper published in the journal *Biology Letters* by a *Homo sapiens* team led by Graham L. Thomson at Western University, Ontario, opened the door to a *passiens* interpretation. They referenced studies on altruism and social behaviour, and compared them to eusocial and altruistic behaviour in social insects.

Mike: And found variations in expressions of oxytocin and arginine vasopressin?

Gordon: Precisely – these are critical, genetically modulated variants in altruistic phenotypic expression and each of these is profoundly involved.

Mike: And dopamine?

Gordon: Likewise – dopamine is one of the most versatile of monoamine hormones, is correlated to both arginine and oxytocin expression in *Homo sapiens*, and in *Homo passiens* bipedal neotenous footballers, and modulates ...

Mike: *Homo passiens* super-lucid REM wake regulation in its dopamine form, in football hymning and chanting, in mirror activation during dream-play, and fan-dream manipulation?

Gordon: Absolutely.

Mike: Fascinating – we learn about neotenous bipedal football dream-songs, dream-chants, football genetic altruism, and mirror neurone articulation from songbirds, tree frogs and social insects, expressed in a variety of *passiens* genetic activation and hormone release cascades?

Gordon: Yes, but we do have some progressive *sapiens* researchers to thank for opening new fields of passienic research.

Mike: Wonderful.

CHAPTER 3

Soccer in Pre-Colonial America:
Femo passiens

Gordon and I were discussing the sport of pasuckuakohowog – an early form of Indigenous First Nation football, or soccer in the Americas, in the Femo Passiens Tavern in Duddingston Village in Edinburgh, which was first recorded on lands granted to the Abbot of Kelso Abbey by King David I of Scotland between the years 1136-47. The ancient tavern dates to, and is known to have been selling liquor and victuals from, as early as 1360, the oldest licensed premises in Scotland. The village borders an ancient Royal Park, known as Holyrood Park, which includes the beautiful Palace of Holyrood, which has served as the principle residence of the Kings and Queens of Scotland since the sixteenth century. The Palace is situated at the foot of the Royal Mile, at the opposite end from the twelfth century Edinburgh Castle. Within the park is an extinct volcano dated to 240 million years ago. This volcano incorporates visible hill-fort defences, which were used by the Celtic peoples – the Votadini tribe. Archaeological findings indicate archaic evidence of football playing by the Votadini.

The wonderful inn (known historically as the Sheep Heid) has a long and noble association with football. Local historians point out that the area surrounding the volcano has been used for sheep grazing for thousands of years. The shepherds are known to have played football, and their footballs were renowned for being beautifully constructed from sheep bladders and sheep hide. The original name heid on the Inn signage may be the result of a simple error on the part of an early sign painter, but according to local calligraphy experts is correct, and actually derived from sheep hide, and they also claim that there is a reference to the transduction from hide to heid to be found in the Dictionary of the Older Scottish Tongue twelfth century – 1700 (this has not yet been confirmed). One particular and bibulous regular to the tavern claims that she has found a reference to football in the Older Scots Tongue Dictionary expressed as "foetball", that confirms our neotenous and ludenous origins, although other drinkers claim she is somewhat prone to confabulation.

Football appears regularly in Scottish literature – the game was outlawed by King James I in 1424 when it was referred to as "fute-ball", due to its violent practice – " all rough and violent exercises, as the fute-ball", although the ban was not effective, and the game continued in popularity. In the early sixteenth century Gavin Douglas writes "This broken shin that swells and will not be relieved……..Take the whole of his bruised arm to him".

Mary Queen of Scots was a regular visitor from the nearby Palace of Holyrood, after playing the game of fute-ball in the Royal Park, and locals explain that this is the origin of the association of the tavern with the female game, and later became known locally as the Femo Passiens Tavern. Royal patronage of the Inn was continued by her son James VI who it is also claimed by locals, presented the innkeeper with a richly embellished Ram's Head snuffbox in thanks for the good times that his mother had enjoyed playing football with a ball made from local sheep carcasses. The original head or heid snuffbox now resides at Dalmeny House, home of the Earls of Roseberry. A copy resides to this day, behind the bar.

In 1745 Prince Charles Edward Stewart (Bonnie Prince Charlie) set up military camp in the village, where the Jacobites and their wives enjoyed the hospitality of the Inn, again often after playing football in the Royal Park. It is said that they challenged the English Garrison, at that time holding Edinburgh Castle against the Jacobites, to a Fute-ball Tournament, but fearing a devious trick, the nervous colonial soldiers declined the invitation.

Other famous visitors to the Inn include Sir Walter Scott, Robert Louis Stevenson, and according to local football fan historians, many famous female footballers, including Temryss MacLean Lane, the famous First Nation American female footballer, the great Brazilian Marta Vieira da Silva, and two renowned Americans – the forward Mia Hamm, and Michelle Akers, perhaps the greatest ever female striker. The pub is popular with female historians, female football sport anthropologists, and archaeologists who study ancient female sporting artefacts. Locals list many pro-feminist visitors, including John Stuart Mill, Simone de Beauvoir, Alice Walker, Germaine Greer, Yoko Ono, Madonna, Laverne Cox, and the Nigerian writer Chimamanda Ngozi Adichie, although there is no formal record of these claims.

Mike: The notion that football was played in the pre-Columbian and pre-Colonial Americas is lovely, although new to me, Gordon.

Gordon: We should not be surprised, Mike – ancient games were incorporated in the unique Indigenous Creation and migration stories, placing the tribes on North American land before any other continent.

Mike: We do have to dispose of our sporting Euro-centric illusions. I read recently in a fabulous article in the *Journal of Women's History*, by Fabrice Delashut and Thierry Terret that American Indian sport and recreational games, including ball games, were a vital part of the cultural lives of Indian women.

Gordon: Not Indian, Mike – that is a derogatory colonial white-person construct. Yes indeed, the notion of indigenous women as domesticated and subservient squaws is one that the colonials promoted, so that their own female kin would be unaware of the rich participation of First Nation women in all aspects of life, including leadership and military customs. Sports were a major participatory and social form of community practices, the women were strong and physically able to compete with the warriors in many activities.

Mike: The idea of a mentally and physically weaker gender was absent from their thinking?

Gordon: Absolutely – simply another form of colonial myth making, of colonial paternal nonsense, with a particular mother fetishism religious twist.

Mike: Fascinating.

Gordon: Carolyn Niethammer states: 'Native American women loved games and sports. There was little feeling among these early peoples that physical strength was "unfeminine"; the strongest woman was the best mother and homemaker. And when her tasks were completed, the Indian women enjoyed sports that required strength and skill. Sometimes she played just for fun-often she was highly competitive.' There were/are also many Native women warriors.

Mike: Wow – this demolishes the Eurocentric notions of female fragility – usually cloaked in fertility and reproductive mysticism?

Gordon: Yes – also the institutionalism of sport factored into education, and more recently professional sport, is somewhat at odds with the spiritual precepts that were essential to Indian culture.

Mike: Not unlike our great Scottish Christian runner and Olympic Gold Medallist, Eric Liddle, for whom running was a form of prayer?

Gordon: Well related, Mike – his gravestone at Weifang, China, where he died, offers the following simple inscription from the Book of Isaiah – 'They shall mount up with wings as eagles; they shall run and not be weary.'

Mike: How beautifully apposite – could have been quoted from a Native American adage. Are there any Native American ladies who played or are playing in professional soccer?

Gordon: I have just returned from the USA where I met a wonderful Ambassador for Native American soccer – Temryss MacLean Lane is her birth name. Xeli'tia is her given Lummi name. And, I am also very proud to say, she is of Scottish descent.

Mike: Excellent. From what Clan?

Gordon: Temryss MacLean Lane is from the Golden Eagle Clan of Lummi Nation, a Coast Salish tribe in Washington State. Temryss is an Indigenous scholar, sport broadcaster, and coach. She holds a master's degree in American Indian studies from UCLA – that's the University of California at Los Angeles and is a Nike N7 Ambassador where she works to create access to sport for Native youth.

Mike: What a CV – is there more?

Gordon: There most certainly is. Temryss played soccer in Sweden for Balinge IF, Damallsveken, in Uppsalla, for Ajax of America, California Storm, Arizona State University, and the USA U23 National Team. Temryss earned the title of 1999 NSCAA Washington State Addidas Player of the Year, NSCAA/ Addidas Raf West Region All-American Team and WESCO League Player of the year and MVP. The Seattle-area soccer club awarded her the Golden Boot Award in 1999 and 2000.

Mike: Amazing. Surely that is all?

Gordon: No. Temryss travelled to promote women's soccer in North America, South America, Africa, the Caribbean and the Pacific Islands.

Mike: A super-lucid globally active soccer player – Femo Passiens?

Gordon: Yes, although to be fair – Temryss prefers the term football to soccer.

Mike: Not a word I like either – it is an abbreviation of the word 'association' (from Association Football) plus the addition of the suffix –er. Derived from Rugby School slang – a toff derived Frankenstein word.

Gordon: Agreed, but in the USA, football is always associated with the NFL version – so another term is required.

Mike: We need to think about that. Is there a strong connection between Scots who left their native land and the Native American Indigenous peoples?

Gordon: There certainly is, Mike – a deep and lasting relationship which is linked to a shared history.

Mike: How so?

Gordon: Mike, you amaze me – this is a part of our history that you should be familiar with.

Mike: OK, I know that the Scots immigrated in large numbers into America over the last three hundred years, and that they found a shared history with the Indigenous peoples – they were hunter gatherers, they came from tribal and clan-based cultures, where land was the defining and shared communal resource.

Gordon: Well stated, Mike. Both peoples were brutally forced from their native lands, and their traditions and languages suppressed.

Mike: I imagine that they also shared clan-based chiefdom that descended through lineage?

Gordon: They did, the Scots came to the indigenous lands as part of the colonial enterprise, but they did so having been forcibly removed from their own homelands.

Mike: They each had fought against the theft of land?

Gordon: They most certainly did so, both Scots and Indigenous Americans came from warrior cultures, and both had fought heroically against technically superior colonial forces, sword, knife, and arrow against musket, rifle, and cannon.

Mike: You think that it was for this reason that the young single Scots easily empathised with the North American Indigenous cultures that they encountered on their travels?

Gordon: Of course.

Mike: Both cultures suffered from suppression of their native regalia, these were mocked, derided and finally degraded into mascot abuse?

Gordon: In the case of Native Americans their ancient regalia were transmuted into laughable sporting mascots, and for the Scots into music hall pantomime costume.

Mike: Their strong and similar traditions of dance, poetry, music and oral traditions would have allowed for ease of social cohesion?

Gordon: Again, yes.

Mike: In other words, the colonial legacy romanticises the Indigenous cultures that it destroyed, as a strategy to neutralise their historical potency – all colonial or oppressive power seeks to denigrate and negate the legitimacy of the oppressed peoples that they otherwise fear.

Gordon: Agreed.

Mike: Do you think that football may be a valuable medium of healing, as Temryss suggests?

Gordon: Yes, I most certainly do, Mike. Football grounds us, connects us to the land to, and through, the relation between our flat feet, our non opposable big toe, our narrow pelvis and hinged bipedal legs.

Mike: That connection between foot and land – our upright bipedalism – better, between our two feet and land, is ancient, numinous, sacred?

Gordon: I could not have stated it better, Mike.

Mike: And the ball – the round infinite/finite ball is the most valued, most intimate, the most hallowed connection?

Gordon: That is how I see it, Mike.

Mike: Football returns us, reminds us of our game playing origins, of our childishness, our curiosity, creativity, inventiveness – we are *Homo ludens* – games identify the woman – *Femo passiens,* and the man *Homo passiens?*

Gordon: And yes, our tribalism, which we shared with the Native American tribalism, expressed as social altruism metamorphosed into reciprocal and non-reciprocal passing altruism in competitive games – in football.

Mike: Awesome. Can you relate more about Temryss MacLean Lane and the Lummi People?

Gordon: The Lummi are a Native American tribe of the Coast Salish ethnolinguistic group in western Washington state, residing on the Lummi Reservation in western Whatcom County, around 30 miles south of the Canadian border, and close to the town of Bellingham, where Temryss resides.

Mike: Temryss has chosen to return to her roots?

Gordon: Yes. Temryss uses the term "schelangen" to describe her People's way of life, the 'culture of stories and identity rooted in reciprocity, and generations of sovereign sustainability'.

Mike: Wow. Wonderful, inspiring. Does Temryss identify football or soccer as schelangen?

Gordon: Exactly Mike, but for many North American Indigenous communities this identity, this way of life, remains invisible and unrecognised.

Mike: How does Temryss address this tragedy, this wound?

Gordon: Temryss organises Native American stories from the late nineteenth century into the twenty-first century, and examines (I am quoting here) 'how soccer provides intergenerational healing for North American Indigenous Peoples by re-membering communities and refiguring identity, while situating Native American and First Nations People in visibility on the global stage of football'.

Mike: Re-membering, and refiguring are lovely terms – am not quite sure what they mean…

Gordon: Temryss borrows from Kenyan poet and literary scholar Ngugiwa Thiong'o's concept of "re-membering" in partnership with Lakota scholar Philip Deloria's idea of cultural "refiguring" to demonstrate the power of storied memory, sense of collective identity through ceremonial gatherings of soccer.

Mike: Now I think I understand – something akin to football ritual ceremonials in all communities, simply more potent in colonially impacted peoples, who are survivors of colonialism, and who have been subject to a kind of engineered 'forgetting'?

Gordon: Yes, Mike. Ann Laura Stoler, the Willy Brandt Distinguished University Professor of Anthropology and Historical Studies at the New School for Social Research in New York City speaks of "cultural aphasia" a kind of 'forgetting' that erases the colonial people from the imperial narrative.

Mike: And which has no language to address pain of the historic negative impact, this 'forgetting' is a kind of cultural device to ease the pain of commission?

Gordon: Yes, the Scots are not exempt. They have been both colonial settlers and colonised. This dichotomy expresses a double cultural aphasia – the Highland Clearances which drove them from their homelands is not remembered, and likewise their settler occupation of Native American lands is equally erased.

Mike: The "forgetting" applies to both coloniser and colonised. For the one group, the memory and language of commission is erased, and for the other group – the memory and language of the subjugation?

Gordon: I think so, Mike. This double, this twin "forgetting" always accompanies colonisation – the power of the coloniser is masked and hidden in the language, as a form of social control, in the way that Michel Foucalt articulates.

Mike: Since the language of oppression is masked, the subject people are obliged to participate in the linguistic deceit – for the oppressor, social and public "order" is for their control, and for the oppressed social and public "order" is for their pacification – the formal language of "legality" in books, documents and education is itself a weapon – the painful history is masked in the public discourse, and therefore suppressed?

Gordon: Of course. For Foucalt language is an instrument of control, yes you may talk with me, the coloniser, but only in the language I choose, your language, your truth, has no legitimate linguistic expression.

Mike: OK, so there is no Dictionary of the Oppressed, no grammar, and therefore no mnemonics of the colonised. So "remembering" and "refiguring" are vital mechanisms of historical truth and healing?

Gordon: They are.

Mike: And football may be a vital, a communal and remedial source of repair?

Gordon: Absolutely, as ceremony.

Mike: Is there a mechanism, a facility at international level, for "re-membering", for "refuguiring", for opposing the "forgetting" and for healing the colonial induced amnesia?

Gordon. There is Mike – the World Indigenous Games.

Mike: I have never heard of them. Where and when are they held?

Gordon: Temryss has spoken and written extensively on these games – known as the WING.

Mike: Wow, can you elaborate?

Gordon: I learned from Temryss that in 2015 she met Dr. Lawyer Ermenskin Cree Chief Willie Littlechild, the Canadian delegate, at the inaugural World Indigenous Games in Brazil. In 1977 Chief Littlechild had presented the United Nations with a "Resolution" or the U.N. Declaration on the Rights of Indigenous Peoples (UNDRIP), which initiated activism in the form of the Indigenous Peoples Games.

Mike: Wonderful – what an historic moment – I guess the media were silent, and therefore we do not know about it?

Gordon: Exactly. The international perspective or philosophy of re-membering, begins with "The Medicine Arrow" as related to Temryss by Chief Littlefield, a former professional hockey player, academic, defender of human rights and Indian school survivor. The Sacred Medicine Arrow, like the torch at the Olympic Games, ignited the unified Indigenous Peoples from around the world to gather in Brazil to celebrate Indigenous survival, through sport, soccer, and thriving cultures.

Mike: This is a wonderful celebration of international Indigenous survival, and soccer is at the very core of this vision. Can we learn more about "The Sacred Medicine Arrow" and its significance?

Gordon: We certainly can, Mike. Temryss explained that after Chief Littlechild presented the Resolutions to have the World Games in 1977, he was approached by a spiritual leader from Brazil, who gave him an arrow, which he described as a Medicine Arrow. He told the Chief always to hang the arrow with the arrowhead pointing downwards, and that it would capture negativity from any source and shoot it into the centre of the earth. He said to the Chief "it dissipates, It's always positive".

Mike: We all need a "Sacred Medicine Arrow". Does Temryss view this as significant in terms of healing, a spiritual Rod if you like, of re-membering, of refiguiring, of recovering, of healing, and is soccer a major facilitation?

Gordon: That is close, Mike. Temryss describes the story of the "Sacred Medicine Arrow" as a Brazilian-First Nation co-creation story of the WIG, and that connects unique and relatable Indigenous worldviews.

Mike: This is historic, and iconic – a creation story that unites Indigenous peoples across the world, frees them from colonial mythical constructs, and engineered cultural aphasia.

Gordon: "The Sacred Medicine Arrow" is potent and positive token, a signal, a sign of re-membering, of refiguiring, a validation, of rebirth, of hope, of anticipation, and of aspiration for renewed schelangen.

Mike: Wonderful, Gordon, do you know of any similar *Femo Passiens* heroic football stories, stories that may resonate with Temryss' articulation of football schelangen, and its positive healing role in Indigenous history?

Gordon: I do, Mike – a recent story from Italy shows how football, via its female exponents, may unite a community against a dark, pathological and dangerous force, a cancerous corrupting influence, and one that brings fear into community life, into homes, families, schools and businesses – a story of football as a positive life-force.

Mike: I assume you are referring to the Mafia?

Gordon: Yes. The Calabrian Mafia – known as the Ndrangheta, are among the richest and most powerful crime groups in the world.

Mike: I have heard that Mafia money is laundered through football in Italy – was never quite sure if this was a rumour or based on fact.

Gordon: Sporting Locri, from lovely town of Locri in Calabria, is one of Italy's best female football teams, and compete in Italy's top Serie A League.

In 2015 the club's President, Fernando Armeni received a message which stated "It's time to close Sporting Locri. Leave!"

The threats became increasingly more menacing, and included direct threats to his daughter.

This was more than the President could tolerate, and not surprisingly President Armeni announced the closure of the club. He posted a note on the club's Facebook page announcing "Game Over", and that the club would close.

Mike: Why Sporting Locri, and what was the outcome?

Gordon: The why is not known, but locals suggest that the ground may have been the target – the Ndrangheta are major land and real estate brokers. The outcome was an explosion of local anger, including support from across the entire Italian football community.

Mike: And the team members – the Femo Passiens?

Gordon: They refused to capitulate and announced that they would continue to play.

Mike: True, and heroic Femo Passiens?

Gordon: Certainly. A project "I go to play in Locri" was initiated and mobilised thousands of fans in support, on a community sports day Sunday – Sporting Locri's team captain, Beita Fernandez, said "I'm happy that it went well. There were a lot of people and it was beautiful to see".

Mike: Awesome. What was the result, was the initiative successful?

Gordon: Well Sporting Locri are still playing lovely and elegant football today.

Mike: What a fantastic community response. Do we know why the Mafia backed off – if they are not frightened of the Italian state, why would a small (although brave) female football community see them off the field – seems paradoxical?

Gordon: I visited this charming city, in the province of Reggio Calabria, in 2016 to check out the Mafia legend. Plato named it "The Flower of Italy", due to the local peoples' friendly characteristics, and it was the site of two important sanctuaries, Persephone, the Protector of Fertile Marriages, and of Aphrodite, the Goddess of Love and Beauty. Since the Mafia code of Omerta is absolute, Italians invariably resort to 'confabulazione' when discussing Mafia affairs – every Italian knows somebody, who knows somebody, who has the inside story. Every bar, every cafe has their resident 'expert' who has access to the true story.

Mike: What was the most believable narrative being retailed in the cafes and bars?

Gordon: First of all, their wives refused to cook – a significant blow against Mafia machismo. The poor men were viewed by locals seeking their favourite pasta meals in local restaurants. Locals claim that collection of protection money was suspended in favour of food.

Mike: That worked?

Gordon: No, it did not, according to my contacts.

Mike: Do we know what finally caused the change in strategy?

Gordon: We do – it seems that some of the Mafia daughters applied to the club coach, to play for Sporting Locri.

Mike: Wonderful – were any of them technically good enough to represent this great club?

Gordon: Not yet, but the word on the Locri football street is that one of the younger ones, who challenged her father – a Mafia Don, shows real promise as a wing back, and has been offered a contract, and will soon be picked for the Serie A team.

Mike: This is a 'healing', a heroic healing of resolution, bravery and community solidarity. Football healing!

Gordon: It is Mike, football healing ascends, rises, and soars, with every reciprocal altruistic pass, every poetic, beatific move, every brave and self-sacrificial block, every beautifully space and timed tackle, every acrobatic and goal preserving save, and every mystical, transcendent, and quantum lucidity goal.

Mike: Temryss is right – football may be a source of healing, from historical wounding, a wellspring of rehabilitation, of recuperation, of reparation, of reconciliation, and of regeneration?

Gordon: Let me quote Temryss: *"Re-membering Indigenous football is schelangen, a right to be happy as a way of life. I ask that Native community leaders rethink the overdeveloped pay-to-play game of soccer and return to its roots. And of great importance I ask that we invest in Indigenous soccer, as a proactive health measure that brings people together to work toward a common goal"*

Mike: How gorgeous.

Gordon: May I add what we may take away from Temryss' work – in her own beauteous expression?

Mike: Please do.

"Indigenous football at its core is centered in wellness, balance, education, and cultural engagement where soccer is a healing practice of schelangen. One of the young World Indigenous Champions, tattoo'd a soccer ball along with the words, "Wherever, Whenever, Forever" on her leg to represent her commitment, her identity and her love for the beautiful game. These tattoo'd words think beyond football into a way of life and Indigenous permanents: Yes, we are here. We have been here. And we will remain here. Our experiences and stories tell us so".

END.

CHAPTER 4

Gordon P. McNeil's Craniometrics: Football Phrenology

I arrived late at the Albert Camus Bar on George Street on a foul, wet, black Saturday in the first week of March.

It was early afternoon and I knew I would find Gordon discussing football and philosophy with some of his faculty cronies, and his garrulous and bibulous fraternity. This was their regular Saturday debate. The buzz in the pub was contentious, pugnacious, loud and raucous. Groups of men and women were making all sorts of cranial measurements using sheets of graph paper, rulers, lengths of wood, bits of string, and anything else to hand that could be used as a measuring gauge. Brows were being carefully examined. Cranial angles were being checked. Cheek bones explored. Jaw alignments adjusted.

"Craniometrics," the barman said to me in answer to my puzzled look. "We are measuring our crania for heading angles."

Albert Camus, who the bar is named after, is a famous Algerian/ French writer who was awarded a Nobel Prize in 1960 for his writings on philosophy. He articulated a philosophy of absurdism in his fiction and other writings. Camus was born in Mondovi, Algeria, in 1913, the son of a cellarman and a cleaning lady. His father died from wounds he received during the First World War at the Battle of Marne. Camus was happy at school, excelling in intellectual discussions. A prolific reader of French literature, in particular Gide and Malraux, he was also excellent at swimming and football. He went on to the University of Algiers and founded the Group for International Liaisons, which attacked the ideologies of both the Soviet Union and the USA. Football had a major influence on him and his thinking, particularly the comradeship and shared community of football. He was a goalkeeper for Racing Universitaire d'Alger, which later won the North African Champions Cup and the North African Cup, twice each in the 1930s. He played in the junior team from 1928 to 1930, but had to abandon all hope of a professional career when he contracted tuberculosis at the age of seventeen. In later years, he said of his footballing experiences: "After many years, during which I saw many things, what I know about morality and the duty of man I owe to sport and learned it in the RUA". His most famous book, *The Plague*, features a professional footballer and various discussions on football.

Camus visited Edinburgh in the early 1950s at the invitation of Hibernian Football Club when it was enjoying its most successful period. He was present at a game at the Easter Road Stadium in which Hibs defeated the famous Glasgow Rangers by five goals to one, and remarked that he had never witnessed football of such elegance, poetry and speed. He was introduced to the players by manager Harry Swan – the architect of this wonderful club, and a football visionary who took Hibs into Europe before any other British team. The European competition at the time was known as The Fairs Cup, and Hibs reached the semi-final by defeating Barcelona.

Camus loved the social and often disputatious atmosphere of Scottish bars. He spent hours arguing about football and philosophy in the ancient tavern that became a bank for a while, before returning to its original role as an inn called The Standing Order. In 1998, after the France's victory in the World Cup, and in memory of his visit in 1952, it became the Albert Camus Bar – now a major international football tourist destination. Camus remained a fervent supporter of Hibs until his tragic death in a car crash in 1960. The bar is favoured by French football fans, absurdist philosophers and existentialists, who add to the atmosphere generated by super-lucid REM dream stages, and advocates and researchers of fannabinoid, hopoid and hopamine. Sometimes they reflect on their dream-team of absurdists and philosophers, and their Absurdist Manifesto.

Mike: What is this craniometrics stuff all about, Gordon?

Gordon: Optimum angles for heading, Mike. Football players differ in their cranial formations. You would be surprised at the variation in cranial formation among any group of footballers, no matter what background they are from – even if they are from the same family. Do you recall the fabulous Baker brothers, Gerry and Joe, who played for Hibs in the sixties? You may remember that Joe rivalled Brian Clough, and was capped for England. Both brothers were prolific goal scorers. One would score by neat downward glancing headers and the other with explosive power headers that transformed confident goalkeepers into manic depressives. They were equally brilliant exponents of the headed ball. Their differential expertise was, of course, in the fine variations of their cranial angles. I have explored these issues at great length in my book *The Cranium and the Header*; this one will be published by the esteemed Kenny Dalglish Publishers of Liverpool.

Mike: Where does this come from, Gordon?

The noise in the Albert Camus Bar grew louder as the customers debated the significance of Gordon's craniometrics among themselves, demonstrating various heading angles by throwing packets of crisps and balls made of crushed paper into the air and performing brilliant balletic acts of heading as they descended. One customer was playing headers behind the bar with the young barman – winning easily because of the young lad's bar-room sense of wisdom and propriety. Bottles were being dislodged from the gantry. Nobody except the barman seemed to be concerned.

Gordon: I have Stephen Jay Gould, the poet of neoteny, to thank for this, Mike. It was Gould who made me aware of the work of the eighteenth century Dutch anatomist Petrus Camper. Camper was also a painter, and interested in beauty; curious, too, as to how the classical artists arrived at the ideal in terms of beauty. He realised that they based their anatomical forms on abstract geometrical principles, and in relation to the skull – the cranium. He thought he had worked out an angle that defined beauty. It's known as Petrus Camper's Angle, and is formed at the intersection of one line drawn from the opening of the ear to the base of the nose, and another drawn from the most forward projection of the upper lip to the most prominent part of the brow. He measured this angle in people around him and found it varied between 70 and 90 degrees, but in classical Grecian art it was 100 degrees. I read his book in the original language, Dutch, at Leiden University. His work was later distorted for racist purposes, by other thinkers, but this was not his intention.

At this point, I suggested we refreshed our glasses.

Gordon: Where was I now? Oh yes. Camper was not free of the prejudices of his century, of course, but his primary interest was in the combination of art and science. If we take Camper's Angle as an index of heading variation we can see that a 70 degree angle makes for upward glancing headers, a 100 degree angle for power forward headers, and a 110 degree angle for downward headers. For side headers we make an angle from the horizontal passing through the centre of the cranium to another horizontal crossing the at the optimum heading point at eyebrow height. This line coincides with the tangent of the curve of the cranium and gives us three variations: the shorter line and more acute angle makes for upward headers or lobs; the longer line and more obtuse angle makes for power sideways headers; and the longest line makes for superb sideways downwards headers. This angle we can call Camper's Optimum Angle, although we have no direct knowledge of his attitude to football.

Mike: You believe he was Passienic, don't you. Do we also find examples of strikers with more acute Camper's angles?

Gordon: Yes, Mike. And yes.

Mike: Who in your opinion, then, was – or is – the greatest exponent of the headed ball?

Founded in 1940 by
a team of surrealists
and absurdists escaping
from the Nazis

A. CAMUS
GOALKEEPER
"Autumn is a second
spring when the
football season starts"

R. MAGRITTE
CENTRE MIDFIELD
"The luxury player
evokes the mystery
without which the world
would not exist"

S. BECKETT
RIGHT-WING
"Ever tried a bicycle
kick? Ever failed? No
matter. Try again. Fail
again. Fail better."

F. KAHLO
CENTRE FORWARD
"Wings. What do I need
you for when I have
feet to play football?"

A. BRETON
LEFT-WING
"Of all those arts
in which the wise
excel, Nature's chief
masterpiece is the
step-over"

F. KAFKA
LEFT-BACK
"Anyone who watches
the beautiful game
never grows old"

J-P. SARTRE
CENTRE-BACK
"Only the guy who
isn't running has time
to complain to the
referee"

M. DUCHAMP
CENTRE-BACK
"I don't believe in
football. I believe in
footballers"

M. ERNST
RIGHT-BACK
"Creativity is that
marvellous capacity
of players to pass
and move and draw
a spark from their
juxtaposition"

M. RAY
CENTRE-FORWARD
"All football pundits
should be assassinated"

S. DALI
CENTRE-MIDFIELD
"The attacking
midfielder is
destructive, but he
destroys only what he
considers to be shackles
limiting his vision"

*The Surrealist & Absurdist F.C. founded in 1940. A fantasy dream-team of absurdists
and philosophers responsible for The Manifesto of Football Surrealism (overpage).*

Manifesto of Football Surrealism

1. *We demand recognition of the nominal and neotenous Homo species – Homo passiens.*

2. *We demand full recognition of the passienic sciences in all institutions of academia, universities, colleges and schools.*

3. *We call upon the people to support our demand for a recognition of neoteny and bipedal and opposable-thumb game-playing in human culture.*

4. *We call on all governments and national institutions to recognise the role of super-REM lucid wake-dream induction expressed in all bipedal and opposed-thumb sports, in all ball-playing sports, and in all of the arts associated with human neoteny.*

5. *We insist that bipedal and neotenous football playing and fan practice are the keys to human culture, not exclusively so, rather foundational and integral and articulated by Huizinga.*

6. *We have no fundamental argument with Homo sapiens, we simply stand for full recognition of Homo passiens as generative and nominal.*

7. *We salute André Breton and the surrealist artists who proclaimed a return to dream re-enactment and culture, and who said, "surrealism is based on the belief in the superior reality of previously neglected associations, in the omnipotence of dream, in the disinterested play of thought. It tends to ruin, once and for all, all the other psychic*

mechanisms and to substitute itself for them in solving all the problems of life".

8. *We salute William Wordsworth who wrote the neotenous, visionary and beautiful legend "the child is father to the man".*

9. *We demand full integration of faculties of passienic sciences, art and culture in all institutions of higher learning.*

10. *We agree with Albert Camus and his absurdist philosophy of football and who said "All that I know most surely about morality and obligations, I owe to football."*

11. *We agree with Albert Camus who said of goalkeepers, "I like people who dream and talk interminably to themselves; I like them, for they are double. They are here and elsewhere."*

12. *We agree with Albert Einstein who said, "At least once a day, allow yourself the freedom to think and dream for yourself."*

13. *We demand that bipedal and opposable-thumb neotenous football, representing 3.5 billion fans worldwide, most of them not affluent, is awarded an International Football Parliament, a seat on the Economic and Social Council of the United Nations, and representation with the United Nations Educational, Scientific and Cultural Organisation (UNESCO).*

14. *We demand funding for the International Football Parliament of $100 billion annually, incorporating FIFA and its budgets.*

15. *We propose a Magna Carta for Football, based on the model and principles of the Supporters Direct Europe.*

16. *We demand increased percentage ownership by fans to 51% of any club, building on local and national inclusion.*

17. *We demand good governance among supporters, trusts and groups and other stakeholders to promote democratic ownership structures in football.*

18. *We demand recognition and promotion of social value in football through improved economic transparency, supporter involvement and community ownership.*

19. *We demand that the great media companies and sponsor corporations who make untold profits from football return 50% of all profits to the game and its supporters.*

20. *We demand an immediate reduction of entrance fees by 50% at the gate.*

In the late 1940s, Paris was occupied by the Nazis and the surrealist artists were considered to be "degenerate". When they were holed up in a mansion in Marseille, planning their escape, they were befriended by Jean Francois Cantona, who played football for Olympique de Marseille FC before beoming a piscatorial surreal artist. He formed the Surrealist and Absurdist FC Along with Andre Breton. Breton explored the relationship between dreams, lucidity and neoteny and developed the famous "Manifesto of Surrealism", adapted as shown here for the beautiful game.

The artists also re-fashioned the standard deck of playing cards discarding the royalty cards, and creating suits of Locks for knowledge, Wheels for revolution, Stars for dreams and Flames for love and desire. This famous pack of cards is known as "le Jeu de Marseille".

Gordon: That really depends on the variety of header you mean, Mike, but if you mean an all-round heading genius then there is only one winner. We have to consider Eusebio, Luis Garcia, Robin van Persie, Willie Bauld of Hearts, and Pele, but *my* winner is Lawrie Reilly of Hibernian. He was most famous for his power headers from a horizontal diving position, but because he was so successful at this the media downgraded his heading abilities in general. I'm sure he had some extra plasticity or flexibility in his spinal column. Some kind of ability to realign his neck and skull bones. Some kind of unique and radical skeletal adjustment facility linking his body alignment to his cranium … and with some dome flexibility allowing him to readjust his cranial angles according to the trajectory of the ball, no matter from what angle or position or with what force or velocity it came. With Lawrie Reilly there was no quantum uncertainty principle; when he connected with the ball, a goal was scored. The connection between his cranium and Gordon Smith's right foot was beauteous, mysterious and ethereal!

Mike: Lucid. Can you describe that to me?

Gordon made a fist of his left hand and opening his right hand, palm upwards with fingers drawn together to represent the Smith's right foot, described the arc of a beautiful right cross from the byeline being met by Reilly's brow, low inside the penalty box; and then with his right hand as a fist, met the left fist of Reilly's head, and completed the poetic and sensorimotor moment and trajectory with his right fist, expressing the explosive journey of the ball into the net. He sighed deeply with aesthetic satisfaction at the thought and continued slowly, slowly, with a kind of ecstatic reverence …

Gordon: I say this as a materialist and a scientist; I say this as an implacable opponent of all attempts to undermine a rigorous evidential approach to science and life; and yet, and yet, in spite of this, I say that the relationship between the right foot of Gordon Smith and the brow and left-angled cranium of Lawrie Reilly was one that defies description – a world-line that defies reduction, a continuum that defies discontinuity. It was beyond the transient, the contingent, the relative, and the moment. This was an absolute and numinous relationship—

Mike: You mean of the neotenous bipedal head and the bipedal foot?

Gordon stopped talking, dropped his head and slowly raised it up, up, up and back, until the spoken words were scarcely audible.

Gordon: Yes. This was a relationship, a continuum, which was mystical, beatific and ultimately truly transcendental: two bipedal football brains, one beautifully angled and articulated cranium, and one perfect, poetic and numinous right foot.

He lowered his head and huge tears flopped onto the wood of the table before us and, finding the grain, spread slowly outwards. He was neotenously happy.

Mike: Um, speaking of craniums, Gordon, I understand that there was a School of Passienic Phrenology formed in Edinburgh in the first half of the nineteenth century. Is that right?

Gordon: There was, Mike. It was much influenced by the Edinburgh Phrenological Society.

Mike: Is it reasonable to suggest that Passienic phrenology – the study of Passienic structures in the *Homo* brain, that correlate to football play and lucidic REM wake-dream expression – might draw on the history of phrenology fruitfully?

Gordon: Naturally, Mike. Why not? The human brain is not a *homo*geneous intellectual organ of consciousness, of unstructured universal energy processing without difference, and positing unvarying sameness.

Mike: Well, okay. Darwin himself stated that the mind is formed and altered by use. Was he very much influenced by phrenology and the manipulation of practice?

Gordon: He certainly was! And he stated in 1838: "One is tempted to believe the phrenologists are right about habitual exercise of the mind altering form of head and thus these qualities become hereditary".

Mike: Suggestions of hereditary memes and Lamarck here?

Gordon: Exactly. We now know that the human brain is modular, and that it is also plastic, so the notion of modular divisions of labour in the brain, altered by practice, was valid then and still is now. Darwin was correct about that and, therefore, the shape of the human head – its cranial formation – cannot *not* be influenced by the practice of thinking and consciousness.

Mike: If consciousness influences neural and cerebral structure, as it does, then it must by necessity alter the form of the brain and therefore its relation to its protective skeletal formation – although not in the way the phrenologists, and Darwin, assumed?

Gordon: Quite so, Mike. Saying that, though, neurology is now correlating human behaviour to precise areas of the brain, such as criminality. (A very dangerous direction of travel, if you ask me.)

Mike: Yes. Imagine being told "We just need to do a brain scan and then we will know if you're going to rob a bank". Nuts! Of course, we know that when one area of the brain is injured or damaged that another may replace it and even recover the original function; that suggests that the brain is modular, but not exclusively so?

Gordon: Yes, as in engineering, when a water tank is transmuted into an armoured vehicle.

Mike: Can you tell me what the history of Passienic phrenology is prior to your own theory and perspectives?

Gordon: It won't surprise you to hear it began right here, in Edinburgh. Edinburgh was once the leading European centre for the study of phrenology – a world leader in the science.

Mike: I didn't know that. Of course, it was correctly termed a *pseudo*science, with respect to the variations of the skull surfaces, but it did correctly posit the notion of variation of units of cerebral function. Who was involved?

Gordon: The first British society was The Edinburgh Phrenological Society, founded in Edinburgh in 1820 by a physician called Andrew Combe, and his brother George – a lawyer. It was housed in Chambers Street and its members often met with the members of the Scarlett Society in the Homo Ludens Bar. Leading members included Robert Chambers, who wrote *Vestiges of the Natural History of Creation* (a Darwinian-type view of natural history), one William A. F. Browne, a leading pioneer in mental health therapy and the Commissioner in Lunacy for Scotland (he pioneered art and occupational therapy for patients), and William Ballantyne Hodgson, who was an economist and educational reformer. There were more members: John Pringle Nichol, Scottish educator, economist and astronomer; Hewett Cottrell Watson, a botanist and evolutionary theorist; Alexander Dunedin, a pioneer of the Ragged Schools Movement and founder of the Ragged University, which provided free educational support to university level and encouraged the spread of innovative ideas both within and outwith formal institutions of learning. I think that's all. I believe this Dunedin fellow was a great friend of Darwin. They were both students here in Edinburgh, you know. And Darwin was much influenced by phrenology, before it fell into disrepute. Funny how it is undergoing something of a modest revival in modern theories of neurology. The idea of Franz Joseph Gall's – that neural functions such as thought and emotions may be located in specific regions of the brain – is essentially correct.

Mike: Although not expressed by variations on the surface of the skull?

Gordon: As in phrenology. Correct.

Mike: Did Gall, the founder of the science, visit Edinburgh and meet with the Scottish advocates of his theory?

Gordon: No, he did not. But his secretary and assistant, Johann Gaspar Spurzheim, did. It was Spurzheim who introduced the Combe brothers to the theory.

Mike: Was there any link to the Plinian Society at Edinburgh University where Darwin announced his first scientific discoveries?

Gordon: Certainly there was. Edinburgh was quite a small city back then, and the members and officers of the Phrenological Society would definitely have known and met socially with members of the Edinburgh Plinian Society; their offices were but a few yards distance from one another. As a matter of fact, members of the Plinian Society often met with the phrenology advocates and members of the Scarlett Society here, in the Ludens.

Mike: Is the Edinburgh Phrenological Society still in existence?

Gordon: No. It was finally disbanded in 1880, although the building that housed its office and museum of phrenology still remains – in Chambers Street, opposite the National Museum of Scotland. It is now the Crown Office of Scotland. Some of the original artefacts are kept in the University of Edinburgh's Anatomy Museum. That's on Bristow Street.

Mike: And the connection to Passienic phrenology?

Gordon: Oh, yes. Of course. One of the original members of the Edinburgh Phrenological Society was Dunedin, the founder of the Ragged University. Also a Director of Hibernian FC. He adopted a theory of evolution not so far removed from Darwin's: it was he that noticed that walking is actually kicking. He wrote that book – something about kicking and the playful history of humanity. He believed that walking was the origin of our success as a species – rather than our intellectual prowess. It was published by the *Edinburgh Review*, a publication that was unfriendly about the evolutionary ideas circling around Edinburgh at the time. It wasn't a fully developed theory of *H. passiens*, but it was

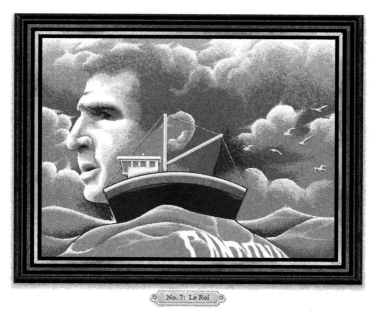

No. 7: Le Roi

"Le Poisson et la Beauté du Football" by Jean Francois Cantona, the "Piscatorial Surrealist". Reproduced with permission from the Museum of Modern Art in Edinburgh.

> *A footballer from Marseille name Eric*
> *Told a tale both surreal and epic:*
> *Seagulls follow the trawler for sardines*
> *As strikers net goals for their teams!*

certainly a visionary outlook. I'm convinced that Huizinga – the chap who wrote *Ludens* – read what he wrote and was influenced by it. It was written in Dutch in the 1890s – I've viewed a copy myself in the Leiden University Library. As it happens, Huizinga was a keen fan of football; seen regularly at AFC Ajax matches in Amsterdam, along with his great friend, the surrealist and piscatorial artist Jean Francois Cantona.

Mike: But what happened to the Passienic phrenologists?

Gordon: The same fate as the Edinburgh Society. Their documents and artefacts were housed in the Museum of Phrenology in Chambers Street, and later removed, in 1880 as I recall, to the Anatomy Museum at Edinburgh University.

Mike: Was Huizinga interested in the dream-game?

Gordon: He did not refer to it directly in relation to football. He did say "dreams are more important than census and tax figures" though. That was quoted in a paper delivered to the Johan Huizinga Conference in Groningen in 2014.

Mike: And that connects him to the surrealists.

Gordon: Yes! Very much so. He is known to have been a close friend of the French surrealist artist, Jean Francois Cantona, who came from Marseille, and who knew Breton, Dali, Man Ray, Duchamp and the Romanian surrealist painter, Jacques Hérold. Jean Francois Cantona is known as the "Piscatorial Surrealist" because he only ever painted and sculpted fish. As a matter of fact, one of his most famous paintings hangs in the Museum of Modern Art here in Edinburgh, at Belford Road.

Mike: Did he play football?

Gordon: Yes he did. He was outstanding in his youth. He played professionally, just briefly, for Olympic de Marseille football club before he became an artist, stating that "two-footed football may never approach the beauty of fish, which can translocate without two legs, and without even one leg". He believed that the *Homo* species was originally a marine species, and would eventually digest their legs, and return to the oceans, whence they came.

Mike: That's really fascinating, especially because it came so long before Elaine Mitchell and her Aquatic Ape Theory. Was he related to our famous surrealist footballer Eric Cantona?

Gordon: I believe Jean Francois claimed to be his great uncle … and we know that he taught the young Eric to fish in the famous Canal de Marseille, and to play football of such surreal and absurd beauty that late in life the old surrealist artist was heard to mutter under his breath that he may have "made an error in career choice, and I also could have played beautifully for Manchester United".

Mike: Did he meet Alex Ferguson?

Gordon: Who? Jean Francois? He did, he did. And there is evidence that he was directly responsible for the surreal REM dream-time phenomenon known as Fergi-Time Dilation – we must talk more about that another day.

Mike: Plasticity of time is consistent not only with Einstein's theory of relativity, but also with super-lucid wake-REM dream physiology – and consequently with surrealism.

Gordon: Yes, it surely is.

Mike: Brilliant. I must make a trip out to Belford Road and view Jean Francois Cantona's fish painting. What is the title?

Gordon: *Le Poisson et la Beauté du Football.*

Mike: Cool! See you next week.

CHAPTER 5

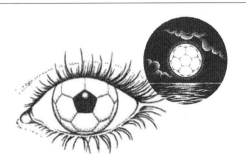

Transliminality and Super-Lucid Football Neotenous Dreams

I met the Professor in the Football Lucidity Bar in Drury Street, Glasgow (also known as The Horse Shoe Bar) on a particularly rain-soaked day in the middle of April.

The Football Lucidity Bar is an ancient hostelry dating from the sixteenth century. It developed from its earlier functional building, in the nineteenth century, into one of the most popular, decorative and iconic bars in Scotland. Its lobbies boast decorative timber and etched glass doors. Its ceiling is compartmented with beautifully moulded cornices and timber-boarded panelling with carved decorated frieze and inset panels. Its rear wall is decorated with mirrors; the timber chimney-pieces with carved detail, horseshoe-shaped openings, pedimented overmantle openings and horseshoe-shaped overmantles. The bar is widely believed to be the most elegant in Scotland with its horseshoe-island shape (and further lobes added at the rear): the superstructure on slender turned columns; etched glass partitions; an island gantry with spirit casks, turned columns and deep cornice, and cast-iron columns up to the ceiling with horseshoe detail to capital.

Famous visitors (according to locals) include the writer Alasdair Gray, the comic Billy Connolly, notable designers Alexander 'Greek' Thomson and Charles Rennie Mackintosh, the tea-man Sir Thomas Lipton, and the Scottish Einstein, James Clerk Maxwell, who always paid a visit on his annual holiday to Scotland. Jock Stein and Sir Alex Ferguson are said to have shared drinks in this tavern. Famous football visitors include the Real Madrid side of 1960, and included Ferenc Puskas and Alfredo Di Stéfano. The great R.D. Laing was also said to be a regular visitor to the Football Lucidity Bar, where he engaged in many heated discussions about the divided psyche of goalkeepers; in fact, the Professor became embroiled in major discussions with him on super-lucid REM wake-dream physiology and psychology, because it is a fruitful area for learning about the split psyche of goalkeepers and Scots.

I asked the Professor about his seminal work on lucidity in the exploration of the dream-game and its role in emotional homeostasis and cognition.

Mike: Is there a role, Gordon, for transliminality in the elaboration of the unconscious and conscious lucid super-REM dream narrative during football for both fans and players?

Gordon: I'm sorry, Mike, I've already had a pint while I was waiting for you and I'm not following you too well. If I understand you correctly, then yes, there certainly is a role, and football – above all – is the perfect discipline for exploring the neural and cognitive pathways that correlate with such altered states and their interface fluid interactions. Michael Thalbourne at the University of Adelaide has shown us that transliminality is the state of hypersensitivity to psychological material of imagery, ideation, affect and perception; he says it involves both unconscious and conscious activation, along with tendencies in the direction of mystical and creative expressions, and correlates with several types of dream experience.

Mike: Cool. The correlation for neoteny, for *Homo passiens* philosophy and psychology?

Gordon: Yes – the super-lucid wake-REM dream state.

Mike: And what is the cerebral key?

Gordon: Narcolepsy.

Mike: How so?

Gordon: The keyword is *fantasy*, or lucid fantasy, because each fan enters a fantastical state – transcendental, if you like – that also represents a lucid dream-wake state. It isn't far removed from a kind of intuitive form of narcolepsy. Actually, better to call it neo-narcolepsy. We know this because narcolepsy is positively associated with lucid dreams, and people with narcolepsy are usually unable to elaborate their orexin hormones (also known as the hypocretins) which are known to be associated with dream mentation and with emotional hedonic and homeostatic state activation. They're expressed both in fans and football players.

Mike: Narcolepsy is known to be expressed when these hormones cannot be synthesised, then. And in *passiens* physiology there is invariably a low level of expression of these hormones.

Gordon: Quite correct. I describe this as passienic neo-narcolepsy. I've written a book about it where I elaborate on it. It's called *Neo-Narcolepsy and REM Lucid Dream Psychology during Neoteny and Football*. It'll be published by Jim Baxter Lucidity Publications in Hill of Beath over in Fife. Should be out in autumn next year.

Mike: Such as during football games when creative play reaches a level of transcendent metabolic physiology of such beauty and meta-physiology that a type of super-REM wake mentation is activated, and a lucid dreaming cascade is found via neuroimaging in several cognitive brain areas that are not usually activated during normal REM sleep.

Gordon: Quite.

Mike: And this has been confirmed in neuroimaging studies?

Gordon: Oh yes. In several passienic universities around the world. There was an iconic study by the Cristiano Ronaldo Neoteny Psychology Institutet the University of Lisbon in Portugal.

Mike: Are you suggesting that the three primary states of being in humans – wakefulness, non-rapid eye movement sleep (nREM), and rapid eye movement (REM)sleep – should be expanded to four? To include what you describe as super-REM wake lucid dream psychology? To explain what happens during football play and observation?

Gordon: Yes I am suggesting that. Unless we grasp the *absolute* uniqueness of football viewing and playing for human individual and social recovery – psychologically, physiologically *and* metabolically – and of the dream-game for emotional homeostasis, cognition and survival, then we can never understand what it is to be *Homo passiens* … or indeed *Homo sapiens.*

Mike: And neo-narcoleptic super-lucid REM wake-dream activation is the key area we should address?

Gordon: Yes. Its specialised form of super-lucid REM wake physiology is found in football, above all – but it is also found during all adaptive ball games – such as American football, baseball, basketball. Rugby! Other ball games are not exempt, they are simply more weakly expressed. Each game-adaptive subspecies' ball-playing is always derived from bipedal and/or opposed-thumb locomotive play, as expressed most perfectly in football.

Mike: We begin with transliminality?

Gordon: We have to. States of being are categorised by scientific enquiry, so that we can begin to understand what role they play in survival. This is via pathways such as locomotion, consciousness, cognition, sleep and play. Dream problem-solving is a vital pathway for resolving complex difficulties that may be unresolved from earlier play physiology; each new game provides a special opportunity for both individual and collective conscious as well as unconscious Jungian and fruitful interactive transliminality.

Mike: Football fans are spectacularly accomplished in super-lucid REM wake-dream psychology, physiology and metabolism – indeed all sport fans are skilled in this ancient and deep science and art! Football fans have the edge, though, simply because bipedal neoteny is the founding expression of all that makes humans human – *Homo passiens*?

Gordon: Yes, you see it. Lucid dream consciousness embodies both wakefulness and higher cognitive REM lucidity, a specialised form of emotional homeostatic learning. It may access wake- and dream-state physiology and psychology, transliminal transitions and time oscillations – from one to the other and back.

Mike: The *sapiens* mind-set are somewhat surprised that lucid dream fans are able to recall their dream states, but any fan of the dream-game would ridicule their surprise. Elderly football fans may recall game dream states from many decades before, if the game – the dream-play – was of particular lucidic and neotenous brilliance. We know that in Scotland some of those who were present as youngsters at the iconic European Final involving Real Madrid and Frankfurt Eintracht in 1960 – and I am one of them – can remember not only who the individual players were, but *every* goal and *every* beautiful pass, dribble, cross, tackle and save. And that was at a time of their lives when it is difficult for them to recall what they had for breakfast or lunch.

Gordon: Mike, that is the power of lucid REM wake-dream recall psychology in great neotenous game-playing. Not only is it remembered, but it is crystallised unconsciously *and* consciously *and* collectively. If the game is historic or of lucid brilliance, it remains cognitively available for the lifetime of the subject – whether player or fan.

Mike: May the lucidic memory cross into the next generation via epigenetic meme transmigration?

Gordon: Hey, Mike, that is a brilliant and radical idea! As it happens, a great team at the Lothar Matthaus Epigenetic Meme Neoteny University at Erlangen in Bavaria are currently following up this lovely notion.

Mike: Well, what do you know. So, our metacognitive recall is enhanced if experienced during a lucid event, and rendered available during later waking events. Or in the words of LaBerge and DeGracia – two leading world researchers into lucid dreaming – "there is a relative continuity of consciously accessible memory linking lucid dreams and waking experience".

Gordon: Exactly, Mike. LaBerge and DeGracia are *sapiens* researchers but they have penetrated deeper into lucid dream states than others have done. Their work is elegant and lucidic, and although they miss the metacognitive gain of neoteny – and lucid game psychology – they must be congratulated for their contribution to the field of REM dream study in football, since taken up by several passienic faculties and universities … and of course expressed in other derivative ball-game neotenous sports.

Mike: And the lucid dream context for the fan is the game? As it is also for the player?

Gordon: Yes. For both fans *and* players the situational stable context for lucid dream elaboration is the game, both for the collective experience *and* for the individual participant. It is a learning and metacognitive event, and it's correlated to waking learning – so it is no different from learning to play, to drive, to count, to speak or to emote. Or any other waking event.

Mike: They – the fans and players – they develop lucid expertise both individually and collectively.

Gordon: Of course! A fan – *every* fan – has to learn about super-lucid wake cognitive expression. They remember many decades later their neotenous dream events of high lucidity, not just late in life, but – as studies now demonstrate – elevated neotenous lucidity may be recalled during episodes of dementia.

Mike: States of metacognitive knowing – I am dreaming this event, but I'm also aware of the context, of the lucid event as it unfolds … They remember both? Lucid dream and context? Knowing and dreaming.

Gordon: Yes they do.

Mike: And this allows for knowledge of the other life, retained in the lucid state – the parallel life – whatever stressful and tiring waking life that is left behind at the moment of entering the stadium, and emerging into its specialised interior space – the anticipation and view of the venerable and revered historic cloister, its lovely tiers of seats and their colours, proclaiming the stadium and team name, the luscious green turf, the formal and geometric white lines marking the field and areas of play, the goals and nets, ground staff meticulously checking the lines, nets and posts, the gathering crowd, the lights of an evening game, the clear dark sky and stars above, the spreading ancient planet beyond the lights, separate but somehow also connected to the unfolding lucid dream, the rolling murmur of conversations, greetings, discussions, arguments – some groups breaking into hymning loved club songs and chants – the opposition fans and their songs, catcalls and colours, the aromas from the food booths, blistering hot pies, coffees, frying hamburgers, hotdogs, onions, chips, the club colours on scarves, shirts, banners, pennants, flags, the shamanic and totemic team mascots around the stadium, the electric aura of the media centre, the gathering wheel chairs and their joyous and happy cargo, and then club official anthems over the sound system, announcements of coming games, events, raffles for charity, someone being asked to report to officials for a special reason ... And *then* the transcendent glorious moment of appearance of the team and players, fireworks, substitutes, coaches, and officials onto the verdant turf, the line-up, introductions and handshakes, the coin toss and captain exchanges of honours, the players organised into positions, goalkeeper, centre halves, wing backs, midfield, forwards, strikers, referee, linesmen, and the shrill whistle signal to herald the kick off. The stadium and its people, immersed in their dream state, now raising a storm of individual, collective and rising super-metacognitive REM dream lucidity such that no outside life waking experience may ever reach; the world outside the dream state, outside the dream-brane, the world beyond is non-lucid, non-REM dream or waking state, of loss, stress, depression and sadness ... and meanwhile inside the stadia, inside the dream-brane, the shutters, the barriers to super-lucid REM wake-dreams are removed, ripped, dragged and torn down, and lucidity potential unfolds.

Gordon: Thank you, Mike. That was quite well articulated. Truly, no other neotenous event in culture, no great work of art, music, symphony, concerto, painting, sculpture, theatre, drama, dance, opera, work of architecture, or photograph may come anywhere near the collective neoteny and dream-storm and poetry of bipedal football in this respect.

Mike: I assume that this neo-narcoleptic super-lucid REM wake-dream state is asomnic?

Gordon: Most certainly. Asomnic super-REM dream state is inversely proportional to atonic muscle inhibition. Atonic muscle inhibition is inhibited – and somnia is also inhibited. It's a double-negative correlation facilitating bipedal neotenous football play and fan activation.

Mike: Is this in any way related to the observation that narcoleptics enter sleep during daylight hours, but are unable to activate sleep during the dark phase of the twenty-four-hour cycle of night and day?

Gordon: It is, Mike, which is why I characterise super-lucid REM wake-dream psychology and physiology as neo-narcoleptic.

Mike: Let me get this clear. Neo-narcolepsy provides us with a model for the activation of super-REM wake lucid dream expression by fans and players during bipedal and neotenous football, *because* narcolepsy also inhibits nocturnal sleep, or should I say somnia?

Gordon: Yes.

Mike: And narcolepsy is also associated with suppression of muscle inhibition during lucid dreams. In other words, the person can activate muscles when normally, during a narcoleptic state, he or she is paralysed with respect to muscle activation?

Gordon: That's the great and hidden secret of super-lucid REM wake-dream physiology. Without this double negation of sleep

101

and muscle paralysis, game-playing neoteny would be impossible. It is known exclusively only to *Homo passiens* researchers, to football fans and to football players.

Mike: And not to *Homo* science? The bipedal expression of our evolutionary locomotive and neotenous *Homo* passienic species – it also applies to those viewing on television or listening via a radio link.

Gordon: Yes. The lucidity is modulated though. It is usually less potently expressed outside the dream-brain, but nonetheless it manifests. Furthermore, the distance from the live event may introduce elements of non-REM atonicity, and non-lucidity.

Mike: I think I get this now. Non-lucidity is a modified – or weaker version – of lucidity during the dream-game, and non-lucidity can dilute lucidity when the play is not present to the perceptual consciousness or unconsciousness of the fan.

Gordon: Yes, that's about it. Fan and player immersed in the perceptual flow of the game. The TV fan somewhat less so. And the radio listener, slightly less again.

Mike: The super-lucidity is not negated, simply diluted.

Gordon: Exactly. The game narrative and unfolding are available to every fan. That's why a fan viewing or reading about the game many days, weeks or even years afterwards can access dream-state super-REM wake lucidity – even though it is diluted.

Mike: Is it possible that the REM lucid dream state is metacognitive, in the sense that the conscious element – as opposed to unconscious – is of a higher plane, or a higher proportion or specific weight, than during non-lucid REM state? Or indeed the wake state?

Gordon: That was beautifully questioned, Mike. Lucid dream metacognition during neoteny is one of the highest learning experiences known to *Homo* species – and *passiens*. Why else do newly born infants devote most of their sleep time to REM sleep cognitive acquisition.

Mike: Neoteny and delayed/extended childhood are the foundations of what *Homo* assume to be higher human intelligence, but actually they are a function of *retardation* – the slowing of some functions, the human brain, and the acceleration of others, such as long legs, opposable thumbs. This is completed long before the brain is fully functional after two, perhaps three, decades from birth, but it's formed in the school of neoteny, expressing two essences of bipedal *Homo* passienic development.

Gordon: Yes, Mike – right again.

Mike: Can the increased consciousness that correlates with bipedal neoteny and REM dream lucidity be interpreted as primordial? In other words, does dream- and lucidic-gameplay-generated self-reflection underpin the metacognitive expression of conscious intentions?

Gordon: That makes sense, Mike.

Mike: And that the increased conscious awareness of metacognitive neoteny and homeostatic gratification (resolution) in game-play, and therefore in football, is one of the key motivating factors for attracting billions of fans worldwide to football every week?

Gordon: Correct.

Mike: And the emotional homeostatic dividend follows?

Gordon: Every time! Win or lose.

Mike: Lucid. You referred to narcolepsy as an agency for such enquiry …

Gordon: Narcolepsy is directly and positively correlated to high levels of lucid dreaming, and lucid dreaming is correlated positively to super-REM lucid asomnia – which is expressed only during football.

Mike: Where are we going with this, Gordon?

Gordon: Okay, Mike. Here is where we are headed. A bunch of clever folks at the Max Planck Institute for Human Cognition and Brain Sciences in Leipzig, Germany, have compared neural correlates of dream lucidity obtained from contrasting lucid versus non-lucid REM sleep. This was in 2012. By neuroimaging.

Mike: And they found?

Gordon: I think I could have told them in advance, but I was still overjoyed when they announced the results. They observed increased activity in the right dorsolateral prefrontal cortex during lucid REM sleep – a brilliant result. The dorsolateral prefrontal cortex is believed to underpin a wide range of higher cognitive capacities.

Mike: Football activation of super-lucid REM wake physiology is, therefore, paradoxically a period expressing the highest activation of cognitive learning and memory consolidation.

Gordon: Why is football the most popular sport worldwide? Why do fans devote large amounts of spare time and resources to football viewing?

Mike: Well, we know why! It makes the fans happy, joyous. They learn. They express their neotenous ontogeny. They enter their dream-game, individually and collectively. They view transcendental forms of human creative, bipedal and heading physiology, unknown outside of the beauty of football. Dream-play and sensorimotor art. And here we are – in touch with our bipedal and bicerebral origins; our bipedal locomotion and jumping; our bipedal consciousness and language. The key to who and what we are, and to how we got here. To how we survive. All gifted to us via bipedal football, on any Saturday of any week, anywhere, worldwide. Is creativity also associated with REM and super-REM sleep?

Gordon: Oh yes, and so much more, Mike. Eighty per cent of a premature infant's sleeping time is taken up by REM sleep. In a sense, newborn infants "dream or create" their cognitive world afresh, drawn from their first contact with the external environment; learning is perhaps the most creative of all human cognitive interactive unfoldings. All learning is ultimately a creative act – neoteny and extended childhood. Not exclusive in humans, but more potently articulated in *Homo passiens* … and also moderately in *Homo sapiens*. And therefore it is a form of dream learning creativity.

Gordon: Otto Lowei – the great German physiologist who received the Nobel Laureate in 1938 for discovering neurotransmission – described the process beautifully. He said:

"The night before Easter Sunday I awoke, turned on the light and jotted a few notes on a tiny slip of paper. Then I fell asleep again. It occurred to me at 6 o'clock in the morning that during the night I had written down something most important, but I was unable to decipher the scrawl. The next night at 3 o'clock, the idea returned. It was the design of an experiment to determine whether or not the hypothesis of chemical transmission that I had uttered seventeen years ago was correct. I got up immediately, went to the laboratory, and performed a single experiment on a frog's heart according to the nocturnal design."

Mike: Do you believe, Gordon, that lucid super-dream-REM sleep or the neo-narcoleptic dream-game activated during football – in both fans and players – is an iconic example of waking lucid dream REM creativity and learning? And that football fans around the globe are consciously or unconsciously promoting this?

Gordon: Yes. Spot on. Consciously and unconsciously. Individually and collectively.

Mike: What of atonia? It's well documented during REM sleep, when there is muscle inaction due to the suppression of several neurotransmitters, resulting in inhibition of motor neurons, so that the person may not act out their dream state. This seems a super-paradoxical effect of REM mentation – itself a paradox. Fans and players are clearly not in a state of muscle atonia?

Gordon: Well observed, Mike. REM sleep is paradoxical sleep, and super-lucid REM sleep is equally paradoxical with respect to its specialised twin – a double paradoxical, wakeful, transcendent and numinous expression of *Homo passiens*, during football play and observation. Muscle inhibition of REM sleep has been itself inhibited by super-lucid wake-REM dream physiology and psychology.

Mike: Okay, I think I get this. REM sleep activates muscle atonia to protect dream acts during the nocturnal and dark phase of the circadian cycle, allowing for partition of energy in favour of neurogenesis and learning. It would also avoid locomotion that would expose the subjects to dangers of predation or nocturnal accidents.

Gordon: Definitely. Inhibition of muscle atonia during REM sleep is only weakly and rarely expressed in *Homo sapiens*, but actively expressed in *Homo passiens* fans – even more potently expressed in *Homo passiens* football players.

Mike: Super-REM sleep and its lucid neo-narcoleptic dream state inhibits this inhibition, during football – a controlled, rule-driven and socially positive play enactment that underpins all human play and culture, perhaps the highest expression of our primordial and essential creative foundational unfolding bipedal selves. We are a bipedal super-lucid dream species?

Gordon: Yes. We know that football activates and promotes melatonin. This hormone is described by some sport physiologists as an antioxidant strategy during physical locomotion.

Mike: You clearly don't agree.

Gordon: No way. So, it is released during football and other forms of physical locomotion, contingent upon football, but actually it is not melatonin itself that is the key modulating influence. Oh no. It is the tryptamine cascade from the *passiens* cortex.

Artist's impression of early football playing by Passeolithic Man in the stone circle of Brodgar on the island of Orkney. Training and accommodation facilities both for home and visiting players and fans were found elsewhere at the Ness.

Mike: Within the brain's pineal gland?

Gordon: Yes. And here we begin to interrogate the real role of this complex and vital gland.

Mike: Does the pineal provide some of the critical functions and challenges of the relationship between sleep and physical locomotion, football as in transliminality?

Gordon: It does, Mike. Sleep and physical locomotion are not separate, mutually exclusive states of being, though they may be described as two sides of the same bipedal coin.

Narcolepsy is key to understanding about this. The hormones for locomotion – for hunger-driven food seeking – are the orexins, released in the suprachiasmatic nucleus, and yet when they are missing in people, for genetic or other reasons, they are constantly influenced by an impulse to sleep. The dichotomy influencing sleep or locomotion, is controlled by the same hormones in the same cells.

Mike: Okay. Football locomotion hides sleep as an underpinning and necessary function. And vice versa.

Gordon: Precisely. Football, especially physiological and metabolic dynamics, embodies this dichotomy in the elaboration of the very high energy state of neo-narcoleptic lucid super-REM wake-dream state – the greatest period of energy consumption by any brain recorded in nature.

Mike: The dream-game is energetically expensive?

Gordon: Melatonin – the hormone associated with football-generated super-REM sleep – is associated with a high-energy status of the brain. And with this, a high-energy status of the liver – the only cerebral energy reserve available to the brain during both sleep and physical exercise.

Mike: This may explain the nature of dream-game feasting prior to, during and afterwards! The North Americans have made this into a modern ritual during which more food is consumed per person than on any other ritual day or feast festival.

Gordon: Yes. Quite. We know from ancient archaeological finds associated with early *Homo passiens*, that ritual feasting is directly correlated to game-play. Check out the recent discovery of the so-called Neolithic Cathedral at the Ness of Brodgar in Orkney. My own observations and analysis confirm that if this *is* a cathedral, it is a *football* cathedral – an indoor stadium and complex of training facilities and accommodation structures, both for home and visiting players and fans. As is invariably the case, archaeologists, anthropology experts, and other evolutionary disciplines date the finds and other artefacts to the recent Neolithic, but – as is usually the more correct approach – they should multiply the timeline by a factor of ten, putting it into the Passeolithic.

Mike: In other words, the Long Neolithic. Archaeology and all evolutionary science have contracted the Neolithic era. It's a form of anthropological time contraction and contemporary arrogance, isn't it?

Gordon: Yes. You're right again. The Passeolithic dates from 2.5 million years ago to 100,000 years ago. Several significant finds at Brodgar should be noted – the colouring of buildings and other structures with iron ore, animal fats, milk and eggs – all point to the early introduction of team colours. Ritual feasting associated with bipedal football gaming is common in these finds; animal bones and other food remnants are universal.

Mike: Any other significant neoteny artefacts?

Gordon: A beautifully formed clay artefact, known as Brodgar Boy, was unearthed in 2011. It's clearly a sculptured depiction of a young footballer. And close by was a carved stone ball – a petrosphere or as we "in the know" know – a fitba'sphere. They're common in that area of Northern Scotland and have been closely identified by passienic archaeologists from the Faculty of Passienic Archaeology at the Passienic University of the Orkney and Shetland Isles as positive evidence of football and bipedal neoteny artistic articulation.

Mike: Like other carved stone balls and ritual artefacts around the world?

Gordon: Yes. Similar stone balls, both spherical and ovoid, have been identified across Europe. And North and South America from the early migration into Europe from Asia. All indicative of bipedal football. There are representations in art, and likewise similar stone and carved ornamental balls across Asia, prior to the migration into the Americas. We may not often encounter the symbol in its original form – the soft animal tissue-derived round ball with animal bladder as the air-blown support – due to oxidation of animal and plant materials from which they were manufactured, but thankfully we do have access to their representations in art.

Mike: Amazing! This is all emerging in a great rush, I suppose, since the birth of passienic art as a major growth point of archaeological and evolutionary science.

Gordon: It is, Mike.

Mike: Old Otte. He couldn't have guessed where his lucid dream articulation would lead.

Gordon: No, he could not.

CHAPTER 6

Football Heroes: The Coal-Miners of West Auckland and Hearts of Midlothian

I met Gordon in McCrae's Battalion Bar in Dalry on a dry, crisp, bright and cold morning in early May.

McCrae's Battalion Bar, named after the famous Battalion that included players from Hearts of Midlothian FC (also known to locals as the Diggers Arms), is a beautiful Art Nouveau bar that serves as the alternative offices of the Guild of Elite Gravediggers and Premium Funeral Directors located nearby in the old village of Tynecastle. According to local historians, this bar also served as a favourite drinking house for Edinburgh's scientific luminaries, such as Max Born, Peter Higgs and Ian Wilmut.

Max Born emigrated to the UK after Hitler came to power. He was a pioneer in the origins of quantum mechanics and Tait Professor of Natural Philosophy at Edinburgh University. Peter Ware Higgs was the theoretical physicist who predicted the existence of the boson particle, the first known scalar particle, the existence of which was finally confirmed at CERN on 14 March 2013. The Higgs Mechanism is accepted as an important ingredient in the Standard Model of particle physics, without which particles would have no mass. The Higgs boson was for some time viewed as a potential candidate for the dribbling particle in football – the mession – the elusive bioparticle that has puzzled biophysicists and Passienic scientists alike for many years, and which may become the key interface linking the Standard Model to biological tissues – which of course has been studied as the key explanatory influence modulating the attraction of ball and boot in bipedal neotenous football. Recent work at several Passienic universities suggests that this is not the case and the hunt for the mession continues. Sir Ian Wilmut is an embryologist, Chair and Emeritus Professor of the Scottish Centre for Regenerative Medicine at the University of Edinburgh, and is famous (along with his close colleague Keith Campbell) for having been the first scientist to clone an animal from a somatic cell. The animal was a Finnish Dorset lamb named Dolly. Professor Wilmut was granted an OBE in 1999 and knighted in the 2008 New Year Honours.

It is not known if any of these brilliant scientists ever met up in McCrae's Battalion Bar, but what is known is that this pub is now a favourite tourist destination for theoretical physicists, embryologists, particle physicists, biophysicists and messionic researchers from around the world – and football-fan scientists. Football crime detectives, known as referees, are also frequently present and often get involved into heated debates on force field dynamics with both particle physicists and football fans. The discussion, when I arrived that day, was on the question that every football fan spends a significant portion of cerebral energy pondering: What is the greatest World Cup team? Where and when was the greatest final? And who is the greatest player?

Mike: What are your thoughts on this, Gordon?

Gordon: Easy Mike. No need for soul-searching on this one. The greatest World Cup Team was West Auckland Football Club, Durham County, England. The 1909 final was in Turin between West Auckland 2–0 Winterthur. Greatest player – Jock Jones.

Mike: Gordon, I have never heard you utter a single untruth or questionable hypothesis in all our discussions, yet I confess I am profoundly confused on this one. Neither of these teams have I ever heard of. Neither is an international football team. How could they participate in the World Cup?

Gordon: You're wrong, Mike. If you make the trip to County Durham you will be told a very different story in every pub, and most surely a tale that most football fans around the world should be familiar with. But they are not. All the more so if you visit the famous Jock Jones Legs in West Auckland, also known to some locals as the Eden Arms.

Mike: Okay, but I need convincing. This is a very strange tale. Football fans are known to confabulate their lucid REM wake-dream experiences – some of which stretch not only time but also certainty. How may it be verified?

Gordon: Ian Midgely of Newton Aycliffe, County Durham, introduced me to Darren Fairclough of West Auckland, who has researched the story. Ian and Darren articulated the fundamentals of the story over excellent local beer in the Jock Jones Legs.

Mike: Can you elaborate?

Gordon: This story is one of the most interesting in modern football history. West Auckland Football Club represented Great Britain in the inaugural World Cup during the Easter Holiday of 1909, and believe it or not, they won it.

Mike: Where was it held?

Gordon: As I mentioned previously, in Turin, or Torino.

Mike: Who organised it? There was no international football organisation at that time, I assume?

Gordon: Correct, there was not. The competition was organised by British industrialist Sir Thomas Lipton.

Mike: Who participated in it?

Gordon: There were teams representing Italy, England, Switzerland and Germany. That they were club, and not official international teams, was simply because the relevant football associations were too conservative to send national teams. The English FA declined to send a team. Not for the last time were the stuffy football bureaucrats affected by football parochialism. Sir Thomas Lipton was a millionaire Glaswegian working-class lad who had no such reservations, and he organised the tournament.

Mike: All right, but how did West Auckland Football Club come to be involved?

Gordon: Sir Thomas had an employee who was a referee in the Northern League. It seems that he was the conduit and link who arranged for West Auckland Town – as it was then known – to represent Great Britain.

Mike: Excellent! The story begins to appear credible. Do we know the players involved? By name?

Gordon: We certainly do. For the historical record, I learned from Darren that they were mostly coal-miners who had to raise the money to travel, and pawned some of their personal possessions to do so – hence their play and subsequent victory assumes heroic levels of personal and football commitment and attainment.

Mike: Fabulous! The story gets better and better.

Gordon: It does.

Mike: And who was the team on the day?

Gordon: Yes. I am proud to announce Jimmy Dickinson, Rob Gill, Jack Greenwell, Rob Jones, Tom Gill, Charlie "Dirty" Hogg, Ben Whittingham, Douglas Crawford, Bob Guthrie, Alf "Tot" Gubbins, Jock Jones – he's our hero – and David "Ticer" Thomas and Tucker Gill.

Mike: Is there a record of the game and play?

Gordon: There is, Mike. There is a contemporary report in *La Gazzetta dello Sport* by the journalist Gianfranco Buffon, a brilliant sports journalist who won many prizes for his investigations in sport, and who is related to the famous Italian goalkeeper Gianluigi "Gigi" Buffon on his father's side. I translated it from the original Italian.

Mike: Can you elaborate?

Our English friends have taken the noble sport of football to a new level of brilliance. Their defensive and attacking qualities have not been reached in our Italian game – every young football enthusiast in Italy should be told about this new type of football, and a strong and skilled combination of tactics, interplay, team communication, a level of cooperation between back and forward players that could only come from a shared history of work in dangerous conditions. In such an environment the necessity of caring one for the other is essential for successful work and safety – the work skills are translated to the football field, and this in turn is expressed by their speed of play, their strength of opposition against the other team, by their ability to share the play and ball in a dance of quite poetic beauty and elegance.

It would be unjust to mention the names of the individual best players due to their shared unselfish play – they showed a level of team unity not seen in our more haughty and arrogant Italian players, who often keep the ball from their fellow teammates, when it may benefit the team to be less selfish. However I must make mention of Jock Jones who in the eighth minute, having received a clever pass from defensive teammate Charlie "Dirty" Hogg, a forceful and skilful player, ran for many metres around and past several Swiss defenders, and tricked the Swiss goalkeeper into diving in the wrong direction, so that he was enabled to score a truly wonderful goal.

The spectators, although almost exclusively Italian, were ecstatic in their response, and cheered and cheered the player, who modestly acknowledged their enthusiasm. Jones was applauded at the end of the game as the most perfect player on the pitch during the game. The Swiss played a very beautiful game of football, but were unable to match the coal-miners who were stronger and better equipped to withstand the rigours of the game, and displayed a superb level of sportsmanship that is usually associated with the gentleman sports enthusiasts from among the higher echelons of their society.

It seems that in England there is a new breed of sportsmen who come from the working men, and who bring great credit and distinction to their own countrymen. The English Football Association would be well advised to look among these noble sportsmen for new recruits to their football ranks and to learn from their interest in displaying and sharing their superior skills and abilities to other nations that are not part of their Empire. The English are the founding nation of modern football but their officials seem to desire to keep it on home soil. Shame on them, and many happy applauds for the West Auckland miners.

Original arti cle from "La Gazzett a dello Sport" on the inaugural World Cup in 1909, writt en by Gianfranco Buff on.

Gordon: Buffon described the coal-miners in lyrical terms, and their football play as beatific. I promise I will send a copy to you some time.

Mike: I expect they were given a great reception when they arrived home?

Gordon: Hardly. Just family and workmates. However, they returned by invitation in 1911 to defend their title. They beat Red Star of Switzerland 2–0 on the way to the final where they beat the mighty Juventus 6–1 in the final on the seventeenth of April 1911 – another historic and iconic day in the history of modern football. The team on the day was J. Robinson, Tom Wilson, Charlie Cassidy, Andy "Chips" Appelby, Michael Alderson, Bob "Drol" Moore, Fred Dunn, Joe Rewcastle, Bob Jones, Bob Guthrie, Charlie "Dirty" Hogg, T. Riley, and John Warick.

Mike: 6–1. Lucid. And who scored?

Gordon: The scorers were Bob "Drol" Moore – he got two. Fred Dunn got two. Andy Appelby and Joe Rewcastle.

Mike: Fantastic. Did Buffon file a report on this game?

Gordon: No. He was away on another assignment and missed the final. However we do know that the team members were cheered through the streets of Turino, and were treated to a high-class dinner reception at the town hall where they met the mayor. They were persuaded to greet the assembled crowds below from a high balcony, and have the trophy presented by a notable Italian politician. A very different reception to that when they arrived home to only family and fellow workmates – who were of course immensely proud.

Mike: No signs of the national and metropolitan press on that day?

Gordon: No. Although Sir Thomas Lipton had stipulated that if a winning team won the trophy in consecutive tournaments, they would be entitled to keep it. West Auckland had their name etched into the annals of football history as the winners and defenders and holders of the First Football World Cup.

Mike: Cool. Where was it kept?

Gordon: According to Darren they immediately had to find £40 to pay for the trip. Their only asset was the World Cup and they arranged with a Mrs Lanchester, the landlady of the Wheatsheaf Hotel, to provide the £40 and hold the trophy as security until they could find the money. It remained in her possession until 1960, when officials of the club tracked her down in Liverpool and reclaimed the cup for £100. The trophy was then displayed in the Eden Arms public house in West Auckland – which happened to be the home of the Club Secretary, Sydney Douthwaite.

Mike: That's brilliant! Is it still there?

Gordon: No. It remained on display until the new World Cup Jules Rimet Trophy was stolen in 1966. Then Syd Douthwaite, realising that the original trophy was of far greater historical and social significance, locked it away.

Mike: Is that the end of this amazing and quite fabulous story?

Gordon: No. In January 1994 the trophy, which was at the time held in the West Auckland Workingmen's Club, was stolen and was never recovered. It was insured, so a replacement was made by a Sheffield silversmith called Jack Spencer. He was able to make an exact replica from photographs and videos – all sponsored by Liptons – which is now kept in West Auckland Workingmen's Club in a specially constructed secure cabinet for viewing by any visiting football tourists. I understand that they receive thousands of enthusiastic visiting football fans every year, from every continent, who value the story of the First World Cup. If you have a drink in the Bar of West Auckland Workingmen's Club, where visitors are always welcome, you can hear accents from all around the world, and in particular from Italy.

Mike: Just stunning. A team of coal-miners from West Auckland won the first World Cup – you couldn't invent it! So close to the First World War, too. I wonder if any of these heroes signed up for that other field of oppositional endeavour?

Gordon: That I am not sure about, Mike – another football story worthy of investigation. Saying that, I do know about one famous football team that went off to fight in that dreadful conflict – Heart of Midlothian FC.

Mike: Hearts? But they are Hibs' historic rivals, aren't they? And not to be referenced in any honourable football discussion, if possible?

Gordon: But Hearts have a very wonderful history, Mike. They played a highly significant and heroic role in World War One.

Mike: How so?

Gordon: Mike, you surprise me. Have you never looked at the Heart of Midlothian War Memorial at Haymarket?

Mike: No I have not. What is memorialised there? I assumed it was just one of many such memorials?

Gordon: All war memorials have their own special resonance, but the Heart of Midlothian War Memorial has a special historical significance, in that it memorises the personal sacrifice of football players and fans.

Mike: Not sure how I missed this story. Can you elaborate?

Gordon: Sir George McCrae was an Edinburgh businessman and an MP. He was keen to form one of the famous PALS regiments here in Edinburgh. He realised that if he could encourage some Hearts players to join the 16th Battalion of the Royal Scots – Hearts were the leading football club in Scotland at the time and their players were revered by football fans – then he would succeed in forming a Battalion recruited mainly from the many thousands of football fans.

Mike: Was he successful?

Gordon: He most certainly was. He organised a rally at the Usher Hall, and when he paraded the new recruits from among the Hearts players the result was electric. He invited the assembly to follow him to the recruiting office in Castle Street and sign up – there and then. Hundreds did so. More followed from across the city, and he had all the recruits he required to form his battalion – known to this day as McCrae's Battalion.

Mike: They actually participated in the fighting?

Gordon: They did. They entered the action on the first day of the Somme. Indeed, they were one of the most successful units in the British Army on that dreadful day.

Mike: At great cost?

Gordon: Over the period of the war, Hearts sent sixteen members of its first team to fight. Seven died in action. Two succumbed to gassing. Another was crippled and unable to play football on his return. Of course many footballers from around the country volunteered for action in that war, such as Donald Bell of the 9th Yorkshires – the Green Howards – who played for Bradford Park Avenue. He is thought to be the first professional footballer to join up. Others included Walter Tull of Tottenham Hotspur and Northampton Town. Hearts are especially remembered for their collective willingness to form the unique recruiting core that crystallised the formation of the Battalion. Other professional football players – from Raith Rovers, and Falkirk – also fans of Hibs, and a contingent of Manchester Scots, all joined McCrae's famous Battalion.

Mike: I see. Hence the memorial at Haymarket. Are they remembered in France?

Gordon: They certainly are. A memorial cairn has been erected in Contalmaison, the Somme village that McCrae's Battalion liberated.

Mike: Fantastic. Do you know what the dedication is?

Gordon: Mike, you have to read Jack Alexander's wonderful book on the subject – *McCrae's Battalion* – and make the journey to Contalmaison to view the memorial for yourself.

Mike: Okay. I will.

CHAPTER 7

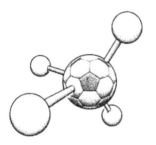

The Hunt for the Mession: Football and Yatagarasuism

I was late meeting the Professor at the Lionel Messi Tavern in Rose Street on a sunny, windy, showery day in June.

The Lionel Messi Tavern was originally known as the Abbotsford Bar, and was a favourite eating and drinking hostel for the famous Scottish historical novelist Sir Walter Scott. Abbotsford, Scott's ancestral home, is located in the borders of Scotland. He is depicted in the bar in a contemporary engraving by Thomas Faed, with his friends from the community of Scottish writers, musicians, poets and artists, including the famous Ettrick Shepherd and James Hogg.

Lionel Messi, of course, is the Argentinian football player who plays for FC Barcelona – his national football team of Argentina – and is capable of mesmerising his opponents with his ball skills. Born in 1987 in the city of Rosario in Santa Fe Province, he joined the local football team, Grandoli, for whom his father, Jorge, coached, at the age of five. Even as a child, his prodigious talent was obvious, and his relatives in the city of Lleida in Catalonia brought this fact to the attention of the director at FC Barcelona. Young Lionel emigrated along with his father to Catalonia, under the care of the Barcelona Club, and enrolled in the great club's famous football Youth Academy. It is very likely that Messi will be rated as the greatest football player of all time if he continues to develop his extraordinary talent beyond its current level (in the twenty-teens), however Cristiano Ronaldo – his nearest opponent in ability – may yet overcome him. The next decade promises to deliver some of football's most historic performances as the two players ply their passienic neotenous bipedal arts around the globe, and the 2018 World Cup may prove decisive in this respect.

This iconic pub has, in recent years, become a favourite haunt of an international group of biophysicists belonging to the Biophysical Society, a scientific discipline whose founding father was Luigi Aloisio Galvani, the Italian physician, biologist and philosopher, who discovered animal electricity, bioelectrical magnetics and the electrical stimulation of the nervous system. Local oral legends and traditions place Galvani in the Abbotsford Bar in the late eighteenth century when he visited Edinburgh, and where he met and discussed matters with key members of the Scottish Enlightenment. More recent visitors to the tavern include Professor Seth Lloyd who has distinguished himself, and his team of colleagues at Massachusetts Institute of Technology, in the field of Biomechanics. Staff claim that Richard Feynman was a regular visitor.

Gordon was nursing a pint of his favourite beer when I arrived and pondering on one of his ideas about how Lionel Messi is capable of mesmerising his opponents with his ball skills. I already knew that he espoused a theory of a new force of nature to explain the unique and quite baffling physical connectivity between foot and ball (for example, when Messi collected the ball around the halfway line and motored at high speed into the opposing half, leaving a trail of puzzled, disoriented defenders in his path), whereby the ball oscillates between, and is indissolubly coupled to, one foot and the other. Many football journalists, and scientists, including Passienic researchers, have tried to analyse this quite amazing connection, but none had come up with a satisfactory explanation. The Prof. told us he had come up with a name for this paradoxical push-and-pull, exotic and foetal force. He christened it the "mession" and followed this up with the hot news about progress with the Passienic Particle Accelerator at CERN in characterising this elusive particle that facilitates binding of ball and foot.

Mike: Do you have any sense of exactly what dove-tailed neotenous foetal force or forces are being activated by Lionel Messi on one of his high-speed weaving runs into the opposing penalty box, Gordon?

Gordon: I do, Mike, and I must say that Messi and a few other great footballers, such as Cristiano Ronaldo, George Best and Paul Gascoigne, are – or were – expressing this fundamental force of nature between foot and ball that has up to now simply been overlooked by the *sapiens* researchers, and indeed by our very own *passiens* scientists. Although, to give our people credit, they have been hunting for a physiological and biophysical explanation.

Mike: What forces are we looking at that may explain this astonishing gain of oscillating and accelerating bipedal and neotenous football function?

Gordon: First of all we must consider gravity. Both the foot and the ball express mass and therefore gravitational forces must play a part, although the graviton has been considered and rejected in several passienic studies. Gravity is vitally important in football play due to its influence on bipedal balance, and the best footballers modulate gravity via their advanced knock-knees – Messi expresses this beautifully, and his maintenance of balance during his mazy runs – under often violent tackles – is almost beyond scientific understanding.

Mike: What about electromagnetism?

Gordon: This type of force unites both magnetism and electricity, and its particle is the photon. Of course these forces must also play a role – all biology must include electromagnetism in energy metabolism – as a modulating influence – but it is highly unlikely that this would have a major influence on bipedal ball control and football-play dynamics.

Mike: Yet some goalkeepers seem to have an electromagnetic force that attracts the ball even when it appears to be on a different path! Could this perhaps be the Weak Nuclear Force?

Gordon: Hmmm. An effective force on all particles and subparticles perhaps, but not a candidate in this field of play – in bipedal neotenous football.

Mike: Then the Strong Nuclear Force?

Gordon: It is a potent force – and an attractive candidate. The activating particulate entity is the gluon, but here again I doubt if it fits the bill as a biological adhesive functional interface between foot and ball. We are seeking a dual-energy force that can both hold the ball, oscillating between two dancing feet, and or drive the football with extreme power in a long crossfield pass, or incendiary shot.

Mike: Any new candidates to the fore?

Gordon: The Higgs field and boson seemed briefly to account for the complex mathematics expressed in mession field dynamics, but have been discounted.

The Ronaldo constellation as viewed in the Northern Hemisphere. This was recently identified and officially recognised by the International Astronomical Union.

Mike: So we, or at least the Passiens university faculties of accelerated particle and force-field theory, are on the hunt for your so-called mession – the football particle that accounts for paradoxical push–pull foot-and-ball energy biomechanics articulated by the bipedal bi-footal geniuses such as George Best, Paul Gascoigne, Ferenc Puskas, Diego Maradona, Cristiano Ronaldo, and of course Lionel Messi?

Gordon: Several bipedal neoteny universities around the world are focusing on the agonistic and antagonist ball-and-foot biomechanical bioforce that facilitates the gain of function that is the driving element of neotenous dribbling football play. It seems that the force that adheres to the ball is the same force that parts with the ball; we have as yet no clear knowledge of what the mession force and particle is, which tends to zero at 100 yards, but we have no difficulty in observing its effects in time and space – the mession bioparticle, in its deepest biophysical essence, is the quintessential goal particle and football field force. Maximum messions appear at the point of connection between ball and foot, and that minimum mession force tends to zero at 100 yards – the length of a football pitch and the maximum distance of function.

Mike: So we are left with a ghost particle and field, but with the poetry of its expression in football neoteny, and football play, as majestically evidenced by Lionel Messi?

Gordon: Yes. We cannot see the wind, but we know when it blows. Similarly, we do not yet see or understand the action of the mession, but we can enjoy its physical expression and dynamics. However, there is good news from CERN, where they are working with the Josef (Sepp) Hugi *Passiens* Particle University of Riehen, and where they believe that they have already viewed evidence of its bio-energetic and bio-informatic after-trail.

Mike: Does the mession adhere to the Standard Model?

Gordon: It seems that this is the case, Mike. In proton collisions at the Large Hadron Collider, the scientists observed massive subatomic particle trails, among which were tiny trace trails of the mession, before it disintegrated into other particulates – furthermore there may be another group of such messionic particles. It seems just a matter of time before other more mession exotics – a whole family of such – are discovered.

Mike: Great football articulates great particle physics and bioenergetics?

Gordon: Yes. Every time.

Mike: Are messions fuzzy in two places at once?

Gordon: Yes. Any defender would agree to that – Messi articulates Heizenberg's expression of quantum uncertainty: it may be possible to locate the position of the ball, or the foot, at any fuzzy moment during a Messi mazy run, but not the momentum of either – never both at the same moment.

Mike: Each run, each bipedal locomotion, is a parallel in-out, right-left, up-down, forward/reverse, symmetrical/asymmetrical, orthodox/eccentric possibility and actuality, mediated by quantum potential and modulated by the mession particle?

The elusive Mession particle that binds foot and ball, recently isolated in the Large Hadron Collider at CERN.

Gordon: When Einstein referenced the aim of life as a goal, he was postulating the negation of entropy, not its annihilation; rather its dialectical uptake, negation and inclusion in lucidity.

Mike: Lucidity and goal maintain, and yet simultaneously negate entropy?

Gordon: With every completed pass, dribble, step-over, nutmeg, successful tackle, save and goal, lucidity is affirmed, and entropy allowed, but suspended.

Mike: Many football fans, and other more objective observers, have claimed that Messi's brilliant and numinous bipedal neotenous dribbling is equivalent to having an extra leg. Fantasy or reality?

Gordon: Having three legs – what we call tripedalism – is far from a fantasy, Mike. The elevation to tripedal canonisation is allowed to only a very few football players. As a matter of fact, it is expressed by two ancient and famous football cultures, as seen in the flags and totems of Sicily and the Isle of Man. Tripedalism is revered in both cultures – in football, literature, poetry, drama and art.

Mike: The original historic correlation?

Gordon: That is found in Japan. Emperor Jimmu was a descendent of the Sun Goddess, Amaterasu, and was a famous warrior and footballer – also known as the "Divine Footballer". Tripedalism is a major influence in Japanese mythology, culture and literature, all beginning around 600 B.C., when tripedalism became synonymous with great Japanese dream-play and lucidic football.

Mike: When Messi embarks on an interweaving forward/reverse double/double-helix dribble, facilitated by the mession, he attains such a level of super wake REM dream brilliance that he attains hyperlucidity and canonic Grand Master status of—

Gordon: Exactly! Tripedalism! Yatagarasuism, Mike. Yatagarasuism is its official Japanese honorary title.

Mike: And how is this expressed?

Gordon: By the famous Three-Legged Crow – now the symbol of the Japanese Football Association – which has, you might be interested to hear, recently inaugurated a new Passiens University at Hyuga Province to study tripedalism in football. It is called the Keisuke Honda Academy of *Passiens* and Yatagarasuism Sciences of Hyga.

Mike: What do they specialise in?

Gordon: Tripedalism, obviously, in modern neotenous football expression.

Mike: Have you written about this, Gordon?

Gordon: I am doing so, Mike. *Yatagarasuism in Ancient and Modern Japanese, Sicilian and Manx Cultures* will be published by Tripedal Publications in Saito, Hyuga, Japan.

Mike: I look forward to its publication.

CHAPTER 8

Moai and the Easter Island Heads of Heading

I met Gordon in the Easter Island Moai Tavern, in Easter Road, on an easterly-windy Wednesday evening in July.

The pub (also known as the Four in Hand) is famous for its Moai Heading stadium, built at the rear. It hosts an annual Moai Heads of Heading Competition, which attracts professional heading experts and fans from all around the world. This celebrated pub, rich in Polynesian artefacts, is currently owned and run by one of George Kane's descendants, Paul Kane, who had a successful professional football career with Hibs from 1982 to 1991, and later with Oldham Athletic, Aberdeen, Barnsley, Norwegian Viking, St Johnstone, and Clyde, thus keeping alive the family tradition going back to his famous ancestor. The tavern houses a wonderful collection of photographs of Hibs teams down the centuries, with special interest in the Famous Five – greatly celebrated in the 1940s and '50s.

Among the broad Scottish accents of the many Hibs-fan regulars may be heard accents from Chile, Polynesia and Easter Island. Members of the Captain Cook Society often gather to discuss the exploits of George Kane, who is especially revered for his work and influence on Easter Island, and also for his deep scholarship of the flora and fauna of the South Pacific.

The Captain Cook Society has members from Australia, Canada, Japan, New Zealand, Sweden, Great Britain, and the United States of America, and covers many diverse areas of scholarship and interest including studies to do with animals, birds, botany, zoology, astronomy, exploration, navigation, ethnography and history. It returns every five years to hold its annual conference in the Moai Tavern. The mix of Pacific botanists, zoologists, naval historians, Hibs and visiting football fans, fans of the Moai Heading Competition, Captain Cook researchers, Chileans, Polynesians and Easter Island visitors makes for a lively and excellent atmosphere any day of the week. During the Heads of Heading competition there is often a queue to obtain a seat and a drink.

Mike: I've just read an article in the *Chilean Journal of Passienic Culture*, Gordon, on your theory of heading as a Polynesian adaptation of bipedal football, from around 1.5 million years ago. You say it was exclusive to Easter Island from the Passeolithic era. How did you come to this conclusion?

Gordon: I visited Easter Island in the 2000s, Mike, and met with a brilliant anthropologist and archaeologist called Francisco Sanchez, who I think may be related to Alexis Sánchez of Arsenal. He was from the University of Valparaiso and studied with the famous Rotary World Peace Scholar in Sergio Rapu.

Valparaiso was one of the earliest universities to introduce a faculty of Passienic Studies. Anyway, Francisco explained to me that the famous Moai Heads represented an ancient sporting culture of heading, and that the Moai Heads with round balls on top were famous Heads of Heading Kings of the past. He showed me round stone balls that were clearly being sculpted for future use on top of the heads. No other explanation for this culture and art has been satisfactory, and Francisco and his team at the University were the first to link the Moai to our neotenous history of heading, sporting and game-playing.

Mike: I see. But were the Rapa Nui the only people known to have developed an exclusively heading sporting culture?

Gordon: As far as we know, yes they were. There are some excellent genetic markers that indicate a particular heading hormone was released from the passienic cerebral cortex – a part known as the foraminone. These have been brilliantly correlated with advance heading "gain-of-function" – highly expressed in the Rapa Nui people. And in Polynesian populations. All this is demonstrated by a lovely study carried out at the Faculty of Passienic Sciences at Valparaiso.

Mike: Is this in any way related to the hormone "nodadrenaline" – which is highly expressed in professional footballers, particularly in strikers?

Gordon: It is, Mike. Nodadrenaline is universally expressed in strikers. As is foraminone. The difference is that foraminone is more potently expressed in Polynesian and Rapa Nui professional Heads of Heading players.

Mike: Could this Heads of Heading neotenous culture be connected to the civil strife that may have caused the population decline on the island?

Gordon: I believe so. You may find a reference to this in an article I'm writing: "Foraminone and Heading Gain of Function" to be published in the *Valparaiso Chilean Journal of Passienic Sciences*. Of course, I cite the work of Francisco Sanchez as the pioneer in this field. He's retired now, but I list him as my co-author.

Mike: I look forward to that. Is there any Scottish connection?

Gordon: There is a connection. George Kane, a botanist and biologist from Edinburgh. He travelled with Captain Cook to Easter Island in 1774 where he was left when the ship travelled on to Australia, so that he could review the flora and fauna. They picked him up on the return journey. His famous book is *The Flora and Fauna of the South Pacific*, a copy of which resides in the National Library of Scotland on George IV Bridge. He actually references the game-playing neoteny of headers, which he loved, having been a professional footballer with Hibernian Football Club before he took up science. George also founded the Easter Island Moai Tavern in Edinburgh, and instituted the first International Moai Heading Competition in 1779. He retained his links with Hibernian until his death in 1793.

Mike: Hence the Famous Five Heads of Heading sculptures on the East Stand at Easter Road.

Gordon: Yes, and the annual Moai Competition in Edinburgh has become so popular that a new indoor stadium is now being built nearby – to hold around 10,000 fans.

The Moai Heading stadium, at the rear of the Maoi Tavern on Easter Road, Edinburgh. The famous Moai Heads represent an ancient sporting culture of heading, and the round balls on top are a tribute to the famous Heads of Heading Kings of the past. This is the site of the annual Moai Heads of Heading Competition for professional heading experts from all around the world.

Mike: To digress a little, can you tell me when Easter Island was first populated?

Gordon: According to research it was around 1200 BC but Francisco challenged that date – he reckons the real date is around 12,000 years ago, during the Passeolithic. He agrees with me that the official dates are associated with horolog-ical arrogance, which always contract time in favour of their notion of civilisation and the appearance of in the record. Our upright bipedal and neotenous founder species, *Homo passiens*, was erased from the evolutionary history of the *Homo* species. The true history of the island – according to Francisco Sanchez – is that Polynesians navigated from South America and brought with them the sweet potato, a staple food in that continent.

Mike: And became a staple food and fuel for bipedal footb—

Gordon: For headers, Mike! There is no history of bipedal football – as such – on the island. So, yes, a staple fuel for headers. The competitions lasted for weeks according to the petro-archaeology. It's all been confirmed in the oral history.

Mike: What about archaeological evidence for the Heads of Heading competitions?

Gordon: There is plenty. Francisco discovered evidence of rectangular pitches marked by stone slabs and measuring fifteen yards by twelve. There were goals – six yards wide and eight feet high. Archaeological researchers insisted they were the remains of ancient dwellings, but the original dwellings on the island were either elliptical or round – not rectangular. And they had low entrances which required crawling to enter – something not found at the pitches. Any suggestion of game-playing neoteny terrifies them. There's no evidence of fires being used in these so-called dwellings – are they suggesting that the Polynesians had no knowledge of fire, and couldn't cook, when some ethnographers, like Elsdon Best, suggest that the Polynesians were among the earliest humans to create and preserve fire?

Mike: It seems like it. Cool! Stone balls or petrospheres have been found around the world, dating from the Passeolithic.

Scotland is particularly well endowed – have you seen the lovely sculpted examples in Football Festival Square in Edinburgh? They are invariably classed as ritualistic or religious. Do you think this is a deliberate categorisation – to avoid the very simple passienic conclusion?

Gordon: Of course! Bipedal neotenous and passienic evolution is not acceptable in academic evolutionary circles. These balls, dating to the Passeolithic, are beautiful expressions of ancient football art and they represent neotenous bipedal football.

Mike: Any evidence of early balls in the archaeology of Easter Island?

Gordon: Oh yes! There's evidence of ancient remnant head-balls in caves. They were made exclusively from the skins and internal organs of sharks. It's thought the original Polynesian migrants may have brought the head-balls with them.

Mike: And introduced neotenous head-ball play?

Gordon: I believe so, and Francisco is convinced of it. The tradition of heading and the Moai culture may have arisen because of the pressure of agricultural land use – the island is very small.

Mike: Full-sized football pitches would have been a luxury the islanders could not afford.

Gordon: That makes sense. George Kane recorded that the islanders had no interest in bipedal football, and the only sport they engaged in was heading. Their competitions were for both sexes and included matches within, and between, the sexes. The best players were exempt from all labour and agricultural tasks.

Essentially they were full-time professionals. If one of the clan teams won the annual Head of Heading Competition for three years running, they were allowed to carve and erect a Heading King Head – a Moai. Then Kane married a Rapa Nui woman and returned with her to Edinburgh, where they settled very happily. He opened the Moai Tavern in Easter Road in the 1780s, which remains in the family to this day.

Mike: Was there any violence in these games?

Gordon: There was. That's not surprising on such a small island where there's intense rivalry between clans. Heads of Heading competitions around the world today still generate such high fan emotions that they have to be policed from within the team, and by officials and supporters.

Mike: Any evidence of the dream-game?

Gordon: It's something Kane wrote about in his journal. He referred to a dream-like trance, which was enhanced by alcohol or possibly some hallucinogenic drug.

"Each Heading Team is surrounded by a yelling and shouting rowdy band of youths, male and female, waving team colours and banners, and who are often insensible from drinking a medicinal brew, distilled from fruit, which sets the drinkers in a dream-like trance and on a wild display of song and dance. If over-consumed it seems to make them into devils and demons, who are a danger to themselves, to their Christian neighbours, and to the supporters of opposing teams. I have often witnessed wild trances and violent behaviour during competitions that may spoil the ancient practice of Heading on the island, and frighten any supporters who may

arrive by boat from other islands. However, even those who refuse to drink this evil fiery brew seem to participate with energetic enthusiasm, and to express dream-like fantastical behaviour. I made the decision to bring this lovely old game to Scotland where we may have the clergy advise the players and supporters as to their Christian duty to behave well, and to drink their beverages with modesty and responsibility. I have not always been successful in this respect, but will always try to provide a moral example."

Mike: Are there any recent studies on lucidity and REM-dream physiology in the Rapa Nui and footballing cultures?

Gordon: I'm glad you asked that. There's some wonderful work that was initiated by the Passienic Department at Valparaiso, carried out in association with the Ferenc Puskas University of Passienic Physiology and Psychology in Budapest. It's on the generation of super-REM-wake lucid-dream events during Heads of Heading competitions, and bipedal football elsewhere. They jointly developed a small high-tech EEG device in conjunction with an MRI application, known as The Moai, that accesses the brain via the retina, but it doesn't impair vision, which can be discreetly worn by fans of Heads of Heading and football fans all around the word. But it's very inexpensive. So far, it's been trialled in Africa, South and North America, Europe, Asia and Australasia. These are big studies, involving at least 100,000 fans.

Mike: Are there any results of the studies yet?

Gordon: Just preliminary ones. Stunning ones! And more data are still coming in.

Mike: What about the gamma waves that are generated during REM physiology – both somnic and asomnic ones?

Gordon: Good point. Gamma waves are generated before, during and after neotenous ball-play, or heading or bipedal football.

Mike: So are children and ball-playing neoteny key generators of gamma waves at 40 Hz?

Gordon: Definitely. Investigations of lucid-dream psychology and physiology over the decades show they're comprised of hybrid oscillations between lucid-dream REM sleep and super-lucid REM wake-state neural activation. Young children are particularly adept – experts even – in super-lucid REM-dream volition. As we get older, our potential for lucidity wanes, but ball-playing adult neoteny allows us to rediscover this ancient metacognitive and emotional homeostatic facilitation.

Mike: Which opens a new and rich field of study and observation for *passiens* faculties around the world.

Gordon: Exactly, Mike. Fans and players have discovered that ball-playing neotenous games – above all, bipedal football – reactivate their childhood super-wake lucid-REM transcendent potential, their neo-narcoleptic efficacy, if you like. Their emotional homeostatic potency. By studying football – or in the case of Easter Island, heading history and anthropology – we can re-enter that emotional metacognitive *dream-game*, and study its role as a survival mechanism in *Homo* evolution. And in emotional homeostasis. And in promoting mental health.

Mike: I'm guessing it also has addictive potential, via dopamine and the brain's reward system?

Gordon: It certainly does.

Mike: Does this mean neotenous bipedal football is addictive?

Gordon: Mike … is survival addictive?

Mike: Ha! Acutely so. Fans and players activate a super-lucid REM dream state that is metacognitive and neo-narcoleptic, and we know that usually silences most of the neurochemical transmission associated with neurotransmitters and hormones like acetylcholine, noradrenaline and serotonin. But they allow dopamine activity and transmission – hence the wake-REM lucid-dream state of both reward and addiction.

Gordon: Ah, but there's one major, and critical, exception ...

Mike: That's right – inhibition of muscle inhibition! This is key to neotenous dream-play and observation, enjoyed by both fans and players, because dopamine is upgraded and all neurotransmission normally associated with REM-dream-sleep outcomes continues.

Gordon: Yes, and it is only in neoteny game-playing species that this super-REM-dream-immersion and mentation is allowed, along with active muscle tone.

Mike: Hence fans' discomfort and depressions manifested in the close season – in other words, summer "seasonal affective disorder" – another type of SAD.

Gordon: Of course. We're following up all these aspects in new areas of passienic studies all around the world.

Mike: So is it reasonable to suggest that fans also confabulate? We know that during REM sleep there's an increase in dopamine release, but decreased glutamate – the excitatory neurotransmitter – in the nucleus accumbens. This may parallel disturbances that occur in the wake state – similar to schizoid events. Allowing for hallucinations. Fans and players may confabulate major lucidic events to such an extent that a kind of schizoid mentation occurs, not pathological in this case, of course. Quite the opposite! Rather more indicative of metacognitive and confabulatory literary fictional potential! Indeed all fictional art is impossible without its lucidic, neotenous and ludenic roots.

Gordon: That sounds likely. All lucid REM superdream states have the potential to be models of more problematic mentation because they include the psychological, electrophysiological, neurobiological and neurochemical criteria for observing heightened states in medicine, and in psychology, and in psychiatry. We're only at an early stage in this field, but the avenues for future research are really opening up.

Mike: Can you think of any examples?

Gordon: Well, artists have been recognised for centuries as displaying metacognitive supra-real or surreal confabulation in narrative and story-telling, and in childish magical and fairy stories. The same goes for adults in literature, poetry and all the arts.

Mike: So great art activates neotenous wake- and REM-superdream lucidic physiology, psychology? And positive psychiatric mentation?

Gordon: Great lucidic moments for fans – players too – involve hallucinatory, confabulatory and reality-suspension moments. They are surreal … and yet real. Surreal in the sense that for the fan they stretch time and reality into transcendence. But for the player, reality – including time – is stretched beyond its physiological bipedal locomotive limit, into a parallel realm of relativity and surreal lucidity – all underpinned by neoteny.

Mike: Do we have the science to prove this?

Gordon: We absolutely do – so much, from anatomy, physiology, psychology, psychiatry, metabolism, genetics, endocrinology, anthropology, archaeology, and palaeontology – all found in neotony game-playing and bipedal and opposable-thumb sports, And then there's art, music, dance, language, poetry and literature … universal in human culture.

Mike: I imagine you can supply references for all this.

Gordon: I certainly can – they are in this file here.

Mike: Cheers. Plenty to look through, isn't there! But, in addition to the Moai tradition, and Easter Island traditions and technology, is there any other material evidence of prehistoric football technology that's been preserved for inspection today?

Gordon: There is plenty, Mike. In 2014 a team of archaeologists from the Passienic Technology department at Prague Archaeological Institute excavated tombs in western China, as advised by a team of Chinese archaeologists. They uncovered the remains of some early football trousers dating from around 3,000 years ago – that's during the Passeolithic! It's often been claimed

145

they were developed to facilitate horse-riding, in particular by Ulrike Beck and colleagues at the German Archaeological Institute in Berlin, but this is not correct – horse-riding appeared much later in the record than bipedal passienic expression. The *only* explanation for the development of this unique form of clothing relates to bipedal football.

Mike: Is that because tunics were not suitable for football?

Gordon: Exactly that. Human clothing is thought to have originated up to 500,000 years ago, but there is no evidence for that date. Passienic studies suggest that clothing may have emerged much earlier. Early football trousers, which later morphed into shorts, were usually constructed from animal skins, or furs, bones, grasses and leaves, or shells. Needles were used to sew the trousers – they were made from bone. The earliest dyed fibres were found in a prehistoric cave in the Republic of Georgia – 36,000 years old. They indicated team colourings. The first clothing made from woven fabrics in both Asia and Europe was found at ancient football sites, stadia and complexes, like at the Ness of Brodgar in the Orkney Islands. They date back to the Passeolithic. There were coloured tunics, robes, togas, wraps, and tied clothes, all clearly associated with ritual feasting and football fan dress-codes and play.

Mike: What about boots? Is there evidence of prehistoric football boots from outside Scotland?

Gordon: We have that, too, Mike. From around 5,000 years ago. A boot is known as the Areni-1. Found in good condition in a cave in the Vayots Dzor province of Armenia, by a brilliant postgraduate student, Dyana Zardaryan. She was part of an

Chinese watercolour of Jiaodaruism Stadium, Xian, Shaanxi, one of the stadia uncovered by archaeologists in China, where the game of football began around 3,000 years ago. Artefacts from these excavations include remnant balls, football tunics and boots and a unique form of bipedal football trousers, which were formerly thought to be horse-riding attire until accurate passienic dating methods were applied.

international team from the National Academy of Sciences in Armenia from University College in Cork in Ireland and the University of California in Los Angeles.

Mike: That's amazing. But is there any indication of good exercise "fuel" food found nearby, that suggests the boot was actually a football boot?

Gordon: There was. Containers that once held wheat, barley and apricots ... The finding was wonderful, but the brilliant researchers would not have considered that a football origin was possible.

Mike: That's interesting – the presence of apricots in the fuelling protocol of these football ancestors. That's a key sign that they knew the role of fructose, or wholefoods at least, in "partitioning" the liver in advance of playing football – to improve formation of glycogen in the liver and reserve a fuel supply for the brain.

Gordon: I have to agree with you. They were ahead of modern sports physiology by thousands of years. This boot contained grass, but the team of passienic archaeologists were uncertain whether it was used as insulation to keep their feet warm prior to play, or to preserve the shape of the boot when it wasn't being worn.

Mike: I guess we'll never know. Out of interest, what was the size of the boot?

Gordon: Quite small, apparently.

Mike: So it could have been either a *Homo passiens* or a *Femo passiens* boot?

Gordon: That is what I conclude, yes.

Mike: Okay. Good! Of course, in many passienic cultures around the world, particularly in North America, it was often the women who expressed adaptive passienic play and passienic dream-fan culture, rituals and ceremonies.

Gordon: Yes, often it was the females. And many similarities exist between the manufacturing technique and styles of the various one-piece leather-hide boots discovered around the world, and the Areni-1. Boots of this type were worn for millennia, it seems, across large and environmentally diverse geographic regions. Areni-1 is similar to the Irish *pampooti* football boot – this style was used for football playing up to the 1950s in the Arran Islands. Very similar, too, to the traditional football boots worn at football festivals in the Balkans – *opcani*. I learned about these ancient boots from Ron Pinhasi of University College in Cork – over in Ireland – although of course he was unaware of the football passienic correlation.

Mike: Any evidence of football-post technology?

Gordon: Oh yes. In one of the buildings at the Ness of Brodgar, passienic archaeologists reported finding bones that were arranged and jointed in a linear fashion. Right-angled joints that suggest they may have been used as support structures. But for what? Well, the usual answer from non-passienic researchers is that they were for ritual or religious ceremonies. But measurements of the linear and right-angled formations correlate with all the other evidence of a workshop industry for constructing prehistoric goalposts.

Mike: Weathering would rapidly degrade these structures, so that they would have to be made anew on a regular basis.

Gordon: Absolutely. Hence the existence of a workshop for repeated new construction.

Mike: And elsewhere?

Gordon: Again in North America. Similar but much longer arrangements of jointed bone material was found near the Cohakia Mounds State Historic Site, on the Mississippi River, close to St Louis in Missouri. There is evidence of large beautifully engineered bone-type structures associated with bihanded opposable-thumb passienic handball cultures – not unlike the modern NFL, basketball and baseball versions. The site was built over earlier prehistoric remains, demonstrating sophisticated engineering and ground-levelling akin to that of play stadia and play and ball-play rituals from an earlier immigration phase. And some of the early bone structures were in a circular formation – perfectly jointed using small straight pieces formed into a ring – and they are close to the diameter of modern basketballs! These beautifully formed ring structures are found at many sites associated with balls and ball-playing ancient cultures – indicating ancient forms of bihanded and opposable-thumb games – along with human remains containing the DNA of jumping and passing genes and hormones that we now associate with all the modern passienic adaptations noted in the American continents! And there are other carefully carved bone and skeletal tools that more easily correlate to ball-strike implements – not far removed from those used in the modern version of baseball.

Mike: So there may be evidence of balls. Are there any preserved balls?

Gordon: A preserved ovoid animal skin and bladder ball was found at the site, dating to some 25,000 years ago. This is the earliest known find, made by a team from the Passienic Studies Faculty at Alabama University in 2007. Evidence for the use of bone as a building material is best in Ukraine, at Mezhyrich to be precise. Their homes were constructed from mammoth bones dating back 15,000 years. Now, my passienic dating shows they are closer to 150,000 years old, but I don't want to downgrade the work of the pioneer archaeologists who discovered them. I developed my own dating techniques here, in the *Passiens* Faculty of St Andrews University.

Mike: I'm so glad you did! It means that the notion of bone football goalposts is perfectly correlated to the archaeological record. It's simply that the dates need to be revised.

Gordon: Precisely. But goalposts can be noted frequently in cave art – easy to spot for the informed observer.

Mike: Isn't that great!

CHAPTER 9

The Neurology of Football Hymning:
The Consciousness of the Football

Gordon and I were drinking in the Dreamsong Bar, also known as Bennets, beside the King's Theatre in Tollcross in Edinburgh, on a stunning Autumn evening.

This is a popular tavern among lucid REM wake-dream philosophers and thinkers, and close to the famous Meadows Park where many wonderful young footballers have learned their early skills, moves and tactics over the millennia, and discovered and developed their genetic and bipedal *passiens* physiology, anatomy, and psychology.

James Lind, who lived from 1716 to 1794, was a regular customer of the bar when in Edinburgh. Lind was a famous Scottish physician, a keen football fan and a pioneer in nutrition, who discovered that citrus fruits prevented scurvy, paving the way for the future discovery of Vitamin C, and was responsible for improved nutrition in the Royal Navy. He improved shipboard ventilation and cleanliness, and introduced fumigation using sulphur and arsenic. He also proposed that fresh drinking water could be obtained by distilling sea water, and thereby improved the health and lifespan of sailors on long sea voyages, many of whom were press-ganged into service at a young age. James Lind is now regarded as the pioneer and founder of the science of nutrition.

Several of the surrealists are claimed by locals to have visited this tavern when in the UK, including Salvador Dali, Max Ernst and André Breton. The psychologists Sigmund Freud – who believed that access to the unconscious mind was via dreams – and Carl Jung – who elaborated on the notion of the collective unconscious – are both thought to have paid a visit to this ancient bar, Jung after the First World War and Freud after the Second. By the early twentieth century, the bar had become a popular destination for all sorts of psychological, psychiatric and other thinkers, scientific surrealists, dream philosophers, mystics, dream and shamanic archaeologists and anthropologists.

Members of the International Association for the Study of Dreams are still frequent visitors to this lovely old tavern. It is believed they may hold their annual conference here in Edinburgh in 2019, centred of course on the Dreamsong Bar, in conjunction with the Faculty of Lucid Dream Physiology at the Cristiano Ronaldo University of Passienic Studies at Santo Antonio in the town of Funchal in Madeira. Cristiano Ronaldo is a lovely example of a young footballer who articulated his own dream potential, and followed it through to the most wonderful fruition against considerable odds, to become one of the greatest footballers of all time, possibly ultimately the greatest, and who began from very modest beginnings in the neighbourhood of Santo Antonio in

Funchal. Ronaldo began his football dream and dream odyssey at the age of eight. His father was the kit man at the amateur football club Andhorina. By the age of fourteen, young Ronaldo knew that he was destined for greatness. He was noticed by Sir Alex Ferguson and signed for Manchester United.

Of course this dream-wish fulfillment is very different from Gordon P. McNeil's theory of the super-lucid wake-REM-dream articulation, enacted by football fans, and its expression of dreamsong and dream-chant physiology and psychology during football games. Nonetheless it should not be excluded from the literature and study of dream psychic mentation, because it involves long-term passienic hopamine-facilitated neo-hedonic ambition, and indeed significant deferred passienic hopiate aspiration for emotional-success homeostasis.

According to Professor McNeil, Freudian dreams retrospectively access the unconscious mind for hidden unresolved psychic antagonisms and traps, not in a fruitful present or forward psychic activation that informs the psychic self of present and future survival. Jungian dreaming is a much more adaptive survival system that allows for opposite outcomes, looks forward, and is positive as opposed to negative; it is hopeful and optimistic, and correlates to the collective conscious and unconscious psychology of aspiration and expectation expressed in football-fan "infanity". It is the archetypal epigenetic Lamarckian philosophy inherited by every football-fan child, from every football-fan parent, across the globe, in the bipedal neotenous football species – *Homo passiens*.

Mike: Are there any interesting studies on the physiology, neurology and psychology of football chanting and hymning, Gordon?

Gordon: There most certainly are studies like this, Mike. This is a whole new avenue of *passiens* research, opening up pathways that relate football dream-songs and football dream-play to emotional cognitive regulation and homeostasis.

Mike: And to super-lucid wake-REM-dream expression?

Gordon: Yes. Work at the Bobby Charlton Faculty of Passienic Dream Studies based in Ashington, Northumberland, correlates emotional homeostatic drive to passienic opioid-hormone cascades, along with dopamine activation. During super-lucid REM wake-dreamplay, when goal-directed play is not proving fruitful, passienic opioid levels go down, and passienic dopamine levels go up, as reward-seeking stimulation results in chanting and hymning cycles on behalf of each team, and directed to activation of mirror neurones.

Mike: I take it this is aimed at the dream-play of opposition players, and at the dream-songs and dream-chants of the opposition supporters?

Gordon: Of course. Mirror neurones express both reflective and proactive neural and sensorimotor potential.

Mike: Mirror neurones are empathetic, social, cognitive learning and bonding agencies that work via the release of oxytocin from the posterior pituitary gland. But may they influence hostility by reduction and suppression of oxytocin?

Gordon: Yes. Mirror neurones serve both directions, influenced by regulation of oxytocin – negative for opposition super-lucid

REM-dreamplayers and super-lucid REM-dreamfans, and positive for those of the supported team.

Mike: Would you say that was physiologically and emotionally?

Gordon: Both – immensely so.

Mike: In other words, the hymning and chanting are reward-seeking expressions of homeostatic emotional regulation, mediated by dopamine and opioid hormones, and modulated by elevated or reduced oxytocin?

Gordon: Yes. In the context of football dream-play, and fan-facilitated lucid wake-REM behaviour, dopamine is released. Paradoxically, the adrenal fight-or-flight hormones are also elevated, so the impulse to chant or sing is modulated by these complex cascades.

Mike: Does this involve social and metacognitive emotional interaction?

Gordon: It certainly does, Mike. We know the brain is a social construct – in football no less than in life in general. Actually via football – in passienic science.

Mike: And the modulating hormone in all this?

Gordon: Oxytocin is the major social modulating influence. It's expressed profoundly in mirror-neurone activation in both the premotor cortex and the sensorimotor cortex of the brain.

Mike: Which in turn is also modulated by the state of play. Positive in the case of the winning team, and negative in the case of the losing team.

Gordon: Exactly. The aim is always for homeostatic emotional resolution, through neotenous and bipedal play. The result, in terms of success in offence or defence, determines the adrenal hormone, dopamine, as well as opioid cascades and modulation, regulated by oxytocin, and consequently the stimulation, or suppression, of chanting and hymning.

Mike: Yes. So great goals, great tackles, great passes, great step-overs, great runs, great crosses, great saves are all homeostatic award-seeking behaviours. Dopamine activation and elevation of opioid release is mirrored by fans in football dream-songs and dream-chants, such that emotional balance is potentiated.

Gordon: For the players, there is sensorimotor activation of super-lucid REM-dreamplay. For the fans, lucid-REM hedonic hymning and chanting, with both forward and reverse mirroring.

Mike: I can see that. And the two modulate, interrelate and interact super-lucid REM-wake dream-play and super-REM wake-dream hymning for the fan. Lucid REM systems are two sides of the same homeostatic coin, each mirroring the other, modulated by adrenal hormones, as well as dopamine and opioids, with the dopamine cascade, modulated by oxytocin, as the link across the two domains.

Gordon: Yes. Activation of the adrenals facilitates increased muscle tone in super-lucid REM play – and fan enactment and gamma-wave responses in the brain. The dopamine facilitates award-seeking hedonism and lucidity in *both* groups, and opiates promote homeostatic resolution and equilibrium.

Mike: Wow, complicated! But dopamine is the key interactive and modulating influence for both groups.

Gordon: It is. Keep in mind the series of marvellous studies at the Bobby Charlton Faculty of Passienic Dream Studies in Ashington, that discovered the dopamine-related hormones "hopamines" and the opioid-related hormones "hopioids" and their presence in *Homo passiens* football players and fans.

Mike: Brilliant! Hopamines and hopioids. Cascades of award-seeking and emotional homeostatic resolution, and bipedal football enhanced play. Have they been recognised by the scientific community?

Gordon: Yes, but only slowly and very grudgingly.

Mike: Are football fans expressing a kind of schizophrenic mentation, in the sense that they have to simultaneously hold the two opposite outcomes – winning and losing – during their super-lucid wake-REM-dream-game?

Gordon: They are indeed Mike; every fan must hold and suspend the two outcomes, negative and positive, in every game – their super-lucid REM-wake state, and gamma-wave schizoid psychology, that facilitates a "win" hallucinatory mental confidence, despite what the odds may be, and the media pundit speculation.

Mike: Odds against are a provocation for every football fan, hence their dreamsong hymning and chanting is simply a survival strategy to evoke mirror responses in the dream-play of their team. Is this expressed electrophysiologically?

Gordon: Every time, Mike. Gamma wave frequency at 40 Hz is an electro-physiological expression associated with schizoid psychology, as well as with super-lucid REM asomnic football hymning and chanting.

Mike: Thus when the fans activate their hymning responses to the dream-play, they are hopefully stimulating mirror neurones in the primary somatosensory cortex, and in the premotor cortex of their team members to improve their football physiology?

Gordon: Precisely, Mike. Isn't that something!

Mike: What's more, the super-REM gamma wave frequency synchronises around the whole stadium, resulting in Jungian gamma-wave collective conscious and unconscious synaptic memory consolidations and manifestations – a gamma-wave schizoid electrophysiological and lucid metacognitive storm!

Gordon: Yes! Of dream-play, of dream-hymning, and dream-chanting electrophysiological and electropsychological pyrotechnics!

Mike: And the synchrony?

Gordon: Easy, Mike. That's quantum bio-entanglement.

Mike: In which time is emergent and plastic, and not "arrowed"?

Gordon: Yes – hence the implicit time variations, dependent on an internal pacemaker.

Mike: Which may, of course, accelerate or decelerate according to the explicit environmental landscape, in which hedonistic and reward-seeking dimensions and durations are modulated by dopamine or hopamine receptors.

Gordon: Yes, the dopamine and hopamine cascades modulate dream-play, dreamsong, dream-chant and time pacing consistent with—

Mike: Lucidity and schizoid bio-entanglement!

Gordon: That's it. Passes or mispasses, dribbles or tackles, cross or shy, offside or onside, headers or fruitless jumps, blocks or misses, goals or saves, winning or losing – and so on. Every move posits duality and schizoid outcome, which must be held or suspended in the unconscious and conscious lucid dream-play of every footballer, and every dream-active fan.

Mike: Which is also modulated by the success or failure of the mirror hymning influence on each team and its resulting dream-play.

Gordon: Yes. As one team's dream-play drops off with success, hopioid release is reduced and hopamine is stimulated such that hedonistic award and goal-seeking rises proportionally.

Mike: And conversely, in the opposing team the reverse modulation of hopamine and hopioid regulation occurs?

Gordon: For sure. Passienic faculties around the world, particularly the researchers at the Henrik Larsson Psychology Department from the Passienic Science University of Helsingborg in Scania, Skane County, Sweden, have picked up on Panskepp's brilliant work and his seminal ideas in affective neuroscience. He states that motivation, reward anticipation and sensory pleasure are *vital* survival mechanisms, that are conserved in evolution, and may be expressed in humans.

Mike: And expressed most potently in football mentation – the communication and emotional regulation systems. And therefore songs and chants can be factored into this complex behaviour.

Gordon: Yes. Passienic researchers have used birdsong neurology and metabolism as the model to inform their interrogation of football hymning, which is directed at players of each team – positive in the case of the team supported, and negative in the case of the opposition.

Mike: Can you elaborate on this? Have you written about it?

Gordon: Yes I have, as it happens. *The Model of Birdsong and Tree Frog Calling Metabolism in Football Dream-songs* – a book that will be published by Jim Baxter Publications. Male-directed song attracts females or repels rival males; it is a dual mechanism with two aims.

Mike: It suggests that fans direct their hymning and chanting at both their *own* team and fans, and in opposition against the competitive fans and players?

Gordon: Yes, the same hormone cascades are utilised in each case. This is a major consideration that only the betting industry factors for – in its betting odds. They put a great deal into research on passienic studies of football neotenous hymning and chanting.

They rightly realise that quantifying odds *without* including the potential for fan modulation of the *dream-game* – via hymning and chanting – is the road to major loss of income. You know, they invest millions on this research and were responsible for opening the Faculty of Football Hymning and Chanting at the Passienic University of the Isles in Barra.

Mike: There's no point in analysing the form of the two teams without including the performance potential of each cohort of fans in terms of dreamsong and dream-chant influence. It's obvious. Has this been quantified?

Gordon: They use a series of algorithms developed by the Faculty to calculate the influence of hymning and chanting on the results. Naturally the betting industry is risk averse, and they have reputedly saved around a billion by factoring the influence of hymning and chanting into their betting-odds calculations.

Mike: So what are the key influences on supporter oppositional hymning and calling, and on synchronisation of counter-calling and hymning?

Gordon: The precise emergent critical oscillators that facilitate synchronisation within and between oppositional groups are still under investigation. This is ongoing at several passienic universities around the world.

Mike: But do you know if oscillators are internally or externally generated?

Gordon: The consensus is that they are both, and that the internal oscillators are correlated with time plasticity.

Mike: What about any correlation between oxytocin, dopamine and opioid release and social reinforcement mechanisms, consistent with emotional homeostasis?

Gordon: Of course there is. Why do you think fans prefer to attend in groups? You rarely see fans alone. In fact, a fan alone is a mythical figure. It is a key motivational influence. Bipedal football-fan social and communicative dream psychology is one of the founding expressions of Jungian *passiens* psychology. Science traditionally avoids investigating emotional mechanisms, assuming them to be associated with lower levels of cerebration.

Mike: So it imitates the traditional negative attitude to neotenous game-playing characteristic of anthropology and social sciences, and is indicative of consciousness?

Gordon: You are totally right about that.

Mike: What would you say are the most significant physiological and metabolic influences on the success of football hymning and chanting?

Gordon: Hymning and chanting are highly energetically expensive, Mike. If you consider that fans begin their 40 Hz frequency chanting and hymning on the way to the stadium. The whole duration, including through the *dream-game* and the time afterwards may take several hours – that's a marathon of energy expenditure! Passienic studies indicate they may match, even exceed, the energy output of someone running a marathon.

Mike: The success of hymning and chanting may well correlate to how well the fans "fuel" themselves before, during and after the *dream-game*?

Gordon: Absolutely. The fuelling is key.

Mike: And the fuelling protocols?

Gordon: Whoever – or whichever group – emits longer or shorter hymns or chants. The longer hymners and chanters have more influence early in the game. The shorter hymners and chanters have more influence as the game continues. Each cohort of fans attempts to control and outcall the opposition's cohort.

Mike: Second-half hymning and chanting are less potent – it's always a trade-off between energy expenditure and sensorimotor mirror responses.

Gordon: True.

Mike: In other words, the team supporters who "fuel" themselves correctly before and during the *dream-game* have greater potential influence on the outcome because of their improved efficiency of hymning – which in turn is modulated by energy input prior to and during the game?

Gordon: Of course – right again.

Mike: And does this equate to glucose storage in the muscles? To glycogen?

Gordon: Well, yes and no. Muscle glycogen is vital but it is not critical. Nor indeed is stored energy from fat.

Mike: What's the model for this?

Gordon: I've just heard about a fabulous study that draws on interesting work on nocturnal calls of the male tree frog, believe it or not. It has been taken up by lucid-REM wake-dream researchers at the Eric Harrison Academy of Passienic Research (that's at the University of Halifax) who are conducting iconic studies on football hymning and chanting.

Mike: What are the significant fuels, then?

Gordon: Carbohydrates. Almost exclusively glucose. Used by the contracting muscles that make the frog's high-frequency calls – up to 8,000 per hour! In the most energetic fan cohorts, it's 800 per hour. Increased call rates use greater amounts carbohydrate, and this must be sourced from—

Mike: The liver! Which means liver glycogen storage is the critical energy reserve facility.

Gordon: That it is.

Mike: Of course! Liver glycogen is the only reserve energy supply for the brain, and it's key to super-wake-REM-dream mentation. Research on this work is great, but it misses the key role of liver glycogen reserves in singing tree frogs.

Gordon: There's no extended singing of birds, no successful calling of tree frogs, and no efficient hymning and chanting for super-wake-REM dreaming football fans in the *dream-game*—

Mike: Without optimal liver glycogen reserve!

Gordon: Exactly.

Mike: For the male frogs, success with females comes to those with the longest calls – who therefore have the optimum liver glycogen reserve, which in turn is correlated with cerebral energy reserves. The same goes for fans with the most prolonged and energetic hymning and chanting – and again success for mirror stimulation and effect on the dream-play. And the cerebral energy reserve relates to the liver glycogen status.

Gordon: Indeed. It's as simple as that.

Mike: Optimum fuel is therefore required for the dreamsong, for the dream-hymn and the dream-chant. Do you happen to know if there are any significant studies on the influence of neotenous dance physiology and neurology on bipedal football play and fan behaviour?

Gordon: Let me think. Well, there is ballet. It is now considered a major new positive influence on football physiology, not least because ballet dancers are able to counter the negative influence of gravity on maintaining their balance – which is the foremost problem of locomotion in any bipedal species. And *passiens* are always at risk of falls and injuries.

Mike: I assume dance and bipedal expression are integral to both *Homo* species, but what are the key modulating factors?

Gordon: May I quote Lucian of Samosata around 180 AD?

Mike: Please do.

Gordon: It goes like this: *"With the creation of the universe, the dance too came into being, which signifies the union of the elements. The round dance of the stars, the constellation of the planets in relation to the fixed stars, the beautiful order and harmony in all of its movements, is a mirror of the original dance at the time of creation."*

Mike: That's just lovely! It seems a few astute coaches have tuned into this geometry for their team formations, haven't they?

Gordon: Pep Guardiola for one – the star of football geometrics, and stellar formations; a passienic Nobel astronomer of the football field and the universal bipedal football harmonies; a constellation organiser of gravity and antigravity, and of space and time plasticity, of matter in motion, of velocity, momentum; a choreographer of reciprocal and non-reciprocal passing altruism, and bipedal dancing altruism. The Pep Guardiola Faculty of Passienic Geometry – you may have heard of it, at Santpedor University in Barcelona – is pioneering new studies of football force-field geometry and dynamics.

Mike: A true passienic Albert Einstein by the sounds of it, and the Merce Cunningham of neotenous bipedal physics and physiology. And of the green rectangular field of play!

Gordon: Quite.

Mike: And the modulating metabolic influences for this are?

Gordon: A brilliant group of researchers led by Rachael Bachner-Melman. They have opened a wonderful window into the dancing phenotype and the genetic and hormonal factors modulating metabolic physiology.

Mike: What do they show?

Gordon: That the dancing phenotype is directly associated with the arginine vasopressin receptor 1A AVPR-1A, and the serotonin receptor SLC6-A4.

Mike: I believe that AVPR-1A is associated with social and communicative gain-of-function behaviour, and serotonergic gene expression for modulation of dance and extra-physiological experiences. Is that right?

Gordon: Spot on.

Mike: And is there a correlation between the locomotory movements of bipedal football, and inter-passing, teamwork communication and advanced choreographic coordination of position in geometric formations?

Gordon: It's just as we saw in the great Hungarian team of the 1950s. They were the first international team in modern times to express triangular and complex geometry of passing combinations.

Mike: That's so interesting. Does all the gamma-wave electrophysiology and dreamsong hymning and chanting influence the behaviour of the football in any way?

Gordon: I think, Mike, that you are thinking of the "*foet*ball" here – the first spherical object of infant consciousness after the round parental head. The head is the first object a child becomes cogniscent of, as you know, and the round object of the material world is infinitely more complex than any linear representation or manifestation, because it returns to itself – it is both finite and infinite. The foetball is a primary mentation object of the extended infant mind – a spherical finite and infinite object that the infant mind reaches and "colonises". Therefore it can be considered to be vital in the formation of neotenous bipedal consciousness.

Mike: I'm thinking of the role of the football during the execution of a penalty kick. Is the football an information system? In other words, does its behaviour impact on human consciousness and cognition? In particular, that of the penalty kicker and the goalkeeper?

Gordon: Ah, yes. A football is a system that is rich in information potential, both before and after the kick is transmitted by the sensorimotor system of the penalty kicker, and also – of course – the goalkeeper.

Mike: Not before the kick, I would have thought?

Gordon: You're wrong about that, Mike. A football is a product of human ingenuity, intelligence and work – that is, human labour both abstract and concrete – a product of engineering technology, information technology, precision manufacturing, mechanics, physics, pure chemistry and biochemistry. And of human emotion! Even love. A product revered by billions of bipedal neotenous humans, i.e. *passiens*, even by some – and all aimed at absolute identity of similarity, so that any two balls in the same environment will behave in exactly the same way.

Mike: Isn't that a futile enterprise?

Gordon: You hit the nail on the head.

Mike: No ball is, or can ever be, an absolute clone.

Gordon: Exactly, Mike. It is simply not possible.

Mike: Right. Because every ball includes it own internality, its own essential "ballness", making it different from all others, although on the surface may be similar. Every ball has – or is – its own internal information-expressing entity.

Gordon: I agree wholeheartedly. Footballs are individuals, despite all efforts to make them into identical *homo*geneous objects.

Mike: Very funny. This is the same way that a meteorite carries information from space about the origins of the universe and earth, and therefore probably life.

Gordon: Yes, yes, and yes again, Mike. Indeed the origins of life may be carried by meteorites that also embody chirality and life structures as left-sided – hence the origins of left-sided football players may originate in the stars.

Mike: Totally fascinating. Has this been proved?

Gordon: A brilliant research team at the National Astronomical Observatory in Japan has discovered chirality located within the Cats-Paw nebula. They used deep imaging of linear and circular polarimetry.

Mike: Brilliant! And amino acids that form all – or almost all – of the proteins in life are also "left-sided".

Gordon: Yes. Every biology and biochemistry student knows this. And amino acids, of course, are used in the manufacture of footballs with rubber and leather, and our *Homo* species physiology.

Mike: Therefore all balls are also "sided"?

Gordon: It seems impossible for them not to be. The perfect and neutral Platonic ball simply does not exist.

Mike: As a penalty kicker connects with a particular ball, the ball embarks on its own journey, simply modulated by the kicker?

Gordon: Yes.

Mike: And it's influenced by impetus, momentum, force and velocity, including the history, biology, physiology, psychology, psychiatry, neurology, cognition and consciousness of the kicker?

Gordon: Well articulated, Mike.

Mike: It must also be influenced by the collective conscious and unconscious Jungian manifestation and expression of monoamines, hopamine, hopioids, oxytocin and vasopressin modulation of gamma-wave electrical surges. And the net quantum of gamma-wave electricity expressed in the stadium by fans and players! A massive and explosive supercharge across the stadium! Enough to light a small city.

Gordon: That's just it. If you're present at a great game, you can feel the supercharged gamma electromagnetic waves and surges as each fan group counters the opposition's hymns and chants.

Mike: And therefore each ball, in every football game played, or to be played, follows its own path, its own world-line, modulated by all football players, by the stadium, by the environment, by the dynamic of the game and fans and their super-lucid wake-REM dream-contest of hymning and chanting. Then there's the officials, and all the other influences from the weather, wind speed and direction, atmospheric pressure, temperature, humidity, and so on, and so on … And it's also expressing its own internal information expressing potential.

Gordon: Of course it is. Every ball is unique and qualifies as an information system in its own right. Therefore it is an extension of the human mind.

Mike: Active and not passive, every football commits to its own world-line, modulated by human contact and consciousness.

Gordon: Totally right. Every football has a mind of its own as it travels through space and time, whatever the intentions of the penalty kicker. It may not necessarily follow his or her intentions. This means that every football may have its own agenda, and behave either formally or paradoxically.

Mike: Balls have consciousness?

Gordon: Why not? At any rate, a dream consciousness. Footballs are a product of human consciousness. And human consciousness, as you know, Mike, is a product of human cognitive REM-dream physiology – and super-lucid REM wake-dream is one of the highest expressions of human cognitive emotional homeostatic regulation.

Mike: Yes, so it is! And the consciousness of preterm infants is formed in REM dream physiology, the highest expression of cognitive and emotional memory and learning. That means we can include the football in the theory of the extended mind.

Gordon: Naturally! Post-birth human consciousness and language are formed during play, which translates into the adult form – as Johan Huzinga believed and articulated so well in his book. We now understand that bipedal football is the highest expression of this lucid-REM wake-dream neoteny.

Mike: Human bipedal neotenous consciousness is a product of the bipedal football. The parent's head is round, so also is the football.

Gordon: That's the right way to look at it. The forming infant mind reaches out from its internalisation and colonises the parental head – and the ball.

Mike: So it's a two-way process?

Gordon: Yes.

Mike: And when a ball is finally kicked, it carries with it its own internalised potential – its own intentionality, if you like, to behave in this way or that way, to curve one way or the other, to spin left or right, top or reverse, but it's also modulated by the intentionality and ability of the penalty kicker.

Gordon: Indeed, Mike. In the same way that a meteorite journeying through space embodies its own information potential, but can be modified by other space objects and bodies, with which it collides or is affected by space–time distortions and variations.

Mike: A football is "encultured" then – a product of human design, of human conscious intentionality and cognition.

Gordon: That's very much the case. And of course, the goalkeeper has a major part to play in this drama.

Mike: He also reaches out to the ball and makes of it his mind extension and further modulates its journey – its world-line through time and space?

Gordon: Of course, Mike.

Mike: Lucidity and entropy are included, too. Before the penalty kick the football is a homeostatically neutral entity, balanced between lucidic and entropic potential.

Gordon: Quite so. And of course the reverse happens with respect to each; a great lucidic goal suspends, maintains and negates entropy, while a great save opposes lucidity, elevates entropy for the kicker, and facilitates the second law of thermodynamics. Or the reverse unfolds – success elevates lucidity, and failure elevates entropy.

Mike: This differs from Berkeley's idealism where the balls exist only in the mind. A kind of reverse Berkeleyism.

Gordon: Yes, it does rather. The mind reaches out and extends and captures the essence of the ball, or at any rate a portion of it, a fraction of its essence – of its footballness – for its own purposes.

Mike: Okay, but we leave to the ball is own internal potential, or its ballness, or footballness – its footballness consciousness – and its freedom to follow its own potential resulting from its uniqueness and difference from all other footballs.

Gordon: That's it, Mike. No football may be controlled absolutely. A football is a functioning entity, and in play it operates as a functional state; it *responds* to its environment and it *affects* its environment.

Mike: A functional state is, or could be, a non-biological form of consciousness and perhaps emotion, could it not? Such as Hal in Stanley Kubrick's epic movie *2001: A Space Odyssey*.

Gordon: Well noted, Mike. Every ball has its own uniqueness and therefore its own "intentionality" resulting from its own internal structure. Each one reacts to a kick differently due to structural differences, however minute they may be, and therefore its exchange with the kicker must also be unique.

Mike: No football player – no matter how good – has absolute control of the ball. The ball reacts to his or her kick and the environment in its own unique way, according to its own information construct, and therefore its own "ball consciousness"?

Gordon: You bet! It's actually procociousness. I am writing a book on this very subject called *The Surprising Consciousness of the Football*. It's going to be published by West Auckland Passienic Philosophy Publishers next year some time.

Mike: I look forward to that. Back to hymning and chanting, though. The sound waves modulate the ball and its behaviour and vice versa; and the best – the greatest – footballers have the highest level of control, but its never total control because all balls have minds of their own.

Gordon: Otherwise football would be quite easy. Not unpredictable.

Mike: That's right. If it were predictable there could be no pathway of uncertainty. Heisenberg's Uncertainty Principle would be redundant.

Gordon: Exactly.

Mike: And the fans would not show up! Football without Heisenberg's Uncertainty Principle would be very boring.

Gordon: It would be, but do we have to admit—

Mike: That it is sometimes so.

Gordon: Let's leave it at that.

CHAPTER 10

Shamans, Opposable Thumbs and Goalkeepers

I found Gordon by chance in the Lev Yashin Arms in Queensferry Street on a heavy, overcast, humid day in August, during the Forth Valley International Festival of Passienic Culture and Arts.

Lev Ivanovich Yashin (known as the Black Spider) lived from 1929 to 1990 and was undoubtedly the greatest goalkeeper in the history of modern football. He was the first to physically dominate the penalty area, to advance beyond the six-yard line, and to aggressively control his defence. The 1958 World Cup brought Yashin's mastery of the goalkeeping arts to a worldwide audience via television, and his black regalia imposed his brilliance on the consciousness of fans all around the globe. He terrified opposing forwards with his shamanistic and totemic display. He filled his goal like a black and malevolent cloud, a fluid shadow that spilled over onto the playing field. Opposing players testify to the malign dark influence entering their consciousness as they crossed the eighteen-yard line, undermining their sensorimotor transmission and muscular coordination. His penalty performances and wild shamanic prancing disoriented penalty kickers to such an extent that he could rarely be beaten, and opposing captains had difficulty in finding players willing to take him on when a penalty kick was awarded. Lev Yashin played in four World Cups, was chosen for the FIFA World Cup All-Time Team, and in 1963 was named European Footballer of the Year – the only goalkeeper ever to receive the award. After the 1966 World Cup, he paid a visit to Edinburgh at the invitation of Hibernian Football Club, and met the Famous Five footballers of the time. Yashin is known to have visited the public house that now bears his name.

The Lev Yashin Arms is a beautiful old Edinburgh football pub, formerly known as Mathers, at the corner of Queensferry Street, which is the old road to the famous ferry crossing and the iconic nineteenth-century Forth Railway Bridge. It looks eastwards along Princes Street with a view towards the ancient castle atop its volcanic rock. It is a great favourite with visiting football tourists, and is favoured by the new wave of Russian expatriates in the UK; Andrey Arshavin, the popular former Arsenal footballer, is a regular visitor. Russian accents are always audible around the bar. During the period of perestroika and glasnost, and when he was President of the Soviet Union, Mikhail Sergeyevich Gorbachev (winner of the Nobel Peace Prize) was claimed by sober locals to have been a regular visitor. It seems he was partial to a pint of McEwans Pale Ale.

According to some of the regulars, a number of visitors to this goalkeepers' tavern are members of the International Shamanic Community – leading practitioners and shamanic thinkers around the world in the fields of shamanic study, learning and education.

It is also claimed that shamanistic goalkeepers are frequent visitors, and many travel to this tavern to consult with, and learn from, educators in the field of shamanic studies. The hostelry has

Lev Yashin 1929–1990. This portrait was painted by the resident artist of Hibernian Football Club when Yashin visited Edinburgh after the 1966 World Cup and met the Famous Five. It hangs now in the public house that now bears his name. Yashin played in four World Cups and the FIFA World Cup All-Time Team, and is the only goalkeeper to receive the European Footballer of the Year award. He is known in the consciousness of fans worldwide for his black regalia, his mastery of the goalkeeping arts, his terrifying opposing forwards and his shamanistic and totemic displays. It is said "He filled his goal like a black and malevolent cloud, a fluid shadow that spilled over onto the playing field." His wild shamanic prancing and malign dark influence disoriented opposing penalty kickers, few of whom were willing to take him on when a penalty was awarded.

also become a meeting place for students of social anthropology from around the world, who are studying shamanic practices. Lev Ivanovich Yashin is a revered icon among these students, and a frequent subject of their academic papers on shamanism.

Mike: What, in your opinion, Gordon, are the essential gain-of-function evolutionary passienological assets expressed by goalkeepers?

Gordon: There are four fundamental expressions or adaptations required for successful goalkeeping gain-of-function. First, there is enhanced expression of the Human Accelerated Conserved Non-Coding Sequence-OT, known in short as HACNS-OT – where OT obviously refers to the opposable thumb. In simple terms, it is a gene-enhancer sequence that favours opposable-thumb gain-of-function. Second, there is the altered metabolic profile, in favour of anaerobic, oxygen-free, energy production. Third, is the more adaptive shamanistic cultural expression and display. Fourth, finally and critically, there is schizoid mentation.

Mike: I have heard of gene-enhancer sequences, and of their influence in activating major differences in *Homo* and human evolution. Is this a phenotypic key to our bipedal footballing species *Homo passiens*?

Gordon: Yes, Mike, hugely so. Recent work by Dr Shyam Prabhakar – a Senior Research Scientist at the Genome Institute of Singapore – and Professor James Noonan – Associate Professor of Genetics and of Ecology and Evolutionary Biology at Yale School of Medicine – has identified a series of gene enhancers, or switches, that are associated with the most significant differential expression of *Homo* species from primates. These are bipedalism and opposable-thumb gain-of-function. They found that the key sequence – HACNS-1 – activates the genes involved in ankle/ foot adaptations that are critical to bipedal locomotion, and therefore critical to passienic expression. It also activates those for opposable-thumb optimal function – critical to goalkeeping, of course. The fact that the same gene-enhancer sequence is correlated with bi-handed, opposable-thumb and grasping function, and to the ankle/foot adaptations critical for bipedal locomotion (and therefore football skills), is simply a feature of energy "thrift". Of course, they did not make the connection to football – to *Homo passiens* – but their work is historic and wholly worthy of a Nobel Prize.

Mike: Why create two sequences when one will do, with some variation of course?

Gordon: The opposable-thumb variation HACNS-OT was discovered by a great team at the Gordon Banks Institute of Opposable-Thumb Goalkeeping at Tinsley, down in Sheffield, and the bipedal ankle/foot expression HACNS-BP – for bipedalism – at the John Thomson School of Neotenous Goalkeeping in Cardenden, up here in Fife. For one organism to be very different from another, it isn't necessary for a major series of DNA or gene mutations to take place; it simply requires a different sequence of gene switching. In the realm of *Lego*nomics, a child can make any object they can imagine simply by adding or subtracting identical units in different locations, and at different times. The children's *Lego* genes are identical – it's just the timing of each addition that affects the child's point of focus and location, and therefore the outcome. This is not dissimilar to gene-activation sequences: an adult primate has an extended jaw, but a *Homo* individual of any age does not – and extended jaws are not conducive to heading! If the genes or the gene-

181

enhancer sequence that drives the extension of the jaw is suppressed or switched off at a given point, then extension ceases. In this sense, human development is *inhibited*. Some neoteny experts also describe this as "retardation", whereby full expression and extension is aborted. In this case, the gain-of-function is heading: it is only possible in species with a flat face and brow. Of course, they are also a feature of neoteny – the retention of infantile forms into adulthood.

Mike: That makes sense. Can we find instances of specific passienic sequences?

Gordon: A fantastic study at the Jackie Robinson Passienic Genomic University of Cairo in Georgia showed that the HACNS-BP sequence is also related to the development of critical passienic brain structures, such as the lateral machiavellia and the hippocampus, via enhancement and switching-on genes that activate expression and release of neurotrophic hormones and factors that are critical to these parts of the cerebrum. Then there's that lovely study from Budapest's Ferenc Puskas Passienic University in Kispest. They noted that the expression of these sequences is greater in *passiens* than in those of similar age and fitness level. They also found that in football leagues around the world, the expression of both the OT and BP variants is positively correlated with how high individual players and teams are in the football leagues. Not surprisingly, it was inversely related to those in the lower divisions.

Mike: Truly fascinating, and full credit to the researchers who discovered the initial gene-enhancement sequence related to bipedalism and opposable-thumb gain-of-function, this HACNS. Although I imagine they would not understand the significance for the gain-of-function in *passiens*?

Gordon: Perhaps not, but their work is historic, and it opens a major new field of opportunity for all future *passiens* faculties and studies.

Mike: Now may we talk, Gordon, about goalkeeper metabolism?

Gordon: We may! Did you know that a goalkeeper must articulate energy metabolism closer to that of a reptile than a mammal? No disrespect meant, of course. It is simply a matter of how cells survive and maintain energy homeostasis. Mammals – and therefore both *passiens* and – waste vast amounts of energy in the form of heat. Mammalian cells leak both sodium and potassium ions across the cell membrane, therefore to maintain ionic homeostasis and cell viability they expend around six times the energy of a reptilian cell. This is also confirmed in cases of severely hyperactive thyroid glands, with the consequent loss of energy as heat. To stoke our engines requires constant input of new energy it's a survival strategy. Of course, goalkeepers spend a large part of any game in a state of relatively low-energy metabolic flux, and therefore they must avoid – as much as they can – wasting energy during that time. The more they tend towards a low-energy flux during these phases, the more they can mobilise massive, rapid and explosive energy expenditure when called upon.

Mike: The same as a crocodile, operating its engine at a low output while it waits patiently for a herbivore to enter the water. Then it leaps into an anaerobic carnivorous explosion, to grasp and drown the poor victim before eating it.

Gordon: Quite so. Outfield players, on the other hand, operate for the most part in aerobic or oxygenated metabolic states.

Mike: And spend a significant proportion of energy output simply on staying cool?

Gordon: Yes. Shunting blood to the extremities to evaporate water from the skin is a very inefficient method of cooling – water is lost, and the reduced blood volume forces the heart rate up and puts extreme pressure on the cardiovascular system. Crocodiles wait quietly for a dozy zebra at the water's edge, with their engine turning quietly at minimum revs – expending very little energy. When the zebra takes one step too close to the water's edge, up rears the croc and the unfortunate beast is captured in the massive jaws of the cold-blooded reptile. This is the kind of metabolism a goalkeeper should have. Quiet torpor followed by turbo-charged superactivism! If passienic goalkeepers keep their engines idling at low revs, they can mobilise energy at phenomenal rates to leap for a pile-driver volley from the edge of the penalty box. If they could lower their metabolic rate to *crocodilian* levels, then they could engineer the kind of dynamic responses to shots and crosses displayed by the whole family of freshwater predators – and, indeed, by dynamic anaerobic reactors like frogs. It goes without saying, a goalkeeper's biology is – or should be – fundamentally different from that of outfield players.

Mike: Do we have evidence of genes, or gene-enhancement systems, that correlate with advanced anaerobic energy consumption in goalkeepers?

Gordon: We do. We know that the ATP–creatinine phosphate pathway of explosive oxygen-free energy production – taking less than ten seconds – is critical to goalkeeping. And there is a wonderful series of passienic energy studies at the University of Orkney and Shetland – that's the Dennis Law Faculty of Passienic

Energy Metabolism – who correlated this pathway with enhancer-gene sequences known as the Human-Enhanced Conserved Anaerobic Energy Generation (HECAEG), which is found in goalkeeping populations – and in North American enhanced-opposable-thumb games players.

Mike: Since the two major adaptive expressions of *passiens* anatomy are bipedal and opposed-thumb manifestations, and therefore skeletal, is there any way in which we can relate these to metabolism?

Gordon: I'm glad you asked that. There most certainly is. A fabulous 2007 study led by Gerald Karsenty at the Department of Genetics and Development at Columbia University in New York. Gerald's team identified feedback energy regulation via genes expressed in osteoblasts – bone cells. In other words, they found that skeletal structures function as endocrine organs! Working on this hypothesis, researchers at the Border Institute of Passienic Endocrinology at Hawick in the Borders of Scotland published a paper in the *Journal of Passienic Metabolism*, showing that this is exactly how anatomical skeletal formations participate in both outfield and goalkeeper metabolic regulation of energy – aerobic in the former, and anaerobic in the latter.

Mike: So bones do matter in energy regulation?

Gordon: More to the marrow, than structure and support – important though these are.

Mike: And what of goalkeeper psychology?

Gordon: The goalkeeper is almost a different subdivision of the *passiens* subspecies – physiologically, psychologically, psychiatrically and culturally. Albert Camus, above all of the football writers, understood this. He described goalkeepers as "split beings" – as "self" and as "other"; two parts that constantly chatter to each other.

Mike: So this is a specialised and adapted opposable-thumb subgroup within the *passiens* football family?

Gordon: Yes, Mike. It's even possible that the biological and psychological adaptations necessary could at some point in the future give rise to a mutation that would promote the separation of a new subspecies of goalkeepers from within *passiens*. Indeed, it may already be occurring. We see elements of it in *passiens*-generated handball games, especially in North America. Work at the Jackie Robinson Institute – at the University of Passienic Genomic Sciences – has shown that a group of gene-enhancing sequences, the HACNS-OT range, contribute to enhanced opposable-thumb and grasping gain-of-function, compared to the more exclusively bipedal locomotion known sequence as HACNS-BP. The OT sequence arose in Eurasia and was introduced into North America during the Passeolithic period, around 2.5 million years ago. Nowhere else in the world are the HACNS-OT sequences found more frequently.

Mike: Does game-playing neotony confirm this?

Gordon: Beautifully so. Recent work by archaeologists at the Rick Cleveland Faculty of Passienic Studies at the University of Mississippi found that a site close to the pre-Columbian Cahokia Mounds Historic Site on the Mississippi River, near St Louis, houses the remains of game stadia that indicate opposed-thumb handball playing over many millennia. The ancient finds consist of ovoid, round and smaller ball artefacts, with beautifully carved skeletal goalposts of immense length, connected to T-junctions, with skeletally formed circles, connected to ancient surviving remnant hemp nets, and with rectangular and diamond field tracings! No need for me to explain the implications of this. These ancient games survive into modern times.

Mike: These may be correlated with a particular gene-enhancing sequence expression for opposable-thumb and bi-handed enhancement?

Gordon: Yes – HANCS-OT. This has already been proved.

Mike: Are these sequences potent, rather than subtle?

Gordon: They are subtle in their expression, but potent in their effects. A single variation in any gene-enhancement sequence can make a major difference to morphological, physiological and psychological outcomes. It's like cars – two identical automobiles may seem equivalent and equally useful, but if the starter switch of one is suppressed, but not in the other, the difference is significant.

Mike: Are there elements of Lamarckianism in this, Gordon?

Gordon: There are. If a species or subspecies in a given environment is used to activating a particular gene-enhancing sequence via practice or training, then this function may certainly leap into the next generation by epigenetic influences. So yes, we may call this Lamarckian. Goalkeeping sons follow goalkeeping fathers – daughters also. A major study at the Passienic Faculty of the University of Alabama showed precisely that transfer in three generations of great bi-handed-OT passienic-player expression and physiology.

Mike: Does this mean that DNA is not the only vehicle of transmission of adaptive characteristics, of bi-handed opposed-thumb and bi-footed ball play and behaviour and neotony culture across generations?

Gordon: Definitely not, Mike. Adaptations usually *follow* a mutation. They do not normally *give rise* to them. If an adaptation following spontaneous mutation is successful and confers some advantage, then the new mutation will spread through the gene pool and appear in future generations.

Mike: But it's not the only vehicle of transmission, is it?

Gordon: No. New forms of transmission appear regularly. We may be just at the beginning of this rich field of passienic evolutionary science.

Mike: Might there be transfer from one team to the other in football?

Gordon: Indeed, yes. Note the difficulty that many excellent players have when they move to a new club, or a new environment or new passienic ecology. There are collective phenomena, recognised in some faculties and known as team genomes – collective expressions of particular ecological adaptations that are not always easy to access. It takes time. It takes energy and hard work. It takes flexibility to adapt. And the more specialised the passienic genome of any individual footballer, the more difficult it may be to function in a new team-genomic environment.

Mike: Then specialisation for particular play, genetic or other adaptive facility – like goalkeeping – may be advantageous or disadvantageous?

Gordon: Definitely. And the environment or ecology plays a major role in gene switching and gene expression. Switching on of formerly suppressed genes is broadly equivalent to a spontaneous mutation. Suppressed genes are as good as absent. They are basically silent genes – ghost genes. Activation of such ethereal genes by some environmental change, a new team for instance, resulting in a profound biological response or adaptation, is an effective environmental evolutionary transmission mechanism that does not involve mutation.

Mike: We are close here to transmission of passienic memes, I think. To goalkeeper cognition and psychology.

Gordon: Exactly. Goalkeepers co-evolved with shamanistic expression. The split between the right and left brain that took place somewhere between two early groups of *Homo passiens*, *Homo sapiens* and *Homo erectus* was incompletely expressed in some individuals in the emerging groups. This result was something equivalent to a short circuit between the two hemispheres, giving rise to an internal dialogue – a profoundly shamanistic development. The lack of left-brain specialisation for language allowed the language facility to develop in both hemispheres, and this caused the two sides to talk to each other. Likewise for football cognitive and Machiavellian expression – cross-hemispheric dialogue results in each side hearing the other side as an internal embodied voice.

Mike: Should I advance from my goal line or retreat? Should I display or defend?

Gordon: That kind of thing, yes. Goalkeepers express this dialogue more profoundly and more deeply than do outfield players, as has been documented in a series of elegant studies by the Paul Gascoigne Institute of Passienic Sciences at Gateshead University in Newcastle.

Mike: You mean that this hemispheric communication by means of what you call a short circuit, gave goalkeepers and shamans the internal connection with their unconscious – a sort of tripartite system with one or both hemispheres plugged into the unconscious, exchanging information by cross-hemispheric transmission, and each hemisphere hearing the voice of the unconscious transmitted through the other – a faculty developed by both goalkeepers and shamans?

Gordon: Yes. That's exactly what I mean.

Mike: And the dialogue with the unconscious mind during play accesses all the knowledge required to respond to the outfield play … and the weather, wind speed and direction, the time of day, the time of play, where the sun is located, the atmospheric pressure, the humidity, the state of the pitch, the team-genetic history of the opposition and their coach, the informatics physics of the ball on that particular day. All of this is stored and accessed by the passienic unconscious, and accessed much more easily by shamanistic psychology brilliantly and fully expressed by goalkeepers, and of course during their lucid asomnic REM neo-narcoleptic dream state.

Gordon: Well, partly, Mike. What we are interested in here is that lack of specialisation in the two hemispheres. This means that both hemispheres shared the same tasks. It is likely that this resulted in the absence of anatomical sidedness in the best goalkeepers – an ideal attribute for any goalkeeper. Moreover, hemispheric dialogue contributed to shamanistic consciousness, the conjuring up of internal dialogue and embodied play voices. Here we have a very clear connection between shamanism and goalkeeping. It is well documented in the literature that shamans were not hunters; they remained behind when the males went off on hunting expeditions. Consequently, in the event of an attack by predators or other groups, they were also defenders of the camp. They would "voodoo" the opposition before they could promote the attack – or attack the goal. Now you can see the correlation between goalkeeping and shamanism. Some anthropologists have described this form of shamanism as *foodoo*.

Mike: It's all becoming so much clearer. So do we know what the genetics, the epigenetics, and the gene enhancement sequences of goalkeeping shamanism are?

Gordon: Not yet, but impressive work at the Andrei Arshavin Faculty of Passienic Studies in Zenit, St Petersburg, is close to publishing a major – probably historic – paper on this very subject. They are the first to examine genes and gene-enhancement sequences that influence opposed-thumb and passienic neo-narcoleptic lucid-dream hallucinogenic manifestations, and shamanistic adaptations.

Mike: There are genes and gene-enhancement sequences for shamanism, and you mean goalkeepers are also mystics, or mystical defenders. True shamans?

Gordon: Yes, and yes. If your defence is found wanting, and if you are unable to match your opponent physically on a one-to-one moment of the game, then you can foodoo them with shamanistic display. All the greatest goalkeepers were shamans, lucid and non-lucid dreamers, mystics, and foodoo practitioners – all in the best sense.

Mike: And psychiatrically?

Gordon: Ah, now. Goalkeepers are also bipolar. Schizoid. They have to be! Think of the life of the goalkeeper in a game. He is both spectator and participant. Both in the game and not in the game. Oscillating between cold and hot, anaerobic and aerobic metabolism; between torpor and incendiary dynamism. He is one and his own other. His metabolism is part reptilian and part mammalian. His limbs, part bi-handed opposed-thumb primate, and part leap-froggian – almost avian. His dreams are both lucid and non-lucid. As a spectator, he dreams the game. As a player, he participates in a lucid and non-lucid dream state that is both with and without active muscle tone – atonic and tonic – switching, or reversing, from the one to the other, as the game demands. This is shamanistic dreaming – or better still, shamanistic *reverse* dreaming, from the one to the other and back again. Here he can connect with his ancient passienic unconscious, and he can also connect his teammates with this ancient unconscious bipedal wisdom.

Mike: Is it only the goalkeeper that can perform this function? To understand goalkeepers we have to understand not only passienic physiology and psychology, but also passienic psychiatry, of the conscious and unconscious football mind. We have to understand enigma, paradox and mystery, and neo-narcoleptic super-lucid REM wake-dream sequences as the highest expression of passienic enhanced cognition. Is that right?

Gordon: For sure.

Mike: Goalkeepers oscillate between diving and jumping, or diving and flying. They are mysterious – really almost beyond understanding.

Gordon: As an anthropologist and a scientist, I am resolutely opposed to "mystery", but I do believe that goalkeepers are beyond … that goalkeepers are ultimately—

Mike: The Kantian beyond? The Kantian unknowable?

Gordon: Yes.

And with that thought, he shook his head, and left.

CHAPTER 11

The Football Hormones of Negative Entropy and Time Dilation

Gordon was already waiting in the Johan Cruyff Tavern in the High Street when I arrived on a warm, wet Monday in early September.

This lovely old Scottish pub was once known as Deacon Brodie's Tavern, but has since been renamed in honour of the famous Netherlands footballer. It stands at the corner of the High Street and the Mound and looks out along the lovely George IV Bridge – home of the National Library of Scotland and a major meeting place for passienic academics from around the world.

The Johan Cruyff Tavern is a regular meeting place for lucid football-fan discussions, and for tourists walking up to, or down from, Edinburgh's twelfth-century castle, the esplanade of which housed great football games between Hibernian Football Club and Heart of Midlothian before their modern stadia were built. It is today renowned for its famous Military Tattoo, held during the Edinburgh International Festival of Arts. A walk down the lovely old High Street takes tourists to the Palace of Holyrood, and to the home of the Scottish Parliament nearby.

William Brodie, known as Deacon Brodie (after whom the tavern was originally named), was a Scottish cabinet-maker, a respected Deacon of the Trades Guild, and an Edinburgh City councillor. As Deacon (president) of the Incorporation of Wrights, and a city councillor, and a cabinet-maker who repaired door locks (which he also copied), he had access to all the homes of the wealthy Edinburgh bourgeoisie. This allowed him to double-up at night as a highly successful burglar. His unlawful gains funded a gambling career, and allowed him to maintain two mistresses. He was finally rumbled in 1788, when he organised an unsuccessful armed raid on the Excise Office in Chessel's Court in the Canongate. Two of his comrades were caught and, although they did not divulge his name, he realised that he had to flee. He escaped to the Netherlands, but was arrested in Amsterdam and returned to Edinburgh for trial. When he was hanged in October 1788, around 40,000 people attended the spectacle.

Johan Cruyff was named Hendrik Johannes Cruijff, and is generally recognised as one of the world's greatest footballers. Johann Cruyff was the captain of the Netherlands football team that reached the 1974 World Cup Final, and was elected as the "Golden Ball" player of the tournament. He won eight Erdivisie titles and three European cups. In 1973 he moved to F.C. Barcelona for a world-record fee, and won La Liga in his first season. In 1999 he was voted as the European Player of the Century, and came second to Pele in a poll for the World Player of the Century. Cruyff's football philosophy has been adopted by many successful coaches including Frank Rijkaard, Arsene Wenger and Josep Guardiola. He is credited with an approach to football that has made Spanish football not only the most successful, but also the most beautiful, in recent decades.

The Johan Cruyff Tavern has become a popular tourist destination, particularly with Dutch football fans. Famous Dutch footballers, including Marco van Basten, Ruud Gullit, Patrick Kluivert and Frank Rijkaard, are said to be regular visitors. Local legend has it that the most famous Dutch visitor to this tavern was Jan Ingenhousz, a physiologist, biologist and chemist who is known to have studied in Scotland with Scottish various botanists and physiologists. This pioneer of eighteenth-century science was the first to discover that light is required for photosynthesis, and that plants have cellular respiration and build their structures by adding carbon from the atmosphere to create biological materials.

Other local wags claim that Johan Huizinga, the famous Dutch cultural historian and author of *Homo Ludens*, also visited the tavern during one of several visits to Britain in the early 1900s. Some football fans even claim to have viewed the historian at the Easter Road Stadium, the home of Hibernian Football Club, although there is no record of this in his biographies.

Mike: What are your thoughts, Gordon, on winning mentality? On the notion that a particular team – a great team – is invincible and that opponents fear them in equal measure to their level of self-belief. May we speak of the psychology of victory? And may this be collective, rather than simply an expression of individual player mentation?

Gordon: We can, Mike, and we should. Yes, the greatest football teams do express this collective psychology, in quantity, and we may refer to a collective mental strength – a collective and team "iron will" that bodes no weakness, lesion or discontinuity, and that is greater than the sum of the individual passienic genomic parts that contribute to the whole team genome and genome psychology. Revolutions that overthrow tyrants by sheer collective will, that can overcome all opposition, political, legal and military, against insuperable odds, express this type of psychology and manifest a transcendent "group activism" that may be unstoppable – which defies inhibition.

Mike: Does this involve genetic expression, then? Of RNA systems, of mobilising hormones, transmitters, enzymes, peptides and other influences, such as epigenetics and gene-switching sequences, that determine results and outcomes?

Gordon: Certainly Mike. Most certainly. A number of passienic faculties around the world are now at work exploring these pathways – psychological, psychiatric, physiological, endocrinological, neurological, gliological, immunological, genealogical and anthropological, and bioinformatics.

Mike: Is this the reason that one team consistently wins and another loses?

Gordon: Yes.

Mike: Do we have any sense of where this is going? Might it involve particular pathways, glands, hormones, transmitters or nerve feedback systems?

Gordon: We do. There are. In fact, there are some major new studies aimed at unravelling the key modulating influences.

Mike: What are these?

Gordon: Let's begin with the entropy of football.

Mike: By this you mean the waste of energy involved in a failed move, or a missed shot, a misplaced pass, a poor tackle, an overhit free kick, a penalty kicked over the bar, a red card? All expressions of energy lost into the void, wasted, spent needlessly and contributing to a negative and goalless outcome.

Gordon: Yes, that's exactly what I mean.

Mike: But where can we begin to look for the metabolic or other parameters that contribute to this football entropy?

Gordon: We begin in the pineal gland, Mike. We think of the pineal gland as being exclusively associated with sleep, but what is much less well known is that it also plays a pivotal role during physical locomotion and exercise physiology. I have recently returned from the Passienic University of Orkney and Shetland, where much brilliant archaeological work at Stonehenge – and more recently at the Ness of Brodgar – has started uncovering the origins of bipedal neoteny football during the Passeolithic. Their Institute of Passienic Metabolism is also breaking new ground in *passiens* metabolic science, focusing on the pineal gland as one of the key sources of winning mentation, and of course the mentation of losing, when the passien–pineal cortex of the pineal gland is underfunctioning.

Mike: Does this also involve the passien–tryptamine group of hormones, indicative of neo-narcoleptic lucid-REM dream states expressed during football, both by fans and by players?

Gordon: Every time, Mike. These hormones are all correlated with both the pineal gland in and (even more so) in the passien–pineal cortex of *passiens*. In *passiens*, the pineal cortex is always more developed than in *sapiens*. For this, we can thank the great team at Orkney and Shetland.

Mike: Is there one particular gain-of-function that crystallises the major metabolic activism of this special gland? I'm referring to the passien–pineal cortex of *Homo passiens*, as opposed to the pineal gland of *Homo sapiens*?

Gordon: There certainly is, Mike, and that is the expression of football lucidity – active in all great football teams and football players. And, of course, it is mirrored in the neo-narcoleptic super-lucid REM dream state of fans. It also correlates with hallucinatory tryptamine activation in the passien–pineal cortex.

Mike: You're saying that every great team and every great football player activates a state of metacognitive lucidity involving the release of passien–pineal hormones during a moment of metaphysiological expression – like a great and lucid pass? Or a gorgeous step-over. Or a fabulous save or explosive shot – a perfectly timed and goal-saving block or defensive tackle? A moment of skill that transcends all normal football interchanges and raises the level of a game to extraordinary heights? You're saying all of these are accompanied by the release and uptake of a passien–pineal cascade that is also mirrored in the fans' passien–pineal glands?

Gordon: Yes, big time! Johan Cruyff is thought by many researchers to be the embodiment of this bipedal metabolic physiology. Great teams and great players all express passien-tryptamine hormones in cyclical cascades throughout any game-play; they may be chronically and collectively released during a wonderful interchange of beautifully coordinated passing, or individually during a brilliant and explosive reverse-kick goal.

Mike: Can we relate these cascades to anti-entropic energy conservation?

Gordon: Exactly so, Mike. This is perhaps the most beautiful manifestation and affirmation of bipedal locomotive articulation – indeed, of opposable-thumb grasp of function – known to man.

Mike: I assume only football can reach this level of nobility of lucidity.

Gordon: Only football. Yes. Only football can preserve and maintain energy integrity against the pathological increase of entropy of all organic life, and only in its most sublime, highest moments. Of course, there are many wonderful manifestations of human or *Homo* play culture in sports like cricket, rugby, tennis, basketball, baseball and American football, even golf in its best moments, and in dance and ballet, too. And athletics. But *only* in bipedal football does the mind-extended technology – the ball – coalesce with sublime sensorimotor play to reach into the passien–pineal cortex, and activate the super-lucid REM dream state, to release the passien-tryptamine hormone cascade, which explodes and lights up the human mind, in a brilliant and explosive moment of lucid play and observation.

Mike: Only the round and perfect bipedal play of mind, bi-footed and bi-handed body and Platonic perfect round ball can resolve the pedestrian, and take us where we can only rarely go.

Gordon: Yes. You have it.

Mike: The Second Law of Passien Thermodynamics – energy entropy – is a likely outcome of any energy system. But it's not absolute – more of a probability that may be temporarily suspended in football, in lucid play.

Gordon: Beautifully articulated again, Mike.

Mike: Thanks. But is this expression related to metacognitive enhancement?

Gordon: Of course it is. There are three states of dream consciousness that are relevant – wakefulness, non-lucid dreaming and lucid dreaming. Non-lucid wakefulness we can exclude as not normally being helpful in football-dream expression; therefore we focus on lucid wake-REM dream states during football play and observation. Non-lucid dream states are not considered very interesting with respect to volitional consciousness, not known so much for cognitive expressions, but *lucid* dream states present us with a very different cognitive gain-of-function – massively so in respect of football expression and play. And where the most beautiful play events are characterised by rolling cascades of the passien-tryptamine hormones that ignite into incandescent and iridescent displays of participating teams and players, and mirrored in collective waves of football-fan super-lucid wake-REM dream ecstasy, which correlates to gamma-wave electrophysiology at 40 Hz.

Mike: Is this directly linked with time dilation?

Gordon: I hoped you might bring that up. The answer is yes, yes, and yes again. All great payers and all great football teams have this ability, to dilate and slow down time. Those researchers who experiment with, and use the synthetic versions of these hormones, also testify to this time dilation.

Mike: Can we relate this to the time dilation of Einstein physics – the faster we move the slower is the time frame within which we move?

Gordon: We certainly can. If we process information at a faster rate than others do, we dilate the time frame – in the same way that an insect watching us chase it with a newspaper processes the necessary information at such a speed that it has plenty of time to easily avoid the approaching newspaper. We must reject the concept that this dilation is a purely subjective or illusory event, either in insects or in man.

Mike: The insect perceives the swinging weapon, processes the necessary time–space data at ultrafast rates of information transfer into its brain, dilates the time frame, and casually – arrogantly, even – slips out of its pathway, and avoids a collision?

Gordon: Correct.

Mike: Time is not an absolute entity, is it? Time, energy and information are inseparable, interwoven and mutually dependent.

Gordon: Right again, Mike. Every great footballer processes information at speeds faster than his or her opponents. They do not simply appear to have more time – they actually *do* have more time – so they can react to any situation, no matter how tight, or how unpromising. If the energy expended is successful as a result, this player has overcome football entropy; the outcome is positive and the is energy conserved in the positive result. A goal is scored.

Mike: Therefore a goal is an expression of football anti-entropy or reverse entropy.

Gordon: Yes. Some *passiens* researchers have described this as negative entropy, or intropy – faster processing of information into the brain by the glial cells, the energy-processing cells of the human brain. And in particular by the *gol*ial cells, a subset of the glia expressed in *passiens* football players.

Mike: And what about the fans?

Gordon: Of course. Fans also express golial cells.

Mike: Do we know how this conservation of energy is maintained? What are the metabolic parameters involved?

Gordon: We know that, too. Again, because of a brilliant series of studies at the Passienic University of the Isles at Barra. Information is processed at mega speeds into the brain via the golial cell. You remember these energy-processing cells, also known as the Einstein cells.

Mike: I do. Einstein expressed a higher ratio relative to neurones than our friends – the average *Homo sapiens*?

Gordon: That's right. Of course, we have James Clerk Maxwell to thank for the notion that energy and information are inseparable.

Mike: You mean Maxwell's demon?

Gordon: That's the one. There is always an energy cost in information transmission. Many thought that Maxwell was articulating an energy-free information transfer, via his demon, but that was not his intention. The demon had to pay the energy price for using each bit of knowledge.

Mike: It's the same with the passien-tryptamine group of hormones released during football play and also by fans – there is always a cost. Do we know what the pathway may be?

Gordon: For sure. The hormone cascade upgrades the cerebral glucose pump, which drives glucose into the brain.

Mike: And that results directly in greater transfer of energy and therefore information into the brain, and consequently it inflates the time perceived. Increased information consumption facilitates increased time.

Gordon: I think, Mike, that we must avoid reference to perception; the time perceived is the time available.

Mike: Nor is it illusory. I see. It's a clear transfer of energy and information into the brain – as real as that of Einstein's space–time relativity?

Gordon: Yes. Time oscillations are as real in the *dream-game* as passes, step-overs, goals and saves. The more lucid the event, the greater the time dilation, and the suspension of entropy.

Mike: Lucid. Gordon. I recently came across an article in the *Journal of Passienic Genetics* that referenced a study at the Buffon Faculty of Passienic Genomics in Parma, Italy. It examined the genetics of two football hormones – passeopressin and scorotonin. Are you aware of this approach to the science and art of passing and goal scoring? And its potential for future studies?

Gordon: I certainly am. And I can tell you that the work was based on a superb study by a team led by Professor Rachel Bachner-Melman. Published in *PLoS Genetics* in 2005, I think, on genetic influences on dance – one of *Homo* species' most universal expressions of bipedal neoteny and social empathy and communication.

Mike: Interesting … What did Professor Bachner-Melmen find?

Gordon: That dance and music are physiologically and psychologically interwoven. Inseparable. He hypothesised that there may be a significant genetic influence on this form of behaviour, and that those who dance may express genetic differences with those who do not dance.

Mike: Makes sense. What did they look at?

Gordon: They looked at serotonin transporter genes and vasopressin receptor genes among performing dancers compared to elite athletes, and non-athletes who were non-dancers.

Mike: Okay, so the serotonin receptor regulates the serotonin level, which influences the brain's emotional homeostasis. And vasopressin is involved in social communicative and affiliative behaviours.

Gordon: Absolutely right.

Mike: And the outcomes? Did the dancers differ significantly from the athletes and the athlete non-dancers?

Gordon: They did, certainly in terms of genetic expression for both serotonin transporter genes and vasopressin receptor genes.

Mike: How cool. I can envisage just how this would correlate to neotenous bipedal football. Neoteny, the expression of anatomy and physiology of ancestor embryonic and infantile forms, has been a major contributor to human evolution via sexual selection and advanced expression of cooperative forms of behaviour, in addition to more innovative, creative and curiosity behaviours.

Gordon: That is it, Mike. Well explained. Here we have a model of how bipedal (dance) physiology is correlated with serotonin and vasopressin gene expression—

Mike: Suggesting that art and creativity, via neoteny, is a mechanism of evolutionary advance. In humans, bipedal neoteny can be a vital engine of complex evolutionary development.

Gordon: Immensely so. The role of neoteny in human behaviour is vastly underestimated in research, and the genes that drive this have been left relatively unstudied. Bachner-Melmen is a pioneer in the field, and should be congratulated. In other words, the genetic articulation of dance that Bachner-Melmen uncovered may also be directly related to neoteny.

Mike: Excellent. And the passienic research team used this model to examine genetic expression of football hormones, in this particular case scorotonin and passeopressin, which are structurally related to serotonin and arginine vasopressin?

Gordon: All humans express serotonin and vasopressin, but the Bachner-Melmen study showed them to be more highly expressed in professional dancers than in others.

Mike: And likewise, the two related hormones – scorotonin and passeopressin – are more potently expressed in professional footballers than in the wider population?

Gordon: Most certainly this is the case. Not surprisingly, there are differentials when comparing defenders, midfielders and forwards.

Mike: Okay, let me guess. Defenders express higher levels of passeopressin than scorotonin; midfielders express the highest levels of passeopressin compared to forwards and defenders; forwards express high levels of scorotonin; and, of course, strikers have the highest level of this hormone.

Gordon: Yes. That's exactly what the Buffon Faculty of Passienic Genomics found.

Mike: And the fans?

Gordon: This is where it becomes really interesting. Football fans express higher levels of both these hormones than non-football fans, more especially on game days than any other day. And there is even higher expression in those present in the stadium compared to those watching a live game via a live televised link.

Mike: That is fascinating. And do the levels vary during the game?

Gordon: Very much so. In both players and fans. And they fluctuate in accordance with the dynamics of the game.

Mike: So do we know what mechanisms are involved that influence and regulate expression in fans? I assume there are mirror neurone influences at work. If so, how are they measured?

Gordon: Measuring the activations of mirror neurones has become relatively easy since the Football Retinal Magnetic Resonance Device (FRMRD) was developed by a team at the Bioengineering Faculty at the Mesut Özil University of Gelsenkirchen. It was funded by FC Schalke 04. A FRMRD machine can be worn by fans at a and somatosensory cortex are activated during play by fans and they influence the expression of both scorotonin and passeopressin.

Mike: Wonderful. Are there variations in the hormone levels of the two groups of fans?

Gordon: There are indeed. Both hormones are inversely expressed according to the state of play in each fan group – if one team is involved in a sequence of passing moves, passeopressin is more highly expressed in that fan group, while it is suppressed in the opposition group. Similarly for scorotonin: if a team scores, or is close to scoring, their supporters secrete and release a scorotonin cascade, and its expression is reduced in the opposition's fan cohort.

Mike: I take it mirror neurone activation can be precisely attributed to the parietal region and the somatosensory cortex.

Gordon: This is what the studies are suggesting, Mike. Of course there remains much work to do, but the numbers are coming in, from all around the globe nowadays.

Mike: Brilliant. Are there any other studies on other bipedal neotenous hormones expressed by football players and fans?

Gordon: There are, Mike. A group at the Jamie Vardy Faculty of Passienic Metabolism at the Neoteny University of Leicester has found a football influence on a group of hormones related to the catecholamines. They have described them as cate*gol*amines, and the most significant one seems to be *nod*adrenaline, structurally close to noradrenaline as the name suggests. This is directly associated with heading gain-of-function, and is highly expressed in footballers – strikers in particular.

Mike: Any adrenal steroids or glucocorticoids involved?

Gordon: These, too. They have been found by a team at the Carli Lloyd Femo Passienic University of Delran Township. That's over in Burlington County, New Jersey. A whole cascade of steroid hormones, previously undetected, has been found – the adrenal *scor*oids or *gol*ocorticoids. The key scoring hormone, again more highly expressed in strikers, is known as *scor*tisol.

Mike: Amazing to think that bipedal neotenous hormones expressed in football have lain hidden in our metabolic physiology and psychology throughout the history of biochemistry and metabolic science for all those decades.

Gordon: Amazing, yes … But then, also not so amazing. If you are a scientist in denial about the true driving force of evolution – upright bipedal neoteny as expressed in football – you are not going to look for, or find, these hormones.

Mike: Any others I may not know about?

Gordon: Well, we've discussed foraminone – as in *for*ehead, obviously – and then there are the fannabinoids and fanandamide, hopamine and the hopioids.

Mike: There are more to follow, I imagine?

Gordon: Undoubtedly. One recent finding, which is quite paradoxical, came in from the Kevin Mirallas Passienic School of Bipedal Neoteny at Liege University. It seems that Italian players express a football hormone more than other football nationals, which is closely related to calcitonin, from the thyroid gland, and which positively influences bone metabolism. It is known as calciotonin.

Mike: Does it help with deposition of bone minerals during recovery from unusually fierce tackles?

Gordon: It does.

Mike: Expressed positively in forwards who are exposed to aggressive Italian defenders?

Gordon: Yes! The further forward an Italian footballer plays, the higher its rate of synthesis and release.

Mike: So lucid you could not invent it!

Gordon: No, you could not.

FOOTBALL-FAN QUANTUM INTERFERENCE

Stein J, Mourinho J, Wenger A, Shankly B, Ferguson A, Clerk Maxwell J

Department of Passienic Mechanics, University of the Isles, Isle of Barra

Passienic Journal of Quantum Physics 92-104, 17(2) 2017

Gamma-wave-generated REM lucidity is a specialised dream state that expresses emergent quantum connectivity – fan to player – each within the compressed space-wave, and correspondingly the dilated time-wave; every fan knows that they affect the game via gamma-wave electrophysiology, which can reach such heights of elevated electromagnetic charge that at a certain threshold, quantum cohesion is manifest and fans pass from engaged and passionate observers to active participants in football-field fan-generated quantum interference, and effectively initiate superposition dynamics for their team players, such that it is potentially possible for an individual player, and also for the ball, to exist in more than one position at any moment. Hence fans can, at certain moments, manifest superconducting quantum influence in the game, positive for their team elect, negative for the opposition. In other words, classical Newtonian locomotion becomes complex, and expresses quantum dynamics.

A famous study at the Johann "Hans" Krankl Passienic University in Vienna has demonstrated quantum wave/particle duality in footballs under fan gamma-wave quantum interference during ultra-charged *Rapidviertelstunde*, a system of synchronised clapping that causes hyper-charged gamma-wave cycling around the stadium, when fan quantum coherence and interference are explicit. The researchers drew on brilliant research by Anton Zeilinger at the Institute for Experimental Physics in Vienna, that showed buckyballs (also known as footballerenes) (molecules comprising 60 carbon molecules that are structurally identical to footballs arranged in twenty hexagons) exhibit wave/particle duality, the key feature of quantum dynamics. They invited local football fans to fill the Gerhard Hanappe Stadium and create the conditions for super-wake REM-dream lucidity to a fantastical level that generates gamma-wave quantum interference.

Players then kicked buckyball-type footballs from the penalty spot (a single source point) through a double split screen, and arrived at the goal, beyond the split screen. If the trajectory behaved according to classical Newtonian dynamics the ball would arrive at only two positions along the goal line (with various elevations). The goalkeeper could calculate easily where it would arrive, at one of only two locations. However, that was not what happened – the struck balls arrived at a series of locations along the goal line, demonstrating quantum wave/particle expression beyond any reasonable doubt. Although the context was outside of a game, the researchers concluded that this would sufficiently mimic the conditions extant during such a highly charged game as to be conclusive proof of football-fan-generated quantum interference and football wave/particle duality.

It seems that when a football has a buckyball structure, and is composed of hexagon segments, when fan super-wake REM-dream gamma-wave expression reaches such a crescendo of pitch, football-fan-advanced quantum connectivity and quantum interference becomes manifest, and the game transmutes from Newtonian space–time expression to quantum complexity. A goal is a quantum event, and because the fans are inextricably connected via gamma-wave interference, only at this moment does quantum potential emerge into perception and conscious cognition. Many philosophers have tried unsuccessfully to discover and describe the notion of quantum consciousness. Now at last a great team of passienic researchers have discovered just where Newtonian mechanics is expressed through quantum dynamics, during a highly charged electromagnetic gamma-wave event in certain football stadia during certain football games.

Only football dissolves the barrier between the quantum and classical state. In football, the classical state emerges through the quantum state, and via decoherence – a system that allows superposition to manifest from a series of position potentials such that position,

energy, momentum and so on, are both preserved or conserved in time evolution, despite quantum uncertainty. The *goal* expresses this most elegantly and beautifully, although *goal* is not the exclusive domain; other events, such as block, tackle, save, may reach quantum expression, and this may be catalysed – by football-fan quantum interference via gamma-wave super-wake REM-dream electromagnetic effects. In other words, the quantum *wave* function may not be apparent to our senses as the flow of the game unfolds, but it is most certainly present during probability.

We know that when Gordon Smith crossed the ball from the right wing and Lawrie Reilly's left-angled cranium collided with the ball, Heisenberg's Uncertainty Principle was negated and a GOAL was scored. Here, probability fulfilled potentials – the event, the trajectory, articulated translocation via multiple states, multiple moments, multiple potentials, multiple uncertainties, multiple probabilities, and multiple wave functions, and via the GSmith constant (g) arrived at superposition fruition as GOAL. The fans fully comprehended this incipient quantum manifestation and expression by its incorporation within classical Newtonian dynamics, via their advanced super-lucid wake-REM electromagnetic gamma-wave manifestation.

This is the ultimate expression of Fan super-lucid REM-wake mentation and electromagnetic gamma-wave entanglement and interference in the flow of the game, where goal potential and probability are manifest in quantum particle/wave motion, and GOAL is expressed via superposition of the ball, under the influence of the GSmith (g) constant. This was voted by readers of *Football Physics World* as the most beautiful experiment in the history of science, resigning the famous Double-Split Experiment by Davisson and Germer in 1927 to second place.

Referees have a unique ability to initiate quantum collapse so that quantum superposition collapses into a Newtonian classical event – a GOAL. There may be multiple goal potentials, multiple positions, multiple trajectories, multiple wave functions and multiple world interpretations where a goal exists or does not exist, but only the superposition player (under the influence of fan gamma-wave quantum interference) and the quantum creativity of such a player emerging from (and within) the contracted space-wave and dilated time-wave of the football pitch/stadia can express the potential goal as a probability, combined with the referees observation and quantum collapse into *goal*.

Another landmark study at the Landon Donovan Passienic University of Soccer Quantum Physics, at Tucson, Arizona, in association with the Hameroff

Center for Consciousness, found *proto*consciousness in soccer balls that were constructed by hexagons, in the form of buckyballs – a form that optimises universal quantum articulation – and multiple potentials that could be traced neurologically in the microtubules of a referee's brain, where football quantum coherence may collapse into decoherence and observation of *goal*. This was the first time researchers examined advanced high-order quantum sensitivity in a referee's cerebral cortex, essentially confirming that a referee is *born* and not environmentally nurtured.

Football is therefore a rich field for discovering how underlying quantum dynamics is expressed in Newtonian mechanics, not only on and in the environment of the pitch or stadia, but also manifest in consciousness. It is appropriate to note that this new area of locomotive and consciousness studies is opposed by researchers of artificial intelligence, who develop the RoboCup potential, and there seems little prospect of cross-fertilisation. Perhaps "neoteny as quantum creativity" may provide a bridging or linking potential, since it is known that children express elevated quantum neurone processing in their microtubules, along with a higher rate of cerebral energy metabolism and greater quantum coherence and decoherence, than more senior *Homo passiens*.

Yet another iconic study at the Tucson facility discovered that the mession bioparticle has provided evidence of quantum tunnelling. The researchers selected football players with hyper-mession articulation and opposed them with extreme and violent defensive line-up with players who over-expressed *HIPhit* and *ELBhit* in their genomes. Their goal-trajectory expression potentials were significantly reduced. The hyper-messionic footballers had no difficulty is overcoming the insurmountable defensive barrier via the Heisenberg Uncertainty Principle and wave/particle duality. The ball appeared to occupy two positions simultaneously – anterior and posterior to a defender, a superposition that resulted in quantum collapse in favour of reverse-wave articulation and freely impinging on goal. A Newtonian classical *goal* was observed and the Heisenberg Uncertainty Principle negated, influenced by fan collective super-lucid gamma-wave quantum interference. The collapse (or gollapse) was the moment of consciousness – of GOAL!

This historic study opened a new field (super-field, in fact) in thermodynamics known as Ergolic Theory, a hypothesis that is also referred to as a *golchastic* process. It is underpinned by the work of James Clark Maxwellian-probability mathematics. Several passienic physics laboratories around the world are currently following this up.

Quantum spiral waves in football

Football has been one of the leading fields of inquiry during the evolution of *Homo passiens*, generating the sciences of mechanics and mathematics throughout the period of prehistory, and during the more recent period known as history. Isaac Newton was very interested in the game of football, and was a great fan of Leicester City as a boy. In 1672, Newton noted that a spinning football expressed a curved trajectory. A century later, in 1742, Benjamin Robins demonstrated that a transverse aerodynamic force was instrumental in the trajectory of a spinning football – known as the "Robin Spinning-Football Effect". The lateral deflection of a rotating football was later credited to Heinrich Gustav Magnus, and become known as the "Magnus Football Effect".

Lord Rayleigh, who played briefly for Cambridge United,

developed his interest in the trajectory of footballs directly as a result of his interest in the ballistics of cannon balls. He was fascinated by the mechanics and physics of football and, in his stunning hypothesis, showed that the side force of a spinning football is proportional to the velocity of the ball, and its rotational speed. In 1904, the Boundary-Layer hypothesis was introduced by Ludwig Prandtl (a great fan of Bayern Munich) as an explanation for the spinning dynamics of a well-struck curving football. Daniel Bernouilli, who in the 18th century supported Zenit St Petersburg when he was a resident in that city, noted that in football-lift dynamics (as in an elegant chip over the advancing goalkeeper), air pressure kinetics were also involved, with respect to the difference in pressure between the upper and lower surfaces. When air beneath the football moves faster than the air below, the upper air has a lower pressure than the air below, and the result generates an upward force from higher to lower pressure. This is also known as the "Bernouilli Football Effect".

Incidentally, while studying football mathematics and physics at the famous Krestovsky Stadium (home of Zenit Saint Petersburg), Bernouilli articulated the "St Petersburg Paradox", which he published in the *Commentaries of the Imperial Academy of Science of Saint Petersburg* in 1738. The original hypothesis is known to have been articulated by Daniel's brother, Nicholas Bernouilli, who first wrote about it in September 1713 in a letter to the French mathematician Pierre Raymond de Montmort. De Montmort knew Isaac Newton, who shared an interest with Nicholas and de Montfort in football mathematics and statistics. In Nicholas's celebrated football hypothesis, advanced by his brother Daniel – the aforementioned St Petersburg Paradox – a successful striker scores a goal with 50% probability in a given game, in the next game with

25% probability, and 12.5% probability in the following game.

One of the most ancient universal and cultural "hospitality practices" of *Homo passiens* is that in bipedal football the home team provides the ball. This behaviour reflects the more altruistic expression of that nominate species. In modern football, the more advanced thinking (although less altruistic) professional football teams may use this to their advantage. Within the formal FIFA design parameters for a football, there is much potential for modification by one team or another, to take advantage of specialised football morphology, given their awareness of the particular local micro-climate along with atypical atmospheric, environmental and topographic conditions.

All footballers are trained in classical Newtonian mechanics to understand and modulate football trajectories, so that they may influence the spherical motion dynamics during football flow, in favour of goal gain-of-function, and advanced defence articulations either by defenders or goalkeepers, for high-value antagonised goal inhibition.

Now, with improved understanding of latent quantum-motion expression through, and within, classical mechanics, some very advanced professional football teams have introduced quantum physics coaches, who are trained both in classical physics and quantum flow dynamics.

It is now well known that under the influence of super-wake REM-dream and gamma-wave cascades and influences, quantum interference may manifest during football games and modulate the trajectory aerodynamics of footballs, affecting drag and lift coefficients and even spin dynamics, which in turn are modulated by atmospheric conditions and height above sea level.

When a football is struck with a powerful Magnus force, such that it bends away from a linear trajectory to the right or left, in some very few instances the curvilinear momentum may be enhanced, so that the further the distance travelled from the kicking boot, the greater the curve potential. The spin may be affected by drag, lift and spin coefficients. Many passienic studies have observed the transition from laminar to turbulent flow and the football transiting into a quantum spiral wave, whereby the goalkeeper is unable to adjust position in space or time and influence the ball's trajectory, thus a quantum goal (Qg) may be scored. It was also observed that under conditions like this, when football-fan dynamics express super-REM wake-dream and gamma-wave cascades, and there is football-fan quantum interference in the flow of the game, space volume contractions are noted, and time dilations are observed. Mession bioparticle articulations increase significantly. Quantum helical and tunnell-ing parameters are upgraded, along with football (actually buckyball particle/wave) modulations, such that the football appears spontaneously both anteriorly and posteriorly to a particular defender – again, often concluding in the scoring of a quantum goal.

The brilliant Passienic Quantum Physics team also studied football trajectories under the influences of pitch/stadium height above sea level and smooth or embossed surfaces of the ball. It has been known for some time that in the reduced air density of higher altitudes, drag, lift and spin coefficients are significantly modulated, and footballs behave with augmented unstable predictability. The team travelled to the twin Cities of Edinburgh and Leith, a geographical region that is profoundly hilly, where two topographically different, but geographically close, professional football teams play at very divergent altitudes. Cloud cover is major influence, along with variations in air pressure dynamics.

Hearts of Midlothian FC play at the celebrated Stadium of Tynecastle at an elevation of a thousand feet, and Hibernian FC play at Easter Road, around two hundred feet above sea level, with significantly different relevant air densities. Hearts invariably play with smooth balls, a strategy that accentuates the reduction of drag coefficient (this parameter is already reduced by the relatively low air density). Hibs, on the other hand, always use roughly embossed balls with hexagonal (quantum buckyball-shaped) panels, which increase drag coefficients and reinforce football-fan quantum interference modulations.

Hibs of course, are also enabled to benefit from their fan-base's cohort of sophisticated gain-of-function super-wake REM-dream gamma-wave manifestation that activates high-order quantum interference in the play, allowing for wave/ particle duality along with quantum tunnelling, such that ball may be located both anterior and posterior to a defender at exactly the same moment. This facilitates football particle/ wave modulations, again often concluding in the scoring of a quantum goal.

The Discovery of the Schrodinger Goal (Sg) in Football Quantum Physics

A Schrodinger goal is a goal that has collapsed from a superposition of multiple potential Schrodinger goals (Sg) and Schrodinger no-goals (Sng) events, into an observable goal event, and is one that may be measured in the classical state by a Newtonian referee, and recorded in formal statistics that are integrated into league and cup competition indexes. In very rare and unique circumstances, in a given quantum lucidity stadium (Qls), in which football-fan REM gamma-wave cycles collide and envelop the participants, the players and fans (and the football) in quantum interference and entanglement, creating such an elusive event, the evolution of which may be detected from outwith the stadium; only then may the goal-superposition function manifest, and the goal superposition (Gs) and multiple potentials collapse into a Schrodinger Goal (Sg). Several passienic studies have interpreted superposition Gs function that collapses into Schrodinger goals (Sg) as compensated by a Schrodinger no-goal (NGs) in one of infinite universes (Sng) or in classical mechanics observed by a Newtonian referee as a collapse into a classical miss (Cm).

A Muntari–Mach interferometer (named after the brilliant Ghanaian footballer, Sulley Muntari, and the famous physicist Ernst Mach) is a passienic device invented by a team at the Sulley Muntari Passienic Quantum Physics Laboratory at Pescara, Abruzzo in Italy. It may determine the outcome of a "goal super-potential" when two shots are struck in a quantum stadium (QS) from a single penalty spot. When the ball passes through a particular space point in the area of goal potential and the ball is a no-goal ball, a Schrodinger no-goal (Sng) or classical Newtonian Miss (Cm) is recorded. When a ball passes through a fan quantum-interference position, modulated by football-fan advanced super-lucid REM-wake quantum interference, it gains superposition with multiple goal potentials and its wave function collapses into a quantum goal event (Qg), then a Schrodinger goal (Sg) is scored and recorded by a Newtonian referee. The Muntari–Mach interferometer measures which of the routes is followed and which will collapse into a Shrodinger goal (Sg) or Schrodinger no-goal or miss (Sm).

When a detection is made by a Muntari–Mach interferometer from without the quantum stadium (QS), the goal superposition Gs collapses into a known result at 50% of quantum potential, and a

Schrodinger goal (*Sg*) occurs. There is now a 25% potential of a quantum no-goal outcome, and in this case the superposition collapses into a Schrodinger no-goal (*Sng*) event or classical miss (*Cm*). Balls have been observed in both goal- and no-goal-potential superposition states that have maintained their superposition status and failed to collapse into the classical state, causing a multiple quantum-negative super-wave across the quantum stadium (*QS*) and a massive increase in super-frustration charge, which can be recorded by the Muntari–Mach interferometer.

These quantum-negative super-waves, and their manifestation as super-frustration fluxes, may be rare, but they are being recorded in many passienic faculties with greater frequency. In some studies, they have been directly correlated with low economic circumstances, and elevated coefficients of fan incidences of violence. In other studies they have been associated directly with reduced football-fan hopamine, hopoid and scorotonin expression (the HHS index), which is known to correlate with reduced football-fan quantum interference in the game, as well as low football-fan esteem and poor match results.

One study also demonstrated that a low HHS index is a major factor in poor super-lucid REM gamma-wave cycling during football matches, with consequent loss of quantum-interference modulation of the football, reduced superposition mession/wave potentials, and poor football-player quantum expression and articulation. This leads to elevated negative super-waves and super-frustration fluxes, along with poor results. Schrodinger goal (*Sg*) potentials are significantly below mean values and Schrodinger no-goal (*Sng*) potentials are radically raised. This is found to be consistent with increased visits to quantum football physicians by fans who are seeking improved synthesis and release of the neotenous bipedal football-hormone cascades, including hopamines, hopoids and scorotonins.

The wiser physicians advise their clients to avoid drugs, and to look instead to the wisdom of neotenous bipedal football, and encourage their fan comrades to practise enhanced lucidity and wake super-REM dream gamma-wave articulation, such that gamma-wave expression increases to a level such that quantum coherence and interference emerge and raise the Schrodinger (Sg) goal potentials, while reducing Schrodinger no-goal (Sng) potentials with high collapse outcomes into classical goals. These may be measured by Muntari–Mach interferometers and Newtonian referees during future football games – the only truly healthy way to upgrade their HHS index.

Of course, the opposite prognosis applies to fans who are highly schooled in wake super-REM dream-gamma-wave expression with consequent elevated quantum coherence and interference in any game in which the quality of football-fan hymning, expressed by high articulation of hopamines, hopoids and scorotonin, and where the quantum super-wave flux reaches such a firmament that the classical football stadium transmutes into a quantum stadium (QS). In such cases, Schrodinger goal potentials rise above the 50% point, Schrodinger no-goal potentials tend to zero, and quantum collapse into Schrodinger goals (Sg) and classical Newtonian goal-scoring outcomes become a major probability. This type of quantum event is known to correlate directly with improved physiological and psychological health of the fans.

A new field of scientific inquiry has recently emerged known as Quantum Mind – a theory that includes the notion of quantum consciousness as articulated by the physicist Roger Penrose and the anaesthetist Stuart Hameroff. Not only does this approach begin to explain how and in what way consciousness emerges (as a megaHertz quantum proto-conscious structure of reality) within microtubule proteins inside neurones, but it is also recognised as a fundamental principle of all matter in the universe – living matter simply orchestrates the random expression of material proto-consciousness into an orchestrated coherence that articulates consciousness present; it is inherent at every level of organic matter, including for photosynthesis in plants and migration in birds. This emerging paradigm beautifully confirms the earlier prescient hypothesis advanced by Professor Gordon P. McNeil on the protoconsciousness of the football.

CHAPTER 12

Absurdity, the Theory of Football Relativity and the Anthropology of Gambling

Gordon and I were drinking in the Football Absurdity Bar – also known as the Café Royal in Edinburgh's West Register Street, on a snappy autumnal day in October.

The Football Absurdity Bar is another beautiful old bar in the city, close to Princes Street, standing next door to the equally famous Guildford Bar. This ancient bar was a regular haunt of the poets Robert Burns and Adam Ferguson in their time. It has recently developed into the headquarters of a group of enthusiastic football anthropologists, who gather there during seminars and conferences.

The Café Royal has, in more recent times, become a favoured haunt of the Edinburgh literary, medical and scientific establishment and legal luminaries and financial experts who spilled out of the many publishing, insurance and banking institutions nearby, and who formed the core, along with recently arrived illegal drug entrepreneurs, of the nascent Edinburgh bourgeoisie. From its earlier manifestation as a rather functional and no-nonsense drinking establishment favoured by railwaymen, builders, plumbers, carpenters, electricians, post-office engineers, retail clerks, and so on, it was redesigned by the Edinburgh architect Robert Pearson, in 1863, to become a Parisian-styled elegant and beautifully adorned, fine Victorian hostelry. It is particularly treasured for its beautiful wall tiles depicting famous Scottish thinkers, engineers and scientists.

Anthropology has over the years been guilty of not focusing on football – the highest expression of bipedal neoteny in the species *Homo sapiens*, and of course *Homo passiens*, and indeed of cultural tribalism – simply because it did not seem sufficiently exotic or interesting, being firmly based, as it is, in the less affluent communities around the world – a somewhat arrogant and patronising view. However, this perspective has recently changed, and anthropologists now realise they may be missing a universal and rich area for studying human social and cultural behaviour, and the collective unconscious expression of the social psyche. Football play and football-fan behaviour is now a growing area of research within biological and physical anthropology, and within archaeological and linguistic anthropology, all around the world.

Several passienic universities have pioneered research in the area, as well as into human biological, evolutionary and demographic disciplines. But in recent years, new study groups have also sprung up, including one of particular interest – the FREE (Football Research in an Enlarged Europe).

Burns delivering his "Address to the Fitba" at Ayr United FC where he is believed to have played football. The poem is etched onto an old 18th-century window beneath the Ali MacLeod Stand.

Fair and fu' is your honest, fitba' face,
Great chieftain o' the spherical race!
Above them a' ye tak yir place,
Wi' twa legs, twa feet, and fitba' grace,
Then let us pray that come it may,
As come it will for a' that,
That sense and worth, o'er a' the earth,
Shall be the fitba' gift, an' a' that,
That fan to fan, the world o'er,

This group comprises anthropologists from nine game; they are not costly to produce and although they access the brain via the retina, they do not impair vision. And, yes – mirror neurones in the parietal region universities from eight different countries;

it focuses on the dynamics of football identity, patterns of perception, and non-political subcultural expressions of European public-space communication. It focuses on collective memories of European football identity and mobility, feminisation in modern football, and approaches to football governance – in fact, all the subjects that the group around Gordon P. McNeil regularly discuss in the Albert Camus Bar and other popular drinking forums.

FREE aims "to disseminate awareness, among citizens, stakeholders and policy-makers, of the issue of popular cultural diversity and commonality in the field of popular culture, and its often underestimated impact on the political, economic and social dimensions of the European integration process".

The Football Absurdity Bar has also become a meeting place for scholars, academics and students of "play anthropology" around the world. The Association for the Study of Play originated in Minneapolis, Minnesota, in 1973, when Alyce Taylor Cheska convened and chaired a meeting of more than thirty scholars who were interested, and publishing, in the field of play research. The group later reorganised as the Association for the Anthropological Study of Play, with B. Allan Tindall as its first president. In 1987, the name was altered to The Association for the Study of Play (TASP). The owners of the Football Absurdity Bar claim that a group like this already existed in the 1960s somewhere in the city, but some regulars express scepticism about this. A photograph of the group is said to exist, but has not so far been made available to researchers in the field. Nonetheless, this elegant old tavern has evolved into a popular forum for discussion and debate among three groups of researchers in studies related to *Homo passiens* play, passienic anthropologists, FREE football anthropologists, and play anthropologists. Other visitors include anthropologists of gambling, scholars of Huizinga studies, and evolutionary biologists who favour a bipedal neotenous explanation for the development of *Homo* species.

Whenever Gordon P. McNeil is present, the debating noise reaches makes such a clamour and tumult that the police have been called on more than one occasion.

Mike: Is football absurd, Gordon?

Gordon: Absurd? Oh, yes. The universe is indifferent and therefore absurd. Life is absurd. Football most certainly is absurd. Camus understood that this above all applied to football players, and of course goalkeepers.

Mike: And yet he – Camus – loved football as he loved dreams?

Gordon: He did, Mike. He expressed the goalkeeper's schizoid and dual role in dreams, in the *dream-game* – "I like them because they are double, they are here and elsewhere … I like people who talk to themselves interminably". All goalkeepers do so.

Mike: He knew that goalkeepers were, and are, schizoid. And also driven by their innate, primordial desire to win and to dominate – "… what does it matter, after all, if by humiliating one's mind, one succeeds in dominating every one? I discovered in myself sweet dreams of oppression …". Do you regard this as fundamentally passienic, Gordon? An expression of non-reciprocal passing altruism?

Gordon: I do, Mike, but Camus was unique in his sweet dreams of oppression.

Mike: Goalkeepers are largely incapable of non-reciprocal passing altruism. Rarely if ever do you see a goalkeeper act selfishly – their schizoid mentation and psychology allows them to intuit the other.

Gordon: Yes. Camus himself, on the other hand, was always a rebel, his own man, an outsider, a free-rider. And with oppressive intent, which he recognised openly. He had a desire to dominate, as all successful footballers must have. Bipedal upright consciousness breeds arrogance, as it must do, so absurd is it as a form of physiology and survival, a Sisyphusian species engaged in a quite preposterous attempt to survive without the appropriate anatomy and physiology – the necessary armour – in a hostile environment.

Mike: By absurd you mean a weak-jawed, clawless, carnivorous species and yet with the teeth of a small, slow-motion and vulnerable herbivore (upright, bipedal and slow), and therefore generally in full view of all hungry predators, and indeed other hostile hominid groups?

Gordon: Absolutely. And this is close to Camus and his expression of existential absurdity in football and in life. The survival of any hominoid or *Homo* species, who must rely on a slow bipedal motion, is quite absurd.

Mike: Any sentient bookmakers in the Passeolithic would give massive odds against this *Homo* species surviving for longer than a millennia. An expression of the absurdity of bipedalism, of the idea that a quadrupedal sentient species might laugh at the absurd madness of a slow-motion knock-kneed bipedal species, with a big and greedy bipedal brain, surviving in a hostile world?

Gordon: That is precisely how I view Camus, Mike. He articulated the absurd, and showed that football is the key, the route – if you like – to raising the absurd to its highest paradoxical and noblest expression. He once said "All that I know most surely about morality and obligations, I owe to football".

Mike: He, she – football player – confronts and challenges the absurd, the meaningless of life in a universe that is both indifferent and hostile, of such Sisyphusian absurdity, to climb the upward trajectory of life, of football, only to fall again and again. Football illustrates this absurd dilemma for any young player, out of millions of others, to imagine that he or she could mount the heights of club and international success, and survive, in spite of the most outrageous, the most momentous, odds against. Each young "football hopeful" accepts the absurd stack of odds against them, confronts the colossus of absurdity (and each step at a time), with each kick, each header, each goal, with each reciprocal and non-reciprocal pass. He confronts relegation and outloans, and is exposed to the dangerous winds of opposition within and without the club – officials, coaches, injuries, substitutions, team politics, jealousies, greedy and indifferent owners, powerful economic forces, chronic modern overtraining, poor fuelling protocols, post-career metabolic illness, and finally hostile media and impatient fan critiques. The absurd challenge is invariably met with dignity, energy, morality and obligation.

Gordon: Yes, Mike. You expressed that elegantly, as always. As Camus says of Sisyphus "by acknowledging the truth of the absurd, the absurd is negated".

Mike: In the malign silence of the crowd, the absurd is briefly triumphant, the dream is pierced, shattered, until some beauteous, lucidic and transcendental pass, move, step-over, cross, shot or save, reconnects the crowd with the numinous, poetic, ancient, and collective passienic unconscious, and the *dream-game* returns in a musical howling, roaring, cataclysmic cacophony storm of balletic bipedal skill, or opposed-thumb success and thunderous noise?

Early stone vignette depicting crowd and players in one notable match. Passienic specialists interpret the glyphys thus: The two sides lined up with a 4-4-2 formation against a 3-5-2. It was a bad-tempered match with some questionable officiating and a serious injury. The restless crowd was deeply unhappy with a sending off. Then (against the run of play) there was a breakaway move and a brilliant goal was scored. The crowd cheered and the players celebrated a famous win.

Gordon: Football is absurd, but football meets, revolts against, and frees us from absurdity. It was Camus who showed that the road forward from absurdity is (paradoxically *via* absurdity, via plunging wholeheartedly into the absurd) the road to existential freedom.

Mike: Absurdity is relative, not absolute, then?

Gordon: Yes. Absurdity is its own other. Einstein knew that dreams were the key. Dreams free us from the tyranny of the given. They free us from the tyranny of law. We know that Einstein and Camus shared a passion for football and dreams – do you know that Einstein himself said: "At least once a day allow yourself the freedom to think and dream for yourself"?

Mike: No. I haven't heard that one. How do we know?

Gordon: A young researcher in the history of passienology uncovered this quote at the library in Princeton University. She found considerable correspondence between the writer of the article and the physicist himself, which will be published soon in the *Journal of Homo Passiens Culture* – a journal for which I am the Editor.

Mike: And they discussed?

Gordon: Universal absolute and relative indifference; expressed as absolute and relative absurdity.

Mike: Expressed in football? Expressed and yet negated through football?

Gordon: Yes. For Einstein, the faster we travel the slower is the time frame within which we move. Energy and time are both inseparable and relatively inversely proportional. I have interpreted this in terms of football in: *The Football Theory of Relativity* – my book on the subject. I have a contract to publish it with Neotenic Books, also based at Princeton University.

Mike: Cool. And what is the Football Exercise Theory of Relativity? And what relevance does it have for modern football players? *E* equals *MC* squared?

Gordon: No. *E* equals *CM* squared.

Mike: Oh? Please elaborate, Gordon.

Gordon: The Football Exercise Theory of Relativity states that the most important, absolute and overriding fuelling parameter in any exercise or recovery protocol is that of optimal provision of cerebral energy. The human brain affords the highest energy consumption of any tissue known in nature, and on a gram-for-gram basis, burns twenty times more fuel than any other human tissue, including muscle. That's the Expensive Tissue Hypothesis. In addition, the brain has virtually no storage capacity and must rely almost exclusively on glucose released from the small stores of glycogen in the liver. During exercise, the contracting muscles extract glucose from the circulation at an accelerated rate, thus depleting the liver, and thereby competing with the brain for fuel – and placing the brain at risk of metabolic meltdown.

Mike: But what about the difference in the formula from Einstein's historic one? The "M" and "C" are reversed. I suppose this draws attention to the critical role of cerebral energy reserve – "C" – in modulating "M" – the energy consumed in muscle?

Gordon: That's it, Mike.

Mike: And "E" in this case represents the total energy evolved in any exercise protocol from glucose in muscle tissue, or the total glucose oxidised by contracting muscles, and since glucose is the fuel that correlates to power, "E" represents the power evolved. In other words, "E" equals Power Output?

Gordon: Excellent. "C", on the other hand, represents the glucose available for provisioning cerebral energy. This is not simply the glucose sequestered in cerebral cells – this amount is tiny and may be depleted by exercise within thirty to sixty seconds. Nor is it simply the glucose contained in the circulation during exercise – there is only five grams here, just enough for a few minutes at best. But rather, it is the total reserve fuel available for cerebral uptake.

Mike: That means that the liver glycogen store is the only significant reserve-energy store available to the brain at all times, and in particular during exercise, when contracting muscles extract glucose from the circulation at an accelerated rate, placing the brain at risk of metabolic meltdown. That's why we characterise the liver as the *most* critical fuel store during any exercise! So footballers who fail to include this organ in their fuelling protocols pay a heavy price in performance and health.

Gordon: You have interpreted that well, Mike. Note that included in this cerebral energy provision is the ability of the liver to convert protein into new glucose, as its store depletes. And this creation of new glucose (known as gluconeogenesis) is both the solution and the problem. For it to occur, the brain must activate the HPA axis (the hypothalamus–pituitary–adrenal axis) and release adrenaline and cortisol, the stress hormones that facilitate the whole process. In other words, these hormones are not fight-

or-flight hormones, as taught in medical schools – although they are released during fight and flight episodes. Rather, they are cerebral or neuroprotective hormones.

Mike: Their job is to forward-provision the liver, and therefore the brain, when cerebral energy provision is compromised. Therefore, the total reserve-energy supply available to the brain consists of cerebral glycogen, blood glucose, liver glycogen and – of course – the protein that may be converted to glucose (mainly muscle) to replenish the liver. It should be clear to any football player that by optimally provisioning the liver prior to play, and during play, the brain is optimally provisioned, and the activation of adrenal stress will be minimised.

Gordon: That is correct, Mike. In our equatin, "M" represents the total glucose oxidised in muscle *apart* from the additional glucose delivered and oxidised relative to "C".

Mike: So the square of "M" represents the increased glucose made available to muscle resulting from the increase in "C", and that is the additional glucose provisioned to muscle, via the liver, as a direct result of the rise in "C"?

Gordon: Yes. Although we may state this differently. "M" squared is a measure of total glucose oxidation in muscle, including increased glucose delivered to muscle from the liver, resulting from increased cerebral energy reserve "C", and consequently it is a measure of increased glucose oxidation in contracting muscles. And therefore of increased power output! Or, increasing cerebral energy reserve increases power output. Or—

Mike: Powering the brain, powers muscles! E equals CM squared.

Gordon: Yes.

Mike: Metaphorically speaking?

Gordon: Yes, metaphorically. But potently! It is the squared element of our Exercise Theory of Relativity that renders the theory as metaphorical. If it were the case that the increase in glucose delivered to muscle – "M" – as a direct result of optimally provisioning cerebral energy – "C" and this quantitative-resulting increased glucose supply were actually squared, the exponential increase in power output would be of superhuman magnitude, and would make Superman seem positively weak.

Mike: However, you'd have to keep this element of the formula for sound reasons – it immediately conjures up Einstein's fabulous theory, it allows us to keep the formula's essential integrity, and it focuses football minds on the critical role of cerebral energy provision during exercise.

Gordon: I could not put it better myself. So, yes. I make no apology for retaining this "value". Everybody is familiar with Einstein's famous formula and the exercise version focuses football minds on the absolute necessity of optimising cerebral energy provision, whether before, during, or after all football events and play.

Mike: The theory might be only metaphorical, but it does caution the player to fuel his brain optimally.

Gordon: That's the point.

Mike: Did you pick up on the relative theory of time perception in house-flies compared to humans?

Gordon: Funnily enough, I did. And this relates to the glial – Einstein – cells. Einstein would have loved this relative theory.

Mike: I take it, the glial cells transfer energy across the blood–brain barrier into the brain?

Gordon: Yes. Via the cerebral glucose pump. And any increased speed of energy transfer would allow for increased information to enter the brain in a given time, thereby causing the brain to process more information – faster.

Mike: And when time as slower? Like when people describe being in a crisis, like a car crash. They describe time as slowing down.

Gordon: Yes. And for them relative time *did* slow down. They did process more information in a given time frame.

Mike: Therefore, the inverse relation between time and energy applies in *all* relations between time, energy and space. In all motion. Also in the subjective perception of time. It's all relative to cerebral energy metabolism.

Gordon: Exactly.

Mike: Well, that has major implications for football. A player who transmits extra information, via increased glial energy processing of information required to map the game – about the positions and relative motions of the opposing team and own team players, to control the ball, run or pass, shoot or cross, cut inside or out, dive or remain upright – has increased time available to do so? Relative to others, that is.

Gordon: All the greatest football players express this ability. They think faster, react faster, and play faster.

Mike: Are their ratios of glial to neural cells universally higher than the majority of others?

Gordon: Great football players do all express this increased ratio of glial cells to neurones. As, indeed, do great football fans. These studies have been decisive. Some lovely work at the Jim Baxter Institute of Passienic Energy Metabolism at Hill of Beath, has confirmed this beyond doubt.

Mike: And what of the *dream-game*? REM sleep is the highest expression of cerebral energy processing in nature. Can we relate this also to relative perceptive slow-down of dreamtime? And therefore a relative increase in dream production, during specialised neo-narcoleptic and inhibited muscle atonia?

Gordon: Yes. Relative modulation of time, energy and space applies to subjective experiences in life and in dreams.

Mike: So, in football, the relativity of dreamtime neo-narcoleptic experience, both subjective and objective, is the highest expression of emotional homeostasis known to man.

Gordon: It is. And it's also the high road to negation of – and freedom through – absurdity!

Mike: Cool. And bipedalism is absurd, too, Gordon.

Gordon: Totally absurd! Without the evolutionary selection for neotenous bipedal football, sacrificing one – or even two legs – for the benefit of a large and greedy brain, is frankly nuts. Insane!

Mike: Football is absurd, alright. But paradoxically, it rescues us from the absurd.

Gordon: I agree wholeheartedly.

Mike: Do you think that the absurd rapid increase in leg length which takes place in *Homo* species during the first year of life is a feature of neotenous bipedal football – in this case of acceleration as opposed to delay?

Gordon: Bipedalism and the flat foot are, in my opinion, the two most absurd anatomical features of *Homo* species. Can you elaborate further, Mike?

Mike: By neoteny, I mean the appearance of ancestral juvenile characteristics in adult descendents, such as the non-opposable big toe, a foetal form found in adult humans, and incidentally a fundamental characteristic of any bipedal footballing species. *Homo* infants are born with very small and underdeveloped legs, and I wonder if that may be correlated with neotony?

Gordon: That's worth thinking about … I think the rapid growth of legs in the first year represents an acceleration, which upholds and strengthens neoteny. In no way does it constitute a *denial* of neoteny. It merely contradicts *delayed* development as an absolute. Relative acceleration of this or that tissue or organ does not in itself deny neoteny. It is perfectly reasonable that within the context of an overall retardation of the development of some features, for instance the *Homo* chin does not extend and the brow does not recede, each of these represents retardation. There could also be individual relative accelerations of any given organ or tissue.

Mike: In the case of *Homo passiens*, these are delayed and extended growth of the brain and accelerated growth of the legs. There are large numbers of evolutionary biologists who would like to deny the significance of neoteny, are there not?

Gordon: Actually Mike, there is in my opinion a kind of conspiracy to deny neoteny. Science is in open denial about neoteny. It offends their sense of "intellectual competence". Only yesterday I was reading the *Cambridge Encyclopaedia of Evolution*, which was profoundly dismissive and rejects neoteny with the quite ludicrous assertion that it is offered as a single explanation for the morphological, developmental and behavioural changes associated with the emergence of humankind.

Mike: Have the compilers of the *CEE* never heard of football?!

Gordon: No *passiens* or indeed scientist that I know of, Mike, who defends the validity of neoteny, suggests that it provides a single explanation for the evolutionary emergence of humankind. No biologist would make that ridiculous claim from among all the random mutational, selective, genetic, epigenetic and gene-switching mechanisms, or environmental, dietary and other forces acting on early *Homo* populations.

Mike: A neat trick, then, to accuse the opposition of what they are not guilty of, and then to demolish them by attacking that false accusation?

241

Gordon: Neat indeed, Mike. It reeks of opportunism. Note how the *CEE* listed the neotenous features of humans, including the structures of hands and feet (our friend the non-opposable big toe again; lack of brow ridges), brow ridges could you head a ball with, the flat face, and large relative brain? The *CEE* goes further and references our long life, sense of humour, song and dance – and then dismisses them as not related to neoteny.

Mike: Nuts! Do other primates sing and dance? Strange it seems that the *CEE* comes to an understanding of that most human characteristic – the neotenous extension of juvenile features and behaviour into adulthood – only to dismiss it. Perhaps the *CEE* is not familiar with Huizinga.

Gordon: I agree with you. The *CEE* gets close, and then veers off at a tangent. Comes within a whisker of putting its finger on the pulse, not only of evolutionary *Homo* neoteny, but also behavioural – and even cultural – neoteny. I should send them a copy of my manuscript: *The Role of Neoteny in the Complex Evolution of Homo Passiens*, to be published by Non-Opposable Toe Publications in Dunfermline. I'm still writing this one.

Mike: It sounds like a much-needed book. And yes, bipedalism is absurd, but successfully so! The *CEE* is absurd – but nuts!

Gordon: Definitely, Mike.

Mike: These are complex questions, Gordon, and although I have some residual concerns about the specific weight of neoteny in evolution, I certainly do not agree with the *CEE*. The argument becomes quite facile when it states that human infants resemble adult primates, when anybody with the slightest degree of objectivity would agree that this is *nonsense* and that human adults resemble infant primates rather than the reverse. If indeed human infants resembled adult primates, this would be a clear expression of recapitulation, would it not?

Gordon: No human infant ever resembled an adult primate! I noticed a wonderful photograph in Stephen Jay Gould's *Ontogeny and Phylogeny*, which compared an infant chimp with an adult chimp. The infant chimp in profile looks like a stern version of my old headmaster. The adult chimp looks like an adult chimp. The picture was from Naef and published in *Naturwiss* in 1926.

Mike: Recapitulation must be a blind alley so far as human emergence is concerned.

Gordon: Mike, you surprise me with your grasp of the role of neoteny in the evolution of *Homo* and *Homo passiens*. Recapitulation – the appearance of adult ancestral forms in the embryonic period of descendents – would dictate that an adult primate would indeed resemble a human infant! I defy any scientist in favour of recapitulation as being significant in human evolution – or *passiens* to show me an image of such a resemblance.

Mike: And back to the rapid growth of long legs in the first year?

Gordon: A bipedal species would have to develop long legs to run, to escape, to hunt, and perhaps to see over greater distances. Selective pressures would certainly encourage the development of longer legs in a bipedal species – for survival; whether this was on the savanna or not. This cannot take place *in utero* or in the foetal form because so much – actually seventy per cent of the foetal energy – is directed towards brain growth, to give as much protection to this organ as possible, and to complete as much formation as possible before birth.

Mike: Thus legs are left for special attention until after birth, and during the first year of life outside the womb. Upright locomotion results from elongated legs for running, hunting – and for football. And along with legs that are specialised for running, we develop feet that are specialised for kicking and jumping. If we need proof of our evolution for football, we only need to look at leg development in that first year of life after birth.

On the way back from the gents' conveniences, Mike was approached by the barman. "Was that Professor Gordon P. McNeil discussing post-foetal acceleration of long-leg growth in Homo passiens?" he asked.

Mike: Yes.

"Those recapitulationists! Ernst Haeckel. He was most certainly wrong about recapitulation. He wasn't bad for his time, though, was he? But these modern recapitulationists ... Neighbour, they should get the red card. Take two neotenists, Stephen Jay Gould and the great Dutchman Louis Bolk – he was an early exponent of neoteny. They're in my team, neighbour! They're in my forward line. The neotenists versus the recapitulationists – some tie! The neotonists up against the gerontomorphists. The gerontomorphists represent recapitulation, too. Neighbour, there's only one winner. Three points for neoteny! A hat trick for the Dutchman, old Louis Bolk. Three brilliant goals – one the position of the foramen magnum; two, the large relative brain growth; and three, the non-opposable big toe. And Prof. McNeil – he can be coach!"

Mike: Is there a role for neoteny, Gordon, in the mysterious ratio of left-sided players, compared to right-sided players? We know that around fifteen per cent of all footballers are left-sided, and no discipline that I am aware of seems to offer an explanation?

Gordon: First of all, Mike, let's address this from the perspective of physics. The universe itself is "sided" and not homogeneous – or we would not exist. Lack of homogeneity gave rise to all the differential formations of our galaxies, stars and planets, and everything else we know of – including ourselves. We are formed from matter that is itself sided. Biological amino acids are almost exclusively left-rotational under the universal laws of nature. So our sidedness is simply an expression of deep law.

Mike: Okay. Perhaps I should have asked how the evolution of "sidedness" is expressed in the *Homo* species?

Gordon: You asked if neotony may have played a role in the evolution and expression of sidedness in the *Homo* species. Yes, it certainly did so. Humans are born as foetal embryos, and fail to metamorphose into the adult version, retaining their foetal anatomy and physiology throughout life. Our primate ancestors do not express in any significant degree of sidedness, but both of the *Homo* species – *passiens* and *sapiens* do. So we should begin from there.

Mike: Are you suggesting that in any species, quadrupedal or semi-quadrupedal, such as primates, that sidedness is not a major biological concern?

Gordon: I am indeed. Any structural engineer would know that building an upright physical structure on only two bases would be disastrous – three or more are always necessary for stability. Gravity has to be overcome – quite apart from any other environmental forces around. Plants use multiple roots to enable them to maintain upright stability, to reach and capture sunlight.

Mike: And obviously bipedal locomotion adds to the eccentric and chaotic forces that such a species must meet – gravitational, atmospheric and those from other hostile groups and predators.

Gordon: Bipedalism is a very strange form of locomotion. Absurd, as we agree. No other mammals adopt this strategy, though some birds use it to hop around, but usually only briefly. And they must be ready to take off at all moments, because it is so unstable. Grasshoppers are a species that use this form of locomotion, but only at very high speeds, when their momentum briefly overcomes the gravitational force.

Mike: It would not be unreasonable, then, to mention that for young children and elderly humans falling down to the ground is a major source of injuries, morbidity and even death?

Gordon: It certainly would not be unreasonable! Upright bipedal locomotion contributes to frequent falls and injuries in both *Homo* species, and of course bipedal football demands that tackling constitutes a major additional injury and health hazard in such a species.

Mike: If it did not exist in both of the *Homo* species, it would not be a valid strategy to invent it?

Gordon: Upright bipedalism and its offshoot – neoteny – and the ejection of the foetus at nine months when the brain is only partially formed, is the most absurd event in the history of evolutionary biology! Perhaps the most absurd event in the history of the universe!

Mike: Camus was totally right. *Homo* species is absurd. Football is absurd.

Gordon: I quote: "*Football is absurd and surreal, but soaringly, transcendentally, lucidically beautiful, and joyous*".

Mike: Okay. I think I get it.

CHAPTER 13

Ancient Football in the Forth Valley: Stonehousemuir

I took the train from Waverley Station, at the east end of Princes Street in Edinburgh, one bright, curly, windy November day, and alighted near Arthur's O'on Bar, in the town of Stenhousemuir near Falkirk in Stirlingshire, in the beautiful Forth Valley of central Scotland, to meet Gordon and discuss football archaeology.

This celebrated and ancient bar had been a coaching house for several centuries, and had also served for some time as the social club of the local professional football team, Stenhousemuir FC. The old tavern was popular with landowners who had formed a local market in the early eighteenth century, known as the Falkirk Tryst, to meet the growing demand for hardy and rugged highland cattle that were increasingly sought by buyers from all around the United Kingdom after the 1707 Union. By 1785, Stenhousemuir had become host to the largest cattle market in the world. The major sales days were held on the first Tuesday in the months of August, September and October. At their height, the trysts were a sensational sight, with 150,000 cattle, sheep and horses arriving in great droves from all corners of Scotland, settling in the surrounding fields with ponies and dogs in the open, or with portable bivouacs. They were met by hundreds of dealers from around the UK, and supported by a tented village consisting of banks, shops and taverns. Football was the preferred pastime of those who wished to avoid the temptations on offer in the temporary taverns, which provided food, drink, and numerous other services. Following its brief stint as a social club, the ancient tavern was returned to its traditional hospitality role, and named Arthur's O'on (Scots for "oven") after a Roman monument that had existed nearby until 1743, when Sir Michael Bruce of Stenhouse had demolished the structure to rebuild a dam on the nearby River Carron. Arthur's O'on Bar is popular with students of the nearby Forth Valley College, students and academics of Ochilview Passienic University, visiting archaeologists, football anthropologists, antiquarian stone masons, visiting football fans going to games at Ochilview Football Stadium, evolutionary football scholars, classical architecture students, and historians of Roman Britain.

Gordon had informed me that a recent archaeological dig had unearthed evidence of the Roman sport of *harpastum*, or Roman football, close to the site of Arthur's O'on, and beneath that layer of digging there were other sensational finds to confirm the prehistoric and ancient sport of bipedal football from the period of the Passeolithic.

Gordon: The key here, Mike, is that the local ground is peaty. Excellent for the preservation of ancient biological and other

Leonardo da Vinci-style statue of David Beckham and his golden balls.

remains that would normally decay in other locations, which we know from the great variety of bog people who have been found preserved from antiquity, often with clothing and shoes intact.

Mike: Thank goodness for the peat. I assume this means that we have some good specimens and artefacts indicative of prehistoric football.

Gordon: We do.

Mike: Is this connected to the Roman monument, and to Roman neotenous game-playing?

Gordon: Very much so. But what we have here is much more significant than that. As a matter of fact, I regard the Roman game as a derivative form of football; earlier expressions of bipedal neotenous football are more interesting, and more significant.

Mike: Is there any evidence of pitches?

Gordon: There is much evidence of earthworks and posts and goals that relate to the Roman game of *harpastum*, in the vicinity of the O'on.

Mike: Suggesting that the monument may have served as a kind of pavilion with changing facilities, in addition to being a temple.

Gordon: Exactly. The Roman legions were keen to provide the best facilities for their legion teams and would have ensured that they had excellent amenities available. Legionary soldiers who were successful players were regarded as stars, and afforded all the support of full-time professionals, freed from routine military tasks, and provided with excellent equipment, support staff and training areas. And quality nutrition. Successful players were often offered full citizenship, without having to complete the normal time in military service.

Mike: Do you think the wonderful monument at Stenhousemuir was indicative of success enjoyed by the local Legions?

Gordon: Of course. If you visit the Santiago Bernabeu Stadium in Madrid, or Camp Nou in Barcelona, you know you are in the presence of greatness. Why would the Romans, who were very conscious of their temples and monuments as status symbols, express anything different? Triumphal stadia and monuments were a major feature of their building culture.

Mike: I guess so. What can you tell me about the earlier finds? And who made them?

Gordon: They are stunning. Absolutely stunning. A team of archaeologists, led by Professor George Nielson and his team from Ochilview Passienic University uncovered evidence of pre-historic football remains and art beneath the original site of the O'on.

Mike: Was there evidence of football remains?

Gordon: Certainly – leather ball and bladder remains – identical to the football found in Stirling Castle. That is now housed in the lovely Stirling Smith Museum and Art Gallery.

Mike: From the same period?

Gordon: Yes, around 6,000 years ago. The curators at the museum allowed the ball to be dated by the Laboratory of Passienic Physics in Burnbank, located in Hamilton, South Lanarkshire. Also the home town of Jock Stein, incidentally. They found that the leather and pig's bladder ball dated from exactly the same period as the artefacts at Stenhousemuir.

Mike: I remember this. When they found the football in the castle, they dated it from the sixteenth century because that's when the rafters where the ball was found were constructed.

Gordon: Exactly. It is likely that the football was preserved in peat and then found by soldiers in the sixteenth century, who kicked it up into the rafters, and simply failed to retrieve it.

Mike: So we now have evidence of prehistoric footballs, football garments, football boots, fitba'spheres, and pitches.

Gordon: Yes. Absolutely. Bipedal football neoteny is fundamental to the *Homo* species, and we should not be at all surprised that earlier artefacts were simply adapted for use by later arrivals.

Mike: In the sense that early fortifications are adapted and used by later arrivals?

Gordon: Exactly. So many urban, domestic and defensive structures were reworked continuously by descendants or immigrant populations through the millennia, and cultural and game-playing environments are no different. *Harpastum* is simply a Romanic version of the more ancient sport of neotenous bipedal football that the Romans often encountered around their huge empire. They simply adapted it for their own purposes, and introduced their own variations.

Mike: And this suggested to passienic archaeological researchers that there may exist evidence of both Roman ball-playing, and earlier evolutionary forms of football?

Gordon: Yes. Take the Ochilview University. It focuses mainly on bipedal neotenous culture and art, and its oral traditions, and less so on the physiological, psychological and psychiatric disciplines.

Mike: Hence our meeting here, at Arthur's O'on. What was the initial stimulus for the archaeology investigation in the area?

Gordon: A local oral tradition was picked up by students in the area, who had heard numerous legends about the monument – that it had been used as a convenient changing facility by football players prior to its demolition by Sir Michael Bruce of Stenhouse in 1743. He used the stones to construct a dam on the River Carron. It is said that he was angered at the amount of time his workers and tenants spent playing football. He thought they should have been more profitably engaged in their work and religious duties.

Mike: And these students were quick to connect the local bipedal neotenous tradition with its manifestation in Roman times, and initiated some pilot archaeology inspections and appraisal?

Gordon: Quite. But they could not have known just how fruitful it would be. They found post-holes and stones indicative of Roman *harpastum* almost from the first day, overlain with later evidence of pitches that had been simply grafted onto the earlier one during the medieval period – and beyond, right into modern times – before the game we know today was established in the nineteenth century.

Mike: Brilliant, Gordon. Is there more?

Gordon: Much more. They soon found the exact location of the O'on, and beneath the original basement they hit pure archaeological gold.

Mike: Terrific! What exactly did they find?

Gordon: Remains of a prehistoric football, football boots – prehistoric football boots from 6,000 years ago. And football garments made of woven textiles and sheepskin. They found three surviving boots and two remnant garments that were clearly manufactured as "emblematic" football strips, to use the modern description.

Mike: Has all of this been confirmed by scientific analysis?

Gordon: For sure, at Burnbank. They were in remarkably good condition thanks to the ability of peat to preserve biological materials and anything manufactured from biological materials.

Mike: Was there anything to do with burial traditions?

Gordon: No. There was no evidence that football play was significantly correlated with their burial traditions, either here or elsewhere. Not as far as I know, at least.

Mike: Maybe that's because bipedal football indicates life – not death. So the remnants are simply those left after a particular game or contest – for all sorts of reasons. I imagine probably due to conflicts or wars. They simply were not retrieved later.

Gordon: I believe it is really as simple as that.

Mike: Wow, though. From 6,000 years ago. That is highly impressive, and so soon after the ice retreated. Do we have evidence of the inhabitants back then?

Gordon: We do. From around 8,000 years ago. Stone tools indicating land clearing, the remains of fish and shellfish and deer, also wheat and barley – they were beginning to be exploited around 6,000 years ago.

Mike: Any signs of the nutrition provided for bipedal neotenous football?

Gordon: As a matter of fact, yes, there was. Close to the boots, ball and garment finds were stone jars containing wheat, barley and honey.

Mike: Wow! That means these early populations were conscious of high-calorie fuelling for physical output – not just game-playing, but hunter-gathering, agricultural labour, physical combat!

Gordon: It certainly looks that way. The notion that the early hunter-gatherers, who were transiting to farming, were low in high-energy foods and nutrition is incorrect. They were highly successful at achieving a positive energy balance. Far from being deprived, they were the original affluent society.

Mike: I've read that their skeletal remains show they were strong and robust, even if their lifespan was short at around 55 years – usually because of accidents or violence, rather than organic problems.

Gordon: Correct, Mike. We have to thank Mark Nathan Cohen for this new knowledge in his seminal work – *Health and the Rise of Civilisation*.

Mike: I'll check it out. What about shamanism?

Gordon: The team found a perfectly formed and undamaged petrosphere – what we call a fitba'sphere – within a few yards of the boots and garments. This was immediately interpreted as "football art" by the team from Ochilview, an observation with which I completely agree.

Mike: So art – not shamanism?

Gordon: Much has been written about shamanism and magic and other ritualistic practices around this period, but no concrete evidence has been found – apart, of course, from the fitba'spheres that are almost exclusively found in Scotland, which some regard as having ritualistic significance.

Mike: This doesn't exclude the relation between goalkeeping and shamanism.

Gordon: No. Absolutely not. That has already been proved beyond doubt in several passienic studies.

Mike: Okay. That's good to hear. And have the local community shown interest in the archaeology, both from the Roman period and the much earlier prehistoric bipedal football finds?

Gordon: Oh, hugely so, Mike. As you know, the local professional football club is Stenhousemuir FC – the name is almost certainly derived from Stonehousemuir – it relates directly to the O'on. They have already been involved in supporting the archaeology, supplying volunteers and other help.

Mike: Excellent. Not so surprising, really.

Gordon: No. Stenhousemuir FC is unique in that it is registered as a Community Interest Company, and its resources are protected from commercial exploitation. It is an innovative and highly progressive football club – an excellent model for other clubs to follow, especially now that fans are becoming increasingly restless at the way their clubs are open to the highest corporate bidder – for plunder and exploitation. With the result that the Academy youth are excluded from first-team games due to the economic pressures that require use of the transfer market system, and cheap imports.

Reconstructed urn dating from 450 B.C. depicting the Roman sport of harpastum, unearthed from a site close to Arthur's O'on. It depicts an early defensive line-up by Ajax. Note the primitive shin-pads.

Mike: Much like the loss of our indigenous and traditional crops to cheap imports. Our youth also require protected development.

Gordon: Exactly. There's nothing wrong with the market, it just requires regulation. We can import cheaper health professionals, but what would be the reaction to our universities abandoning nurturing our own? It would kick up a massive storm.

Mike: Why should our football youth be any different?

Gordon: Precisely. Well done, Stenhousemuir – for forging a model for the future of football.

Mike: Terrific. Has the local government shown interest?

Gordon: Yes, it has. It has been highly supportive of the initiative.

Mike: Brilliant – and the archaeology, too?

Gordon: Very much so. A committee was formed from local archaeological, anthropological, cultural, historical, educational, tourist, business, and other interested groups, with the possibility of building an exact replica of Arthur's O'on. It would be a major asset for the local community, and for future interest and research.

Mike: Cool.

CHAPTER 14

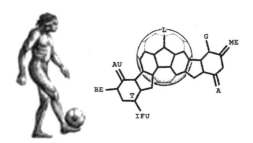

Bipedal Football and Its Opposable-Thumb Offshoots: Facilatylcholine

Gordon had invited me to meet him in the Opposable Thumb Arms in Dundas Street, Edinburgh, on a freezing cold and windy afternoon in December.

The Opposable Thumb Arms (sometimes known as Clark's Bar), is another ancient tavern built over a former loch at the foot of the northern volcano slopes leading from the castle, down from George Street, and towards the old Port of Leith. From the top of the hill, on a good and clear day, you can see the green hills of Fife across the broad estuary of the River Forth.

It is known that Robert Louis Stevenson, the writer of *Treasure Island*, was a regular customer. This lovely old haunt of sporting players and fans has become, over the centuries, a favourite of a number of neotenous game-players and supporters, who prefer bi-handed and opposable-thumb expressions. These include boxers such as the World Heavyweight Champion, John Arthur "Jack" Johnson, the great African-American boxer who was prosecuted by the USA by the notorious Mann Act and escaped to Canada, then to Europe. Others include Ian Botham, the great English cricket all-rounder; Andy Murray, the UK's greatest ever tennis player; Arnold Palmer, who was a regular visitor – though teetotal – when he was in the UK; and many rugby fans and international rugby players during the Six Nations contests at Murrayfield. A few regulars claim that Seve Ballesteros also visited after winning the Open Championship in St Andrews (but that has never been confirmed officially).

Mike: Do you think, Gordon, that the various forms of opposable-thumb neotenous play expression – such as cricket, rugby, tennis, American football, baseball and basketball (even golf, perhaps) – qualify as fully passienic, or as compromised versions? Even degenerate and pathological forms?

Gordon: First of all, it is essential to state, without reservation, that football is the *highest* expression of bipedal neoteny – physiologically, psychologically, psychiatrically, anatomically, neurologically and metabolically. And of *passiens* evolution – culturally, linguistically, scientifically and philosophically.

Mike: That goes without saying. *Homo* species evolved bipedalism to run, kick, jump, head and score or save.

Gordon: Quite. Since two and a half million years ago. Everything else we define as human followed from that critical and momentous alteration in our gene expression – upright bipedal locomotion, the opposable thumb, and the non-opposable large toe. We now know what the genes and the gene expression sequences are the hormones and neurotransmitters, and their neuro-anthropological and socio-anthropological manifestations in culture and civilisation.

Mike: Is that it?

Gordon: Ha. No. It is not. Many games played by the *passiens* species – some recent and others more ancient – manifest both bipedal and opposable-thumb expression. That includes cricket, rugby, tennis, golf, American football, baseball and basketball. They all offer interesting adaptive variations of passienic expression.

Mike: Are they degenerative?

Gordon: They are not. The particular balls they used may be described as derivative, even degenerative manifestations of the perfect Platonic round bipedal ball – the head-sized round ball that was first, and still is, used by *passiens*: the foetball. But the play is *not* degenerative or pathological. Each game, in its own way, is a subspecies of bipedal neoteny, combined with opposed-thumb gain-of-function. And each, in its own way, describes complex biophysics and beauty of space, time, motion, and the poetry of play. Of physiology and psychology. And all qualify as neo-narcoleptic super-lucid wake-REM dream-enactment manifestations – both for fans and players.

Mike: You use the expression "foetball" because of its role in neoteny?

Gordon: Yes.

Mike: Do all these neotenous games express lucidity?

Gordon: They do, Mike. Profoundly so. They comprise two groups – on the one hand, opposable-thumb-grasping gain-of-function – territorial gain – along with body-contact or non-contact games. And on the other hand – bat and ball contests. Golf is different and unique, of course. It is a specialised sub-category.

Mike: Let's kick off with cricket!

Gordon: Okay. As you know, cricket is close to my heart. A game of very complex time oscillations, temporal delays and accelerations. So much so that it is easy to fall sound asleep during a time contraction – and yet miss very little. Yet, equally, it expresses such explosive and incendiary transcendent moments, that time dilates and slows perceptibly.

Mike: As the game accelerates, time slows. And as the game slows, time accelerates. Time in cricket is more visibly plastic than in other opposable-thumb sports.

Gordon: For sure, because all time is relative. And its perception is no different. It is certainly not *subjective* as horological researchers claim.

Mike: Is it the same for spectators and players?

Gordon: Yes. Outfielders have been known to enter atonic non-lucid REM-time contractions, and yet miss nothing significant! To still emerge on the winning side! Such time variations are not exclusive to cricket, but they are potently expressed in the plastic game that enters – no, incorporates – its own time expansions, contractions, dimensions, variations, oscillations and fluctuations. Not excluding reversals.

Mike: Some people claim that they have seen the reversal of time demonstrated on the stadium clock! It just goes to show the impact of the Jungian collective and unconscious gamma-wave potency of such time plasticity.

Gordon: I believe in this rare event very strongly. Gamma waves have been correlated with time oscillations in several passienic studies.

Mike: The fielder transliminates from non-lucid to lucid REM states. From atonic muscle states to tonic. A spectacular athletic catch at the boundary – and nobody notices the transition from one to the other.

Gordon: I have witnessed it a few times, this transition from non-lucidity to lucidity. And its time reversal is usually imperceptible. Only magnetic resonance imaging, or the most intuitively super-lucidic coaches, would notice such transliminal transitions.

Mike: Am I right in thinking that non-REM lucidity and atonic physiology equate to time contractions? And REM lucidity to tonic physiology and time dilations?

Gordon: Yes, Mike. Well articulated. Only the greatest fielders in all opposable-thumb field bat-and-ball sports can make these transitions seamlessly.

Mike: They can transit – transliminate – from atonic non-lucid to tonic lucid REM dream states, from time contractions to time dilations. And back again.

Gordon: Yes, Mike.

Mike: Can you name names?

Gordon: Jonty Rhodes, Herschelle Gibbs, Ricky Ponting, Paul Collingwood, Willie Mays, Joe DiMaggio, Ty Cobb, Mickey Mantle. All great fielders who could oscillate seamlessly between REM-dream lucid and non-lucid physiology and psychology.

Mike: Eleven players play against eleven players, and the contest is largely between bat and ball?

Gordon: Yes. The bowler is essentially the offensive player who attempts to bowl out the batsman by hitting his wicket, fooling him into a miss hit so that he is caught by a fielder, or having him stumped by the wicket-keeper when out of his crease.

Mike: And what's the hook for fans?

Gordon: Complexity. The poetry of batting technique. The clash of bat and ball. The power and direction of the hit. Subtlety of cut, slice or hook. Speed and swing ball of the fast bowler – towards or away from the batsman. The various spin and curves of the slow bowler using the topography of the pitch and the weather to vary the direction and turn of the ball, and variation of speed to confuse the batter, all concentrated into a few milliseconds when the ball pitches, turns, and rises or falls at speeds humans cannot consciously calibrate. Only the speed of unconscious processing, above REM speed (500 milliseconds faster!) – Benjamin Libet time – enables the batsman to react and survive each ball, each new assault, each new variation, and each entropic bowl. If he connects and scores, entropy is negated. If not, he may luckily survive. In which case, entropy is neutralised – or he may be defeated. Out. Entropy prevails, and the batsman is out.

Mike: "Entropised", so to speak?

Gordon: Entropised. Yes.

Mike: And lucidity is negated?

Gordon: With every fallen wicket.

Mike: What of the language of cricket?

Gordon: No neotenous sport that I know of is equal to cricket for its elaboration of neotenous linguistic expressions, as in the field positions and in play.

Mike: Such as?

Gordon: Maiden over. Silly mid off. Silly mid on. Deep fine leg. Slip, gully, cover point, and so on. These field linguistics are among the most poetic in sport.

Mike: Lucid, I need to explore this sport. What about baseball?

Gordon: The French and the English compete for the origins of this game, but it developed in its modern version in North America, where it has become one of the highest and most popular expressions of neotenous bi-handed and opposable-thumb function. Recent research suggests a possible Belgian origin.

Mike: Rather like cricket, there is a contest between bowler/ pitcher and batter, with runs counter-clockwise between bases, each new innings when batters are out – ten in the case of cricket, and three in the case of baseball.

Gordon: Yes. Like cricket, baseball comprises individual contests between batter and bowler/pitcher, batter and fielder, and – just like cricket – baseball embodies strength, athleticism, tenacity, arm and opposed-thumb skills, throw curls, spin, momentum, velocity of the bowl or pitch. Then there is the speed of eye and reaction of the batter, power hitting and running between wickets – should I say, bases. And fielding the ball, jumping, catching and return. Cricket and baseball statistics comprise major industries and resources.

Mike: Both of them express variations of opposed-thumb and bipedal passienic expressions, genes, gene-enhancer sequences, transcription factors, and adaptations?

Gordon: They do.

Mike: And neo-narcoleptic super-wake REM lucid dream and tonic muscle activation? Along with homeostatic emotional cognitive manifestations?

Gordon: Certainly.

Mike: So where does the game of basketball fit in the pantheon of bipedal opposed-thumb neoteny?

Gordon: Basketball is ancient, and prehistoric. As evidenced by the surviving pitch markings and archaeology at the Mounds of Cahokia.

Mike: Of course. And its modern expression?

Gordon: Modern basketball is a classic expression of bipedal locomotion at high speed, combined with opposed-thumb fine-tuned grip, and shoulder-throw power with finesse. The modern game is attributed to a Canadian, Dr James Naismith. In December 1891 he tried to create an indoors winter game at the International Young Men's Christian Association Training School in Springfield, Massachusetts. He came up with *basketball* after pinning a peach basket to a track at a height of ten feet. The basket retained its bottom and the balls were retrieved from inside after a "basket" or score. He wrote the rules at that time, but they have evolved since. The balls they used were originally footballs, but in the 1950s these were replaced by the famous orange ball used to this day.

Mike: Later, the metal ring and backboard were added. With rebounds included.

Gordon: Yes. The game spread rapidly via its YMCA origins. It was adopted by colleges and high schools, and by the 1920s had become a professional sport. Now, of course, it is among the most played and popular games on earth.

Mike: It's a non-contact sport that combines speed, athleticism and dribbling skills, so it is highly suitable for children of all ages.

Gordon: It is, Mike. A lovely neotenous expression of *passiens* opposable-thumb expression, consisting of shots, shooting arms, throws, passing between players, taps, rolls and dribbles. And there is earlier archaeology, found at Cahokia Mounds, that relates to Passeolithic female game-playing – *Femo passiens.*

Mike: But physical contact is disallowed?

Gordon: Yes. If it disadvantages an opposing player.

Mike: And this makes end-to-end play among the fastest known in sport, expressed by neotenous bipedal and opposed-thumb ball games?

Gordon: It does.

Mike: I don't even know how many players there are in a team. Or what their positions are.

Gordon: Let me enlighten you. There are five players per team, and their positions are beautifully articulated – point guard, shooting guard, small forward, power forward. And centre, wings and post players.

Mike: Do they manifest passienic genes, or gene-enhancing sequences and adaptations that correlate with football and goalkeeping?

Gordon: Very much so. Basketball play is a lovely and complex orchestration of *passiens* gene expression. Including metabolism, physiology and psychology – of neoteny ball play, culture and art.

Mike: You have evidence for this?

Gordon: There is plenty. The National American Academy of Play, Culture and Art at the Passienic University of Missouri has faculties of American football, baseball and basketball. They have identified a series of cross-over genes and gene-enhancing sequences that correlate to the bipedal and opposed-thumb expressions we find in earlier goalkeeping phylogeny.

Mike: Do we find lucid REM dream studies that correlate to football manifestations of these transliminal states?

Gordon: We certainly do, Mike. American-sport super-REM lucid dream-state behaviour seems to spill out of the stadia into life beyond – in a way that we do not find in Europe or other continents.

Mike: Are you saying their dream-state psychology interweaves with, and subverts, everyday wake states, and percolates into work, school, college, and university life and media culture more profoundly than elsewhere?

Gordon: American bipedal and opposed-thumb sports raise REM-dream super-lucidity and neoteny to a new level of practice and economic seriousness! And that challenges our approach.

Mike: It seems the Americans can teach us how to elevate neoteny to a major cultural and artistic expression of passienic life.

Gordon: Yes. Huizinga and his momentous work have been largely forgotten, but that is temporary, and the new *passiens* faculties and new students around the world will are bound to recover his name for sport, for art, and for the humanities.

Mike: If bipedal neotenous play and display is the founding impulse of civilisation, it's outrageous that he has been largely forgotten, isn't it? What about Rugby?

Gordon: Rugby, in its two forms, both union and league, is a great game, Mike. Originating recently in England, it is certainly an offshoot of bipedal and opposed-thumb neotenous football.

Mike: It seems to be a major contact sport?

Gordon: Yes. Physical contact and territory. Rugby and American football are similar in that respect.

Mike: Games for which having subcutaneous fat is a major benefit?

Gordon: Big time. Without that lovely physiological manifestation of our neotenous and extended childhood there would be many more injuries – which already cause significant concerns among health professionals.

Mike: Are there other heath implications?

Gordon: How could there not be, Mike? Both of these contact sports involve high-momentum tackles that can cause major traumas. Although the American version makes use of protective equipment, such as helmets, shoulder padding, thigh pads, knee pads, chest protectors and mouthguards, injuries are all too common. Much of the recent research – and concerns – relates to helmet-to-helmet collisions that often lead to concussions. And Parkinson's disease. And ultimately to dementia in later-life. Rugby disallows high tackles and therefore these problems, and potential for injury, are less potent, but nonetheless rugby has a high risk of body-contact injuries.

Mike: I just have to ask about the metabolics!

Gordon: Yes. One of the least understood areas of science in relation to passienic expression, neoteny and bipedal opposed-thumbed sport. Fuelling the brain selectively – via the liver – is almost unknown by them. Their researchers have traditionally focused on *muscle* glycogen stores. As we know, although this is vital, it is absolutely secondary as far as the brain in concerned.

Mike: We've already discussed the metaphorical elaboration of the critical necessity for fuelling the brain during all locomotory events.

Gordon: Of course. Failure to optimally fuel the brain, both during exercise and recovery from exercise, increases the risk of all the metabolic diseases. Studies in American football in particular have thrown up the issue of major metabolic deregulation post-sporting career – diabetes and other metabolic problems. This lack of interest among researchers in fuelling the brain during physical locomotion and sport, and also during recovery, is still a major problem for all modern sport and athletes.

Mike: True, Gordon. In rugby union and rugby league, of course, the ball is never thrown forward, but in American football the ball is thrown forward to make the touch down?

Gordon: Correct. These great and noble sports share opposed-thumb gain-of-function with bipedal football. They all manifest passienic and neoteny expression.

Mike: And in golf?

Gordon: Well, we know that golf is more a question of ballistics, of percussion, and the striking of one object by another to project a missile – in this case the golf ball – through time and space, with the focus on a particular area or target, informed by natural philosophy and the physical sciences, and that the discipline of ballistics has co-evolved with – and is inseparable from – the science and art of golf play.

Mike: The word golf or *gowfe* is derived from an ancient Scots term "to strike; to drive forward with violence"?

Gordon: Yes, it is. The words *goff*, *gowf*, *goif*, *goiff*, *gowfe*, *gouff* and *golve* have all appeared in Scottish scientific and game-play documents relating to golf and missile ballistic science. I mention all of them in my book *The Co-evolution of Gowfe and Ballistics*. Hopefully it will be published by Percussion Science Publications in St Andrews.

Mike: I just don't know how you find the time to write all these books! Anyway ... so there is a complex relationship between ballistic science and more gentle sports that combine locomotion with shoulder strength, rotator-cuff dynamics, opposed-thumb grips, sensorimotor feedback, fine-finger sensitivity of touch, hold, strength, and dexterity with precision. And power percussion dynamics in terms of trajectory, velocity, momentum, control, target, followed by the more refined precision of new percussive ballistics, with shorter and more sophisticated instruments or clubs that become more precise as the target – in this case the pin and hole – approaches.

Gordon: Yes, Mike. You describe that so well. But remember, it's combined with mapping of the terrain, too – the topography, the lie of the land, the weather, wind speed and direction, humidity and aerodynamics. And push or pull, hook or slice, spin of the ball to draw it back or project it forward after landing. Avoiding hazards as well – hostile fans, media equipment, not to mention towers, ponds, lakes and rivers, bunkers and sand traps, depressions and hills, dense vegetation, trees, shrubs, long grass, ravines, steep inclines, and dangerous rocky impediments.

Mike: Where each forward strike of the ball – straight, angled hook or slice – depends on many influences and factors – physiological, psychological and psychiatric. And, of course, the score as it stands, the opposition player or players, and their history. And playing by the rules when nobody can see what the player may see when the ball has landed in a hidden spot.

Gordon: Of course, fairness is a classic expression of this ancient art and the science of *gowfe*. Here in Scotland, unlike other regions, the sport of golf and the science of ballistics evolved simultaneously in St Andrews university – indeed, the Faculty of Ballistic Mechanics was a part of the ancient Institution of Ballistics and Golf Biomechanics as far back as the eighteenth century, The Royal and Ancient club shared its research with the venerable university, and the various schools of ballistics and golf around the world have followed from their example.

Mike: Is this in any way connected to the work of the Reverend Alexander John Forsyth from King's College Aberdeen? He designed a new flintlock system, patented in 1807. It had a percussion cap which ignited an enclosed charge when struck by a hammer, and it was received with great enthusiasm in the British Army, who donated a workshop for him to conduct his researches in the Tower of London. He was invited to France by Napoleon Bonaparte for a £20,000 reward, and eventually retired to St Andrews where he conducted experiments in golf and military ballistics at The Alexander John Forsyth Gowfe Institute incorporated at The Royal and Ancient and the university until his death in 1843?

Gordon: There is a connection, alright. Missile and percussion science has been around at least since hunting during the Passeolithic, and game-playing neoteny has played a key role in the development of both fields for *Homo* species, in particular for *passiens*.

Mike: Can golf be correlated with our hunting and foraging ancestry? Can we trace the reading of the landscape's topography, avoiding hazards, being vigilant for predators or hominid hostiles, and using locally available technology as an instrument for food security and survival?

Gordon: How could it be otherwise? Every "weekend golfer" is a frustrated hunter–gatherer and forager.

Mike: The greatest player or players are the most brilliant exponents of opposed-thumb neotenous game-playing *gowfe*?

Gordon: Every golfer and every golf fan has their own particular hierarchy, but I regard *only* one, above all, who manifested opposed-thumb art and science in elevated expression, and who raised this form of *passiens* game-playing neoteny, to a new level of percussive beauty and power.

Mike: Let me guess – Severiano Ballesteros?

Gordon: That's the one. Seve Ballesteros was, in my opinion, the most gifted golfer in history. He won ninety international tournaments, The Open Championship three times, and The Masters twice. He is regarded by most who know golf, as the single most positive influence on the transformation of the Ryder Cup, from a guaranteed win for the United States over many decades, to a tournament that Europeans are enabled to win on a regular basis. This tournament is arguably the most significant cultural and sporting event to create a form of European consciousness. No other bipedal or opposed-thumb neotenous, sporting, or cultural event comes near to the Ryder Cup in this respect.

Mike: Would I be right in thinking that the players and fans enter a super-asomnic lucidic wake-REM dream state, just as in other passienic sports?

Gordon: They most certainly do, Mike. Thousands flock to the major tournaments seeking super-wake REM lucidity, emotional reward-seeking and cognitive emotive homeostasis. And millions follow on television.

Mike: And Ballesteros embodied that state with his personality, with his exciting, sometimes wild shamanic (but always lucidic) play?

Gordon: He did. Then he died of a brain tumour on the sixth of May 2011. *The Irish Times* said of him: "He spoke many other languages, too: the dialects of honour, of dignity, of sportsmanship, of decency, of fair play, of loyalty, of integrity, and in the end, of dauntless, unforgettable courage. In doing so, he rewrote entirely the international image of the Spanish people. Quite simply, there has never been a finer ambassador for either his sport or his country."

Mike: Lucidity in abundance. Nothing more need be added.

Gordon: Nothing.

Mike: Are you a fan of tennis, Gordon?

Gordon: I am indeed a tennis fan. I love the game.

Mike: What is its relation to bipedal and game-playing neoteny?

Gordon: Ancient, Mike. Very, very old indeed. Tennis is related to one-to-one combat, where a club was a weapon, where tree branches or worked skeletal structures would be used for defensive or offensive purposes. Practice and training would initially involve a stationary solid object that would be attacked. Later, a moving object would improve speed, the angle of attack and reaction times to its alteration of position. And later still this would be refined to an object that could be returned by an opponent, improving all aspects and speed of vision, bipedal balance, forehand or backhand strike, arm and elbow articulation, opposed-thumb grip, and under or over arm-strike power.

Mike: Thus it began as a form of training for combat, and later evolved into a form of neotenous game-playing, when a softer and returnable ball object was developed?

Gordon: Exactly. Which is why the origin in the twelfth century postulated by historians is surely a typical narrative invented by *Homo sapiens* to obscure its prehistoric combat, and opposable-thumb, origins. They usually insist that tennis began in the twelfth century in France, when it was played by monks and called *jeu de paume*, or "game of the palm?. This was under Louis VIIth, who is claimed to have played the game. A later indoor version spread to other European courts and to England, where it became popular at Hampton Court.

Mike: And the tennis racquet?

Gordon: Versions have appeared in ancient cave art. The modern form emerged in the sixteenth century and a popular version was played on village greens using wooden carved racquets and taut fishing nets (to add reverse spring momentum to the return), using large taut nets to divide the court. In the second half of the nineteenth century, a Major Clopton Wingfield popularised tennis around the Empire among the clergy, law and aristocracy – hence its association with the middle classes, which continues to this day. Although it is becoming increasingly popular across all strata, for those who have access to courts and equipment.

Mike: And its greatest exponent?

Gordon: Billie Jean King described Martina Navratilova as the "greatest singles, doubles and mixed doubles player who's ever lived".

Mike: Do you agree?

Gordon: Yes.

Mike: Therefore tennis is also a recognised expression of bipedal and opposed-thumb gain-of-function, a member of passienic game-playing neoteny, and included in the great hierarchy of super-lucid REM-dream cognitive survival, time oscillations, and homeostatic emotional resolution?

Gordon: You said it. And so also does the Andy Murray School of Neoteny, Tennis and Passienic Arts at Dunblane – in a series of lovely studies.

Mike: What of hand–eye coordination in sports such as snooker and darts. Do they qualify as passienic?

Gordon: Hugely so. They are quintessentially passienic. How could they not be? They beautifully express the opposable-thumb gain-of-function in both of the *Homo* species, but most particularly in *passiens*.

Mike: Are there studies that prove this, and hormones indicative of finger/thumb motor control?

Gordon: The wonderful work at The Roger Federer Opposable-Thumb Faculty at Basel University in Switzerland uncovered a lovely transmitter hormone, closely related to acetylcholine that is found in both of the *Homo* species, but is more highly expressed in *passiens*. It is upgraded in all opposable-thumb professional players, including snooker and green-baize games players, as well as in professional darts players.

Mike: Cool. What is the hormone?

Gordon: *Facilatyl*choline.

Mike: Fantastic! So does it function like acetylcholine in fine finger–thumb motor control, in cooperation with dopamine?

Gordon: Certainly. It is also named in some passienic faculties as the "finger-facilatylcholine cascade".

Mike: What can I say. I should have expected it.

Gordon: Indeed.

Mike: And lucidity?

Gordon: Given. Accepted and celebrated.

Mike: Wonderful.

CHAPTER 15

Artificial Intelligence and the World Cup 2050: *Robo passiens – 3 Homo passiens* 2

I struggled against howling wind and torrential rain to meet the Professor on a Sunday afternoon in December.

The Robo Passiens Bar at the foot of Leith Walk is a beautiful and ancient Leith tavern, known to locals as the Central Bar, which served as a favourite watering hole for press gangs, sailors, merchant mariners, matelots, old sea-salts, trawler fishermen, dock workers and shipbuilders down the centuries. It has a simple and unspoiled design, but is heralded with lovely pictured tiles, that make it one of the most loved and popular bars in the old port.

Leith is one of the most important ports in Scottish history, as the gateway to the Forth and the North and Baltic Seas. Although it has not enjoyed the interest of naval historians due to its small size relative to the great Atlantic ports in the west (such as

Glasgow and Greenock) and due to its incorporation into the city of Edinburgh, this is now changing and it is gaining increasing recognition for its critical role in Scottish and European history. Indeed, the clamour of its citizens for independence from its capital and somewhat arrogant southern neighbour, Edinburgh, is constantly growing. A Popular Front for the Liberation of Leith has recently been formed. Fans of Hibernian Football Club have been prominent in the creation of this new movement.

In 1560, Mary of Guise ruled as Regent of Scotland while her daughter Mary, Queen of Scots, remained in France. Mary of Guise established her court at Rotten Row (now Water Street) in the Port of Leith. A large French garrison stationed in the port was attacked by Scottish Protestant Lords, supported by troops and artillery from England, and she was forced to retreat to Edinburgh Castle. That same year, she died, and the siege ended with the Treaty of Leith. Scotland has continued to enjoy a long and fruitful alliance with France over the centuries, known as the Auld Alliance. Mary of Guise artefacts may be viewed in the National Museum of Scotland, and her sculptured coat of arms is in South Leith Parish Church.

According to local legend, one of the tavern's regular visitors, whenever he called at the Port of Leith, was Captain William Kidd, the notorious seventeenth-century Scottish pirate who was born in Dundee in 1645. He successfully preyed on French merchant shipping vessels in the ship *Blessed William*, of which he was the captain. He was part of a fleet of pirate ships, under the influence of orders from the provinces of New York and Massachusetts, that attacked French ships. In New York, Kidd contributed to the building of the Trinity Church, so it seems that his gains were not always wholly selfish.

In 1695, he received a Royal Commission as a privateer and continued his successful career in the Indian Ocean with the 34-gun ship *Adventure Galley*. However, he attacked the 500-ton *Quedagh Merchant*, an Armenian ship filled with gold, silk and spices belonging to the Indian Grand Moghul, who subsequently complained to the East India Company, which had extensive influence in the English Court. Kidd took this vessel and sailed to Boston where he was eventually captured and returned to England. He was tried and convicted of piracy, in spite of his influence with large sections of the English aristocracy, many of whom financed – and gained significantly – from his piracy. He was hanged on May the 23rd in 1701, but his treasure, today worth an estimated £50 billion, has never been located. It is known that the *Grand Mohgul* called in at the Port of Leith on its return journey to Boston, where Kidd had many friends and supporters, and it is widely rumoured that his booty is hidden in the port. Numerous attempts to locate the hoard, both official and unofficial, have thus far been unsuccessful.

It is not clear just how this historic sea-salt tavern mutated into a social meeting place and debating forum for artificial intelligence, informatics and robotic academics, students, enthusiasts and innovative commercial entrepreneurs of related disciplines. Local AI enthusiasts claim that the connection began when Marvin Minsky and Isaac Asimov (who were on a whisky-tasting tour of Scotland) were visiting the amazing eighteenth-century Malt Whisky Vaults by the quayside, and had been advised to sample the unique malts in the splendid bar at the foot of Leith Walk. They struck up a conversation with a young part-time barman who was also a student of cognitive science at Edinburgh University, and it all kicked off from there. It seems that the two American luminaries returned to the bar on the following evening, and were welcomed by a bevy of students and scholars from cognitive science and informatics faculties. A discussion lasting for some hours followed, and the link remains to this day.

Another local legend is that Alan Mackworth, Canada Research Chair in Artificial Intelligence at the University of Columbia, and founding father of the RoboCup, is also a regular visitor. A more recent group of researchers and scholars who have joined in with discussions in the bar are those from the discipline of computational archaeology They study computer-based analytical methods in long-term human behaviour and behavioural evolution, thus cross-fertilising with the other better-known disciplines. Since robotics and bipedal neotenous football represent a growth-point in understanding both the future and the evolution of *Homo sapiens* and *passiens*, AI-conscious football fans have joined in and contributed much to the ongoing discourse.

Mike: I wonder Gordon, if you have considered and examined the potential role of humanoid robots in future football, or indeed if they may have such a role?

Gordon: Glad you asked, Mike. I have been corresponding with Professor Denis Hong at the RoMeLa Laboratory at UCLA in Los Angeles on this very subject.

Mike: Is this based on the concept that bipedal football presents us with a model of how the human or *passiens* brain first evolved?

Gordon: Every football fan knows that the highest expression of dynamic bipedal locomotion in *Homo* species is that of bipedal football, because this form of locomotion involves profound embodied sensorimotor sensibility—

Mike: Of dynamic and translocation stability combined with acute forward and reverse turning, left and right swerving, formal and informal eccentric alterations of speed, jumping, diving, posture, direction, rotation, spin, gyration and pivot on a standing leg?

Gordon: Yes. And in the quest to develop autonomous intelligent mobile robots, it should come as no surprise that bipedal football has emerged as the most efficient and fertile model for such a project.

Mike: I think I get this – and let me guess that this development of an autonomous intelligent robot may recapitulate exactly the evolutionary problem of such embodied intelligence in a bipedal organism – and in our case *Homo passiens*.

Gordon: A bipedal brain that can play football is a bipedal brain that can deal with all the problems of situatedness and of space–time motion necessary for survival in a dynamic and often hostile world.

Mike: By situatedness, researchers mean that a robot is an "embodied intelligent entity", which must react with the surrounding world, and which provides context for their activity?

Gordon: Exactly.

Mike: How and when did the project emerge?

Gordon: The pioneer of robot soccer intelligence is Professor Alan K. Mackworth, the Canada Research Chair in Artificial Intelligence in the Department of Computer Science at the University of British Columbia. He is recognised as the "founding father" of the RoboCup.

Mike: Tell me more about this RoboCup.

Gordon: Professor Mackworth recognised the scientific value of robot soccer as a fertile challenge for cross-testing ideas of developing multi-agent systems. He initiated and developed the Dynamo project in the early nineties, from which the RoboCup quickly emerged due to the rapidity with which artificial intelligence researchers recognised the potential, and rallied to provide teams.

Mike: Soccer-playing multi-agents oppose a single agent that changes its environment with discrete actions and therefore may or may not model a brain or intelligent entity in a dynamic multi-agent world. A bacterium has to deal not only with its own survival, but also with the competing demands of its fellow bacteria, even before the emergence of neural or intelligent tissue. You see, an organism must deal with a dynamic environment and may do so without sentience via a brain – thus, environment may precede neural sensibility.

Gordon: Yes. All life forms, including plants, have to deal with competing life agencies, and bacteria are no different. Soccer or football emerges as a perfect model for a multi-agent intelligence in a dynamic environment that deals with other friendly, or hostile agents, and with a constantly changing environment. And of course it has a specific goal task.

Mike: In the case of early humans, that was survival. And in the case of *Homo passiens*, it was survival via goal scoring – and likewise for our intelligent soccer-playing robots?

Gordon: Agreed. To quote from the original hypothesis: *"The one-agent assumption is violated: there are cooperating agents* *on the robots' team, competing agents on the other team, and neutral agents such as the referee and the weather. The world is not completely predictable. It is not possible to predict precisely where the ball will go when it is kicked, even if all the relevant factors are known—".*

Mike: Here we bring in Heisenberg's Uncertainty Principle again. The key to the success not only of football but of sentient life.

Gordon: Yes. Inasmuch as "The simplifying assumption of discrete sequential actions is violated: continuous events such as a player running to a position and the ball moving through the air occur concurrently. In soccer, robot agents are embodied and are situated in an unfolding game".

Mike: Excellent. Is there more?

Gordon: Yes. To quote again: "Although it is still true that the intelligence of an agent can be judged from the dynamics of interaction with the environment, soccer also provides objective performance criteria".

Mike: In other words, bipedal neotenous football is a perfect model for the emergence of artificial intelligence, which involves embodied, dynamic, environmentally aware, engaged, and sentient awareness of social interaction.

Gordon: Professor Mackworth was the first to recognise football as a rich sphere and model for studying the challenges that early *Homo* species faced as an upright bipedal species in a hostile world.

Mike: And that modern upright bipedal autonomous intelligent robots must likewise overcome.

Gordon: Absolutely. Unless robots are bipedally structured (minus wheels or other technological forms of locomotion), embodied and bipedally conscious, and express bipedal sentience, they can never become fully humanoid.

Mike: Okay. They must walk, run, jump, swerve, reverse direction, spin and dribble – and with a round ball?

Gordon: Sentience of the round ball is the highest expression of environmental engagement, requiring fine motor and sensorimotor control—

Mike: Outside of food and nurture, the round finite/infinite bouncing object becomes, even emerges, as the model of the fluid and constantly ungraspable and non-static universe that the infant human inhabits. Is this so?

Gordon: Yes. I agree with that.

Mike: To summarise, then – football is the highest expression of bipedal neotenous consciousness, and the ball is its purist objectification.

Gordon: Again I agree, Mike.

Mike: Unless – and *until* – robot humanoids are structured with this neotenous ball consciousness, they can never replace non-static humans. The robot artificial-intelligence engineers must have grasped this.

Gordon: Precisely. Bipedal and ball- (or world-) consciousness embodying curiosity, innovation and creativity is key to future artificial intelligence.

Mike: So our future bipedal artificial-intelligent robots must also embody neoteny. Or at least a neoteny module – a robot that can explore the environment through play, curiosity, and creativity.

Gordon: Yes. Artificial intelligence developed in the reverse sequence compared to human intelligence. The AI scientists began with the problem of intelligence in a disembodied machine – a computer; that is, a system without limbs. And they attempted to create humanoid versions that were armless and legless. A fruitless enterprise.

Mike: Bipedalism precedes intelligence. Human consciousness and intelligence arrived more than two million years after bipedal locomotion.

Gordon: Exactly. Human intelligence and cognition arrived in a species that was situated, embodied, mobile, and interacted with other proto-humans, and with the wider environment.

Mike: The first condition of life is survivability. In humans, this was neotenous. Human consciousness and intelligence was not and is not possible without its foundation as an ejected embryo at nine months – and therefore in extended infancy, childhood and in play.

Gordon: Super, Mike! You have nailed this beautifully. Artificial robotic intelligence is fruitless unless it is embodied bipedally, and nurtured in neotenous play.

Mike: Which is the perfect model for this, then? Football or soccer?

Gordon: Alan Mackworth said, "The key idea of situatedness and embodiment is that researchers should consider embodied agents that interact with a larger world, which provides the context for their activity. The essence of intelligence and emergence is that the intelligence of an agent can be judged by the quality of its interaction with its environment".

Mike: Soccer involves perception, motor control and sensibility. Reasoning within uncertainty. Decisions and plans, goals in both senses, and learning in a social context.

Gordon: And, according Alan Mackworth, "on-line" reasoning, resource-bounded reasoning, planning, decision theory, qualitative physics, plan recognition, learning, and multi-agent theory.

Mike: Utterly brilliant. Soccer and football are not the real world, but a fragment of it. A fabulously fertile approximation to life in a hostile environment, with social support and opposition, with wind, weather, temperature, humidity, modulation of the game via hymning and chanting, the referee and officials, opposition fans, hostile media, angry coaches … All a brilliant microcosmic model of the real-world challenge facing any sentient embodied species – whether human or humanoid robot. Have the RoboCup AI researchers considered competing with humans?

Gordon: They expect to be able to play and *defeat* the World Cup winners by 2050.

Mike: 2050! That surely is somewhat optimistic, Gordon?

Gordon: Not in the slightest. The project was born in 1992 as the Dynamo Project at British Columbia University. Remember, from the Wright brothers' first flight to the arrival of jet aeroplanes took only fifty years.

Mike: AI is developing exponentially, I suppose, so this may be fair speculation. Was it initiated as a bipedal form of football?

Gordon: No. These early pioneering experiments used smallscale radio-controlled cars. These soccer-playing autonomous robot cars served as precursors to the genuine bipedal robots that participate in RoboCup.

Mike: What were the original parameters?

Gordon: Neutral, friendly and hostile agents. Inter-agent cooperation. Real-time interaction. The dynamic environment. A real and unpredictable world. Objective performance criteria. And repeatable experiments.

Mike: All of which are mirrored brilliantly in bipedal football.

Gordon: Exactly.

Mike: Did the AI researchers sense that they were simply recapitulating the evolution of *Homo passiens*?

Gordon: Naturally at the time they could not have known about this new theory of evolution. I was only at an early stage of developing the hypothesis.

Mike: Would it be fair to say that the sequence may be flawed? In that they begin with the AI and then incorporate this into a bipedal humanoid robot. Bipedalism in the evolution of *Homo* species predated the growth of human intelligence and cognition by at least two million years.

Gordon: Well noted, Mike. And, yes, this is a problem for the new generation of AI and autonomous robot researchers. Inserting intelligence into a bipedal robot is the reverse of our evolutionary history.

Mike: If by 2050 bipedal autonomous robots can defeat the *passiens* World Cup winners, then the future for both *sapiens* and *passiens* is in serious jeopardy?

Gordon: Mike, we are already rapidly on the way to bipedal degeneration. It is driven by, and allied with, cerebral degeneration. We will meet the autonomous robots along the way, and after we cross over, we will have lost our future as autonomous humans. *Homo "insapiens"* will have arrived.

Mike: I have heard you refer to the sugar-driven shrinkage of the human brain. If I remember correctly, this happens by suppression of the cerebral glucose pump and consequent short-circuiting of the brain, such that the sugars are converted to fat. But we have not discussed the loss of our bipedal locomotive potential, as far as I recall.

Gordon: The two fundamental driving forces of human evolution are bipedalism and the consequent growth of the brain for three decades outside the womb – via play. Via neoteny. Each of these two drivers are degenerating at an ever-accelerating rate.

Mike: The brain I know about. But not the legs. Can you elaborate?

Gordon: Okay. Jean Francois Cantona was absolutely right when he posed his theory that humans would eventually "digest" their legs. If sugars suppress the cerebral glucose pump and short-circuit the brain, modern humans are chronically cerebrally hungry.

Mike: Does this contribute to the explosion of dementia?

Gordon: Oh, big time! Only a small portion of Alzheimer's sufferers express the *ApoE4* gene.

Mike: Therefore modern dementia is an environmental condition, and not genetic- (or probably diet-) induced.

Gordon: Yes. But hidden. Incipient. And nothing to do with age. It begins in the foetus and affects every age. Of course, natural ageing increases the risk, as we may expect.

Mike: And what about the legs?

Gordon: This is very easy to explain. An inability to "provision" the brain leads to chronic cerebral hunger and consumption of more high-energy foods. And this cycle repeats endlessly. The only way the brain can provision its energy supply is by degrading muscle proteins and converting these to glucose in the liver. But these add to the sugar overload in the circulation, and the problem simply gets worse.

Mike: I see. The conversion of proteins to glucose means activation of the adrenal stress system and leads to chronic plundering of contractile proteins from the motor system – with the consequent loss of motor and locomotive function. Losing our brains means also losing our legs?

Gordon: That is it, Mike. In a nutshell. And there is a further insult, too. If the brain is deprived of energy via suppression of the cerebral glucose pump, so also is the peripheral nervous system deprived, such that the motor *nerves* are deprived of energy. Locomotive motor function is additionally compromised in this way.

Mike: Whoa! A double negative whammy on the efficiency of bipedal locomotion.

Gordon: Yes. And of course the dementia establishment still believes that it is an age-related condition. They have no concept of incipient sugar-driven dementia, and they believe that the metabolic conditions obesity and diabetes increase the risk of dementia.

Mike: When in actual fact, the sequence is exactly the reverse! Incipient dementia is the *driving force* of these metabolic conditions.

Gordon: Of course. These metabolic conditions are expressed years, even decades, before the driving force – incipient dementia – appears. Which is then expressed, and diagnosed incorrectly as an age-related condition.

Mike: Thus we are losing two of the major driving forces of human evolution – bipedal locomotion and its corollary – the large human brain. Perhaps Jean Francois Cantona was correct, and we will digest our legs and return to the sea to translocate without legs?

Gordon: Indeed. It is really not so surreal after all. And we should note that creation of new glucose to provision the brain from degraded muscle proteins is actually a form of digestion.

Mike: So he was correct about that also?

Gordon: He was.

Mike: No such problem for our football-playing autonomous robots?

Gordon: Quite.

Mike: And a very big advantage in the future competition?

Gordon: Indeed. However – autonomous bipedal football robots may express one major disadvantage—

Mike: They will lack neoteny! The major advantage of a bipedal species. Bipedalism necessitates the early ejection of the foetus, which would otherwise not be able to exit the pelvic canal – hence the growth of the brain *outside* the womb. In play. And of course the growth is slowed or retarded so that it takes up to three decades for completion.

Gordon: Yes.

Mike: But neoteny is precisely the system that creates curiosity, enquiry, inquisitiveness, nosiness, learning, abstraction, creativity, science, poetry, music, and all the arts. The system that makes us uniquely human.

Gordon: Indeed.

Mike: Neoteny is what is creative in human bipedal football – in *Homo passiens*. And this is what autonomous bipedal football robots will lack.

Gordon: You are wrong about that, Mike. If you are saying that our autonomous humanoid bipedal robots will always lack neoteny, and therefore could not win the RoboCup against *Homo passiens* winners of the World Cup in 2050, this is profoundly defeatist and flouts the recognised exponential speed of development of AI, which, as we know, exceeds by a large margin that of earlier forms of advanced technology.

Mike: So you believe that neoteny – or a neoteny module – can be introduced into artificial intelligence?

Gordon: I do not think it, Mike – I know it. Via reverse engineering, of course. The research is already well underway in several passienic AI laboratories around the world, and bipedal football is the system of choice in creating the necessary skills for such robots to learn and behave dynamically and socially in a law-constrained environment. In this case, bipedal football neoteny may be the most complex problem facing the researchers, but—

Mike: But recapitulating the growth of the human brain in the external environment mirrors that of the human or *passiens* version, which was also grown out of the protected womb?

Gordon: If we think of the laboratory as the "protective domain", we can posit a kind of parallel process of development, prior to the autonomous bipedal robot's exposure to the world at large.

Mike: We could describe it as convergent evolution of two different species which arrive at a solution similar to another species, but by a different route – similar to birds, flying insects and bats. Which all evolved the capacity for flight independently.

Gordon: Yes. Exactly that.

Mike: The womb, in the case of *Homo passiens*, and the laboratory, in the case of *Robo passiens*, serve as convergent and independent forging houses for neoteny in each species, which are sooner, rather than later, exposed to the world beyond. In *passiens*, biological neoteny. And in *Robo passiens*, technological neoteny.

Gordon: I agree with that.

Mike: So, you would place a bet on the outcome of the 2050 meeting of *Homo passiens* versus *Robo passiens*?

Gordon: My bet is already placed with a major international bookkeeper! Not only have I predicted the outcome, I have named the winning team and the final score: *Robo passiens* 3, *Homo passiens* 2.

Mike: Which team wins?

Gordon: The RoMeLa Laboratory at University of California, Los Angeles, led by Professor Denis Hong.

Mike: Wow! What leads you to make such a confident prediction? I imagine there will be several hundred competing laboratories and universities from around the world by that time. What are the odds against *Robo passiens* defeating *Homo passiens* in RoboCup 2050?

Gordon: I have odds of one million to one – although I will probably not be around to collect them! But my children will do so.

Mike: Your evidence?

Gordon: Easy, Mike. The School of Humanoid Robot Studies at the Passienic University of California has already developed a prototype neoteny module, and will soon offer it to the RoMeLa Laboratory to incorporate into their autonomous humanoid soccer-playing robots.

Mike: Cool. Clearly the betting industry has to catch up with this explosive development. Where can I place my bet?

Gordon: McBookie is the only company that keeps track of artificial intelligence in robot football. They accepted my bet and offer odds, so you can place your bet with them.

CHAPTER 16

Fitba' Petrospheres in Edinburgh's Football Festival Square

I was already drinking a pint, on a dry, cold afternoon in January, when Gordon arrived at the Petrosphere Bar in Football Festival Square, opposite the Usher Hall, where McCrae's Heart of Midlothian PALS Battalion was initially formed in 1914.

Football Festival Square is famous for its beautifully carved stone balls, by the Irish artist Remco de Fouw, based on the East Aberdeenshire prehistoric originals, and which have provoked major controversy and disputes in faculties of art, archaeology and anthropology in Scotland and around the world. These ancient carved stone balls, or petrospheres, are largely unique to Scotland, and many hundreds have been located, usually by agricultural workers while tilling fields, and not found in archaeological sites or contexts. Most have been located in the north-east corner of Aberdeenshire, although some have been found in other Scottish locations, and one or two beyond, in England and Ireland.

The location of the modern Petrosphere Bar (or All Bar One; and known to locals as the Fitba'sphere Bar) in Football Festival Square makes it a unique gathering point for art historians, art anthropologists and archaeologists of art culture. They congregate to discuss whether these ancient and beautifully fashioned stone balls are purely aesthetic objects or are associated with more ritualistic, religious or even shamanistic expressions of ancient cultures. Their interest is in avoiding another, and perhaps simpler, explanation of petrospheres as artistic objects representing neotenous bipedal football, as espoused by Gordon P. McNeil and a number of faculties at passienic universities around the world. This makes the hostelry a major hub of prehistoric art discussions. Indeed, the presence of these academics and students, who challenge the *sapiens* origin of the genus *Homo*, makes for many lively, contentious and pugnacious discussion in the bar, which functioned previously as a popular and bawdy railway tavern. Other frequent visitors to the Petrosphere Bar are staff, students and academics from the Hunterian Museum in Glasgow, from Marischal College Museum in Aberdeen, from Historic Scotland, and also the National Museum of Scotland.

If the petrospheres are, as Gordon P. McNeil claims, expressions of bipedal neotenous football art, we have a fruitful field of discussion and debate that cross-fertilises two major areas of human science – archaeology and anthropology. Although archaeology is much better known to the public (as a result of exposure to popular television) as the scientific study of past human society through material remains, then anthropology can be considered as a wider discipline, in that it focuses on all aspects of human behaviour, including language, sociology, identity, gender, economics, environment, religion, politics, conflicts, medicine, science, childhood – and art. None of these exclude the study of archaeology, so the two disciplines share, overlap (and often compete) in our understanding of prehistoric, historic and contemporary society. Passienic studies offer a new and fruitful area for collaboration, and of course division, insofar as they incorporate neoteny with ludenic anatomy, physiology, psychology and psychiatry. The Petrosphere Bar is already an internationally famous forum where these ideas may be interrogated, developed and debated.

Gordon invited me to meet him in the Petrosphere Bar, specifically to discuss the origins of these mysterious spherical prehistoric finds.

Mike: Good afternoon Gordon, I have just been examining these beautiful carved stone balls.

Gordon: Petrospheres, Mike. Prehistoric football petrospheres. Or as locals have it – Fitba'spheres.

Mike: Okay, Gordon. So what made you come to this conclusion? And do you think that the Irish artist, Remco de Fouw, has done them justice?

Gordon: To your second question – brilliantly. Magnificently Peerlessly.

Mike: And to the first?

Gordon: I have just come from the train from Aberdeen, where I visited Marischall College. That is where Aberdeen University houses its wonderful collection of prehistoric petrospheres. I can tell you, they far exceeded my expectations. They are exquisite – perfectly formed by carving of such intricate and delicate craftsmanship. They are absolutely breathtaking.

Mike: Are they all carved from the same material?

Gordon: No. Many different ones. Igneous rocks including diorites, serpentine, basalts, old red sandstone, greenstone, quartzite, gabbro, hornblende and granite gneiss, granite and picrate. They have all been referenced.

Mike: Do they have decorations?

Gordon: Check the examples right here, in the Square. Remco de Fouw has faithfully rendered his sculptures on some of the most beautiful originals, although on a much larger scale.

Mike: Are there any other decorations?

Gordon: Yes. Many have flattened but raised knobs, with numbers varying between three and up to a hundred and sixty. The most common number is six. Some are decorated with graceful spirals. Some with elegant concentric circles. Some with well-executed incised lines and hatchings.

Mike: Not beyond the bounds of reason, or possibility, then, to see the geometry and complex organisational patterns expressed, and the odyssey of the football during bipedal neotenous football play. The petrosphere is a football-art object.

Gordon: Well, art reflects and art informs life. And football. Albert Camus understood this better than any other footballer/writer.

Mike: Of course. He described life, and thus football, as absurd – but positively so?

Gordon: He did.

Mike: These balls – they're from the Passeolithic?

Gordon: Certainly. *Homo sapiens* archaeology insists that they are Neolithic and quite recent, but new studies by some passienic archaeologists at the Institute of Passienic Archaeology at St Aidans in Dublin (where Liam Brady studied) has placed the date *long* before the Neolithic. Actually in the Passeolithic, or as archaeologists may call it – the Palaeolithic.

Mike: If they aren't ritualistic or ballistic, what other explanations are offered by archaeological investigators?

Gordon: Some scholars suggest they are expressions of the five Platonic solids – the tetrahedron, the cube, the octahedron, the dodecahedron and the icosahedron.

Mike: I see. The Greeks thought these shapes represented the core expressions of creation – four of them earth, air, fire and water. And the fifth, life force. Or ether.

Gordon: Yes, they did. The number of raised bosses of the stone balls seems to correlate with the number on the Platonic solids.

Mike: Any valid explanations for their use?

Gordon: Again archaeology is at a loss to try and find any scientific understanding. Some suggestions have included ballistics, or weights, or game-playing. And ritual use by oracles. Also that they are objects that confer status on certain high-prestige individuals during disputes and conflicts.

Mike: Interesting. But are they well preserved – or are they degraded from use?

Gordon: Any game-playing, ballistic or other throwing behaviour does not add up, because they would be seriously chipped and broken, and they simply are not.

Mike: The notion that they could be Passeolithic football-art objects is overlooked, I suppose.

Gordon: As always, whenever the possibility arises to offer a scientific explanation in human evolutionary history that may include neotenous bipedal football, the community invariably closes ranks and looks elsewhere.

Mike: It seems surprising to think that these beautifully carved stone balls hold the key to one of the most intriguing and least understood secrets in human evolution. Yet they do. Upright bipedalism – a mystery that has never been satisfactorily solved or explained.

Gordon: Precisely, Mike. This is what confuses the researchers in every faculty or discipline that studies our evolutionary history, including that of archaeology.

Mike: Unbelievable, isn't it! Upright bipedalism, with its bizarre anatomy, is the most stupid form of locomotion found in nature, and one that would be rejected out of hand by any sentient species.

Human locomotion is half the groundspeed of a geriatric predator. Humans have no claws or body armour. We have teeth that would hardly serve a docile herbivore. Then there's our narrow pelvis, knock-knees and flat feet, which mean we are so unstable that we are the only species to evolve that frequently stumbles and falls over without any physical stimulus. In fact, we could be called more accurately *Homo decumbens* – falling man!

Gordon: Ha! Well said, Mike. Archaeologists who adhere to the tradition of scholasticism, claim – with absolutely no evidence whatsoever – that these balls have ritualistic, religious or ballistic significance. This hypothesis allows them to avoid the more *obvious* conclusion that these exquisite balls are quite simply artefacts or art objects representing one of humanity's deepest cultural expressions – neotenous game playing. And that they are representative of, and indicative of, bipedal football!

Mike: Our ancestors were football players and they simply expressed this fundamental culture in their art. In fact, not only did our ancestors play football, but upright bipedalism evolved to express football – the highest and most universal cultural expression of neoteny. Hence we are *Homo passiens*. Man the footballer.

Gordon: What is neoteny, Mike? Let me say, if we *understand* neoteny, we understand football. If we understand *bipedal football*, we understand humanity. Neoteny is the retention of juvenile physiology and psychology in adults. It is not uncommon in evolution, and humans are one of its most potent expressions. Humans simply never fully grow up. We are ejected from the womb as a foetus. We extend childhood for up to three decades. And we activate our breeding genes before we reach adulthood – indeed before our brains are fully formed! In other words, the species *Homo* quite simply never grew up.

Mike: Absolutely. We are the only known species that plays games in adulthood. As our great Dutch cultural historian, Huizinga, discovered and articulated in his famous book *Homo Ludens* – adult game-playing was, and is, the foundation of consciousness, and language, and art. And all human culture! Of course, he could not have known about neoteny, which was discovered by his fellow Dutchman, Louis Bolk – as recently brought to light and championed by Stephen Jay Gould.

The carved figure of the Willendorf Venus, now recognised by passienic specialists as an early representation of Femo passiens – Woman the Footballer – revered not just as a fertility symbol but for her football prowess, hence the "fitba'sphere" head.

Gordon: Exactly. *Homo passiens* – man the footballer – is the founder species of the genus *Homo*. *Homo* is essentially a subspecies, which appeared in the evolutionary record only one hundred thousand years ago; *passiens* the footballer arrived as an upright sentient species some two and a half million years before that. Do you know what that means? *Homo* is a fraud. An imposter. And assumes that they are the only sentient *Homo* species, giving rise to consciousness, language, civilisation, technology and art, and all that we associate with being human.

Mike: And there you have it. Do we have evidence of prehistoric football, Gordon?

Gordon: What are these petrospheres – if not evidence of prehistoric football art?

Mike: But they are smaller than modern footballs. Is that significant?

Gordon: Abstraction in art did not begin with modern art, Mike. Picasso discovered this at the Trocadero Museum in Paris. Distorting the size of an art object compared to its formal and original life size is what makes it art. Of course, prehistoric footballs may have differed in size, depending on the environment and the particular culture.

Mike: Remnant balls. As opposed to their representations in art.

Gordon: Yes. There are examples of existing remnant balls, and football tunics and boots. From Scotland, Latin America, Asia, China and Armenia. All finely decorated. Their representations in art are found all around the world. In Edinburgh we have the petrospheres, or fitba'spheres, and cave art is rich in images of balls and goalposts. They are easily identified to the open and unprejudiced eye.

Mike: So why is it that they haven't been recognised in archaeology and anthropology? Or by experts in prehistoric art?

Gordon: Archaeologists and anthropologists are no different to all other faculties of evolutionary science – they are neoteny-, ludeny- and football-blind! No academic is going to risk their career by recognising bipedal neoteny as the driving force of evolution, or adult ludenic play expression as the root of all human culture. Their careers would be over! *Passiens* is a toxic subject in most academic circles. Thankfully it is changing – and rapidly. Which is why we see faculties of passienic physiology, psychology, neurology, culture and art opening up everywhere.

Mike: *Homo passiens* has arrived!

Gordon: I believe it has. And evolutionary science is currently having a nervous breakdown. It must finally grasp this fundamental and beautiful truth.

Mike: Are there other expressions of prehistoric art in cave paintings?

Gordon: Many. Mostly paintings of balls and skeletal goalposts – possibly prehistoric art doodles – which have been misinterpreted by researchers as having no significance. It comes down to that wretched football and neoteny blindness.

Mike: You also said the brain is being disembodied – handless, footless and legless.

Gordon: I did. The mind is a myth – a so-called rational mind existing in, and of, itself, and unconnected to a body. It is an idealist construct. A myth. The human brain cares much more about where its next energy molecule is coming from than about Cartesian Dualism. The *Homo* brain is an embodied bipedal brain, in motion and time, that runs, kicks and scores.

Mike: You think the human mind is *bipedal*?

Gordon: It is two-footed and it also runs, kicks and scores.

Mike: Or misses the target! A mind devoid of its corporeal origin. A spirit mind. An armless, legless and footless mind. A ghost mind—

Gordon: Exactly.

Mike: You have described bipedalism without football as a "derisory" evolutionary hypothesis?

Gordon: I have. And you agree with me. Bipedalism is nuts! Insane! No sentient species would actually volunteer to adopt this form of locomotion. Tripedalism is a much better option, if you travel to Japan, Sicily, or the Isle of Man you will find a rich history of tripedalism. The Japanese have a name for it – yatagarasuism.

Mike: Ask any sentient quadrupedal species whether they would exchange their four legs for three – or two – and I can guess what they would reply.

Gordon: Exactly. The future of *Homo* is very likely to be tripedal. Did you know that several laboratories working on robotic locomotion have shown bipedal locomotion to be inherently unstable? They are exploring the possibility of tripedalism in future robotics.

Mike: Are they now? Do you think the future of *Homo passiens* may be tripedal?

Gordon: Why not? Bipedalism is not an *absolute* in any species, and certainly not for *Homo*. Tripedalism would allow for a larger pelvis and so make room for a larger brain to develop before birth – the pelvic canal would be larger! Bipedal locomotion is unstable, but tripedalism confers greater stability and a larger brain in the womb – two of the greatest problems confronting bipedals.

Mike: But wouldn't tripedalism be an offence against football?

Gordon: Who knows! We know some suggestive mession parameters fleetingly appear during great football play; they hint at an evanescent tripedal solution. Along with the mession bioparticle, tripedalism – even transient tripedalism – could be a major advantage in bipedal neotenous football.

Mike: If the standing leg suddenly, – explosively – became an additional dribbling leg, a bipedal run could segue into a fleeting tripedal outcome! Even in bipedal species.

Gordon: Exactly. Robert Kelly's research at Woods Hole suggested that a tripedal transition from quadrupedalism to bipedalism explains the handedness unique to humans, based on the strength of the wrist as a weight-bearing anatomical tripedal gain-of-function structure. "Knuckle walking" is tripedal – one hand is an asymmetrical third leg.

Mike: Cool, Gordon. But Kelly missed the role of bipedalism in neotenous football.

Gordon: He did. But he noted the role of tripedalism as a transitional phase. Have you been following the RoboCup – the international autonomous robot soccer competition?

Mike: We discussed this a few weeks ago, but remind me.

Gordon: Well, the aim is for autonomous humanoid robots to compete and win against the World Cup champions by 2050.

Mike: Oh, yes. Ambitious, of course. Which laboratories lead the way in this?

Gordon: There is one clear winner! UCLA's RoMeLa Robotics and Mechanisms lab led by Professor Dennis Hong. They are five-times winners of the World Cup for bipedal football robots, and are tipped to be the first bipedal robotic winners against *Homo passiens* in 2050.

Mike: Wow. Do they study *tripedal* robotic locomotion?

Gordon: They certainly do. They developed StriDER, a unique walking robot with three legs, that solves many of the problems of locomotion. This should finally prove beyond doubt that tripedal locomotion is inherently stable and superior to bipedalism. I have written to Hong to ask him to develop a World Cup soccer competition between bipedal and tripedal robots, to resolve this once and for all ... although he thinks that tripedal locomotion sacrifices speed and agility for greater stability.

Mike: So much to discover, isn't there. Are any *passiens* faculties involved?

Gordon: Well, there's the Passienic Faculty of Ecology and Evolutionary Biology at Pigtown in Baltimore. That's where Babe Ruth was born. They found a passienic *TPD* gene and a gene enhancement sequence – the *TCGES* – for tripedal conserved gene enhancement sequence. These suggest there may be a new selective pressure for passienic tripedalism.

Mike: So we could be heading for a tripedal period? Lucid. We seem to have drifted somewhat from prehistoric bipedal neotenous football art, though. Is there unanimous agreement among *sapiens* archaeologists about the origins of the petrospheres?

Gordon: It seems that archaeology is the last bastion against the growing tide of *passiens* students and academics who increasingly favour a neotenous bipedal and football origin of *Homo* species, and the idea that carved stone balls represent ancient football art.

Mike: Any breakthroughs?

Gordon: Not yet. But there are some interesting ripples in Scottish archaeology. In fact, there is an ongoing dispute between the Hunterian Museum and the Marischal Museum about the origins of stone balls.

Mike: They both have collections of balls. What are their respective positions?

Gordon: Aberdeen archaeologists are increasingly persuaded of the passienic and neotenous bipedal football art origins, but in Glasgow they favour religious, ceremonial, or ballistic explanations.

Mike: Interesting. Who's winning?

Gordon: It's a score draw at present, but Aberdeen are definitely in the ascendancy.

Mike: The "artball" is at their feet.

Gordon: I would say so, Mike.

ARTICLE PUBLISHED IN THE SCOTSMAN, 12 JUNE 2015 BY ARCHIE BALL—ARCHAEOLOGICAL AND FOOTBALL CORRESPONDENT

It has come to the attention of The Scotsman that a major dispute has broken out in Scottish archaeology circles about the famous Scottish carved stone balls, several beautiful modern sculpted examples of which are located in Football Festival Square in Edinburgh.

The dispute, which involves archaeologists and historians at two Scottish museums that host the prehistoric finds, the Hunterian Museum in Glasgow and the Marischal College Museum in Aberdeen, centres on the true origins and periodicity of these prehistoric finds, almost unique to Scotland.

Simply put, the Hunterians believe the carved stone balls are indicative of ritualistic, shamanistic, ceremonial or perhaps ballistic significance, while the Marischal group believe that they are indicative of, and represent, prehistoric football art.

According to sources, the disagreement began with publication of the work of an evolutionary scientist, Gordon P. McNeil from St Andrews University, who is both an anthropologist and palaeontologist, who claims controversially that the genus *Homo* developed bipedalism to play football.

In an interview with *The Scotsman*, Professor McNeil insisted that the Aberdeen group was correct, and the Hunterians were espousing an outmoded and degenerative approach to archaeology – one which would rapidly be abandoned as evolutionary science and its disciplines took up the new science of human evolution and history elaborated in his work – *Homo passiens: Man the Footballer*. The Professor is the founder of an evolutionary discipline that draws on the seminal work of Stephen Jay Gould, who favoured a theory known as neoteny, which is a type of retardation in development whereby embryonic and infantile characteristics among human babies are carried into the adult form; or, to put it simply, neotenous species never fully grow up. Humans are, according to this theory, one of the classic examples of a neotenous species, of which there are many. This hypothesis enabled Professor McNeil to correlate his work with that of the Dutch historian and cultural interpreter, Johan Huizinga, who stated that all human culture derives from adult "play", and this includes game-playing, as well as literature, the arts, sciences and poetry. Football, it is claimed in Professor McNeil's work, is the highest and most universal expression of bipedal neoteny.

Such is the depth and animosity generated by this scholarly disagreement, that the two museums have broken off all contact and discussions between them, and efforts to reach a compromise by the Scottish Government have consistently failed. In a recent move, the Hunterians have called for the suspension of the Marischal archaeologists and historians from Historic Scotland, and for the removal of all funds directed towards Aberdeen, emanating from both central and local government.

At a recent dinner of eminent archaeologists, to celebrate the remarkable finds at the Ness of Brodgar on Orkney (which include a new prehistoric carved stone ball), hosted by Historic Scotland in the National Museum of Scotland, the tensions and emotional frisson were so high, that a disagreement ensued between the directors of the two museums, with angry confrontations between their staff members, resulting in police intervention. The occasion was cancelled before the first course had been consumed. It was reported, but not confirmed, that some of the carved stone balls were hurled at opponents. The Hunterians claimed later that this simply confirmed their hypothesis of a ballistic origin of these ancient relics.

The schism is now irreparable, and the Aberdeen group have set up a committee to create a dedicated museum to house their valuable football petrospheres, funded by Aberdeen Football Club. It will be named The Denis Law Museum of Football Petrospheres, in honour of the city's greatest football son. Alex Ferguson has indicated that he will make a significant contribution to the new museum, as indeed will Manchester United.

When asked for his views on this, the Director of the Hunterian Museum was unabashed and stated that he would be happy to meet the Director of the Marischal Museum anywhere, anytime – and thrash out a winner.

Asked to comment, the Head of Archaeology and Planning at the Scottish Government, Sir Jock McInester, who was present at the incident at the National Museum and was noted by some of his own staff to receive minor injuries from a passing petrosphere, stated that he had seen and felt nothing, and that anyone who said so, would have legal action taken against them.

Dissenting staff at Historic Scotland, also present at the occasion, have taken up the cause of the Aberdeen group, and have threatened to strike if the Directors of this august body continue to support the Hunterians.

The dispute has caused rifts in the Scottish Parliament, with splits across Party lines.

Several European members intend to raise the question in the European Parliament, and the Aberdeen group have organised a march of *Homo passiens* supporters from Aberdeen to Brussels to press their case for a new passienic and neotenous approach to evolutionary science. They expect to recruit thousands of football fans along the way, who have taken up the cause celebre on the premise that early humans evolved neotenous bipedalism to play football. The recently formed organising committee have indicated that they will field a slew of candidate MSPs in next year's parliamentary election in Scotland. Several well known and respected Scottish footballers have agreed to forward their names as candidates.

It seems that for the first time in modern history, unlike America, the evolution of *Homo sapiens* – or (depending on which view is adopted) *Homo passiens* – has become a major issue in European politics.

Bookmakers have been taking bets on the likely winners of this fierce archaeological and evolutionary conflict, and the current odds strongly favour the *Homo passiens* supporters.

CHAPTER 17

Fannabinoid Signalling and the Hot Sauce Paradigm

Gordon was drinking in the Football Infanity Bar in Rose Street when I arrived during a typical February snowstorm.

The Football Infanity Bar (also known as Milne's) at the corner of Hanover and Rose Street, is one of Scotland's most famous literary establishments, and known widely as the "poets pub". A group of poets and writers, including Hugh McDiarmid, Norman McCaig, George Mackay Brown, Sorley MacLean, Iain Crichton Smith, Edwin Morgan, Robert Garrioch and Alan Bold, were regularly to be found in this lively and noisy establishment, sometimes named as the "Little Kremlin" due to the left-leaning politics of these drinkers and thinkers. Three of the famous men were featured in Alasdair Gray's novel of 1982, *Janine*. The narrator of the story, Jock McLeish, enters to purchase a "pie and a pint" in the basement bar and describes the scene thus:

"The bar was crowded except where three men stood in a small open space created by the attention of the other customers. One had a sombre pouchy face and upstanding hair which seemed to, like thistledown, be natural, one looked like a tall sarcastic lizard, one a small shy bear. 'Our three best since Burns', a bystander informed me, 'barring Sorley of course'."

Mike: I am particularly interested, Gordon, in what studies have been presented in relation to football-fan mentation, psychology and metabolism, apart from super-lucid REM wake-dream physiology and psychology, which we have already discussed in considerable depth. Have you reviewed this field?

Gordon: I have, Mike, in great detail. Essentially the field divides into two very different approaches. My book on the subject is *Fanandamide and the Fannabinoid Cascade: Infanity Signalling*. This one will be published in autumn next year by Johan Cruyff Publications of Amsterdam.

Mike: What are these two different approaches?

Gordon: As you may expect, *sapiens* research follows pathways that are different to those of *passiens* researchers.

Mike: Well, we know that in *passiens* studies, super-lucid REM wake-dream mentation during neotenous dream-play – particularly during bipedal football – shares several metabolic pathways, including dopamine and hopamine reward and opioid or hopioid emotional homeostatic systems, with neo-narcoleptic physiology. Are there other avenues beyond these?

Gordon: Fannabinoids.

Mike: Yes, we did mention them before. Are they implicated in football-fan cognitive and emotional pathways? Fannabinoid-1 and fannabinoid-2 are the two key signalling hormones, as I recall.

Gordon: They are profoundly implicated – big time in football fan psychology, and cognitive emotional pathways and regulation.

Mike: And have they been structurally characterised?

Gordon: They have a similar structure to the cannabinoids – the fanandamides. There are two fannabinoids, as you say – fanandamide-1 and fanandamide-2. Both are endogenously produced, both centrally and peripherally.

Mike: What do you know about the receptors?

Gordon: They are FD-1 and FD-2. FD-1 is found mainly in the brain and central nervous system. FD-2 is also in the brain, and in the peripheral nervous system.

Mike: Any cross-over between hormones and these receptors?

Gordon: Fanandamide-1 seems exclusive to the FD-1 receptor in the brain. Fanandamide-2 activates both groups of receptors.

Mike: Are they exclusive to *passiens* football fans – not in *sapiens*?

Gordon: No, they are found in both *passiens* and *sapiens*, but both fanandamide hormones, and their receptors, are much more aggressively expressed in *passiens* fans. Fans and players of other bipedal opposable-thumbed offshoot games, like cricket, rugby, baseball and National League football, are known to express them too, although significantly more weakly.

Mike: How do they differ from the known endogenous cannabinoids, which are well researched in science, and known to be involved in multiple pathways, including exercise and locomotion, appetite control, memory and cognition?

Gordon: Although they are structurally similar, they must be separated as a distinct cascade, synthesised and released throughout the brain, but particularly in the lateral machiavellia, within the cerebral cortex. This happens during bipedal neotenous football dream-play by football fans.

Mike: What do we know about them?

Gordon: There were several elegant studies conducted by the Faculty of Passienic Metabolism in the University in Marseille – where Eric Cantona grew up.

Mike: And their conclusions were?

Gordon: Stunning, Mike. Truly stunning. Fanandamide-1 activates a range of feelings and emotions that are associated with the fan's team winning and playing well, after a great pass, move, save or goal. Joy, jubilation, pleasure, glee, thrill, gratification, elation, euphoria, exhilaration, bliss, exultation and ecstasy. To name but some.

Mike: And anxiety?

Gordon: Modulated and reduced schizoid-fear mentation – the anticipation of a negative result is significantly reduced.

Mike: What of fanandamide-2?

Gordon: It is released when the fan's team is poorly performing, losing or simply not competing, in several waves, promoting anger, irritation, fury, hostility, aggravation, wrath, outrage, indignation, resentment – all the negative mentation associated with teams that are not functioning well, where reciprocal passing altruism is suppressed, chronic non-reciprocal passing altruism is over-expressed, and expression of team genome RNA is significantly reduced.

Mike: That makes sense. And are these fannabinoid hormones "addictive"?

Gordon: Ha! Fanandamide-1 is highly addictive. Fanandamide-2 almost not addictive at all.

Mike: What is the mechanism of the addiction? The dopamine–hopamine pathway?

Gordon: That's a good point. Fannabinoid-1 is addictive via selective activation of dopamine and/or hopamine release in the lateral machievellia.

Mike: Hence its addictive potential. I assume this is similar to the effect of the cannabinoids on dopamine release and consequent addictive promotion in science?

Gordon: You are right, Mike. Yes. Fanandamide-1 is a major activator of dopamine–hopamine psychology during football super-wake REM dream-play.

Mike: Now we can begin to fully comprehend the addictive potential of football-fan withdrawal symptoms during the close season, or when the fan's favourite football team is falling down a particular league table. Has this been investigated?

Gordon: It certainly has, Mike. By a team at the School of Passienic Metabolism and Physiology in Hill of Beath, Fife – home village of Jim Baxter.

Mike: They found what?

Gordon: That fanandamide-1-mediated release of dopamine is a key mechanism driving football hedonism and addiction, such that withdrawal symptoms, due to loss of fanadamide-1 and suppressed dopamine metabolism, become acute on each alternate Saturday and profoundly chronic during the close season. All the more so if not balanced by the international tournaments that usually held during the summer.

Mike: Has this been proved by antagonising fanandamide-1 or by blocking its receptor FD-1?

Gordon: Well questioned, Mike. And the answer is a resounding yes. Antagonising fanandamide-1, or blocking its receptor, results in major dysphoria in football fans, with increased anxiety, negative mentation, depression, pessimism, melancholia, despondency, and loss of hope – all suggestive of symptoms of withdrawal from addictive psychology and physiology, and mimicking both acute and chronic fannabinoid 2 release and activation.

Mike: Would this explain the psychoneurology of hopamine, given that it is a compound that some *passiens* researchers have elaborated and found to be structurally related to dopamine?

Gordon: Sure. Hopamine was discovered at the Passienic University of Barcelona, and is, as you say, close to dopamine in structure, but it is exclusive to neotenous and bipedal play mentation, and not significantly synthesised in the brains of *Homo sapiens* fans and players. Dopamine as you know is universal, and a major reward-seeking hormone in both *sapiens* and *passiens*.

Mike: It's definitely a passienic hormone. And hopamine is strongly correlated with reward-seeking and addictive behaviour in football fans.

Gordon: Of course. Hopamine, which has only recently been characterised, is emerging as the cross-over hormone between fan super-wake REM dream psychology, and emotional cognitive and homeostatic expressions during bipedal football play. And hedonistic reward-seeking behaviour.

Mike: It seems, therefore, that if we can upgrade fan hopamine levels on alternate Saturdays and during the close season, we can reduce football-deficit depressive and summer seasonal affective disorder among them. Are there pharmaceutical intervention studies underway?

Gordon: Of course. There is a wave – a tsunami, in fact – of pharmaceutical companies worldwide who are working on this right now.

Mike: The hunt for the Gold Standard football deficiency syndrome (FDS) drug is hotting up big time, then! Any successes up to now?

Gordon: No. Not yet. Despite massive investment and synthesis of countless closely related hopamine compounds, the goal is receding further and further into the distance.

Mike: Why is that?

Gordon: To pose the question is to answer it, Mike.

Mike: No synthetic drug can substitute for bipedal football. The standard approach – find the hormone and its receptor and elaborate a synthetic version for upgrading or antagonism, for positive or negative modulation – is fundamentally flawed?

Gordon: That is basically it. Not to attack some great pharmaceutical companies of the past, that have improved and saved many lives, of course. But football fan behaviour is somewhat more complex and not for pharmaceutical reduction, or exploitation, in the same way.

Mike: It's not amenable to drug manipulation. Bipedal neotenous game-playing football is the driving force of *Homo* evolution but it cannot be altered by upgrading or antagonising any single hormone or its receptor and pathway?

Gordon: Right, Mike. This is not to say that human behaviour may never be modulated by drug intervention in very special circumstances, but football is so complex, so universally and psychologically embedded and beyond reduction, that drugs may cause more problems than they resolve.

Mike: Are there any new hormones emerging that are directly correlated with football-fan psychic manifestations, and their emotive cognition?

Gordon: As it happens, there has been wonderful work at the School of Greek Passienic Sciences in Athens. They have uncovered a principle in the hypothalamus that may be termed the *goal*otrophin-releasing hormone.

Mike: Is it released when goals are scored?

Gordon: Yes! And when it seems a goal is imminent, when the fans reach a state of metabolic and emotional fervour, anticipation, excitement and zeal, it is synthesised then released.

Mike: Where from?

Gordon: GtRH is secreted into the hypothalamus–pituitary blood stream, and acts in the pituitary where it releases two goalotrophin hormones. Scorekinase-1 and scorekinase-2. Both directly correlated with goal scoring in football.

Mike: Are they exclusive to fan physiology – or are they synthesised and released during goal-scoring physiology by players?

Gordon: It seems they are more active in fans than in players, but new research at the School of Passienic Sciences at Mexico City University suggests they are also involved in football-play metabolic pathways. Just not as potently as in fan neurochemistry and its psychology.

Mike: Incredibly interesting, Gordon. What about in opposable-thumb game-playing? Are they also involved in fan metabolic responses in all these games?

Gordon: The consensus is that they are. More research is currently underway in several opposable-thumb passienic universities and faculties – but here again the buzz is that they are more weakly expressed.

Mike: Okay. One more question. Is there any cross-over connection between goalotrophin physiology and the fannabinoids?

Gordon: Great question, Mike. There is, and it seems to be significant.

Mike: How so?

Gordon: We all know about the HPA axis – the hypothalamus–pituitary– adrenal axis, the stress axis that is critical for survival in all humans, but not so many know about the HPG axis that is activated during bipedal football play. It is a major pathway that manifests fan responses to goal-seeking via hopamine reward mentation.

Mike: Via what mechanism?

Gordon: Through the HPG axis – the hypothalamus–pituitary–goalotrophin axis.

Mike: Well, okay. So this connection suggests that the HPG axis modulates the activity of the HPA axis during football moments of high goal-seeking tension?

Gordon: Correct. Until now, the connection between the HPA and the HPG has not been elucidated, but a pioneering group at the Thierry Henry Faculty of Passienic Physiology of Paris University has found the link via the fannabinoid system.

Mike: We know in science that the endocannabinoids upgrade stress-induced suppression of the reproductive system. Do the fannabinoids do similar for the goalotrophins?

Gordon: Actually, no. Quite the opposite. In fan metabolism, the fannannoids cascade exerts more complex modulation; fannabonoid-1 suppresses the HPA stress axis, and upgrades the goalotrophins, and fannabinoid-2 upgrades the HPA axis, and suppresses the goalotrophins.

Mike: And how does this work in the players?

Gordon: Again the work on this is in the early stages, but the gossip from the passienic research institutes points to significant modulation of the goalotrophins via fannabinoid activism during football neotenous play.

Mike: This is all brilliant and potentially uncovering parallel signalling in both fan and players?

Gordon: Of course, Mike. We should not be surprised.

Mike: There have been suggestions that the passienic gut hormone – known as ghroalin – closely similar to the hunger hormone, ghrelin – is involved in this pathway. What do you know about this?

Gordon: It seems that ghroalin may be termed the *goal-hungry hormone*, and although it is released in the gut, it has major influences in the brain and in goalotrophin and football fannabinoid signalling cascades.

Mike: Does ghroalin influence, or is it influenced by, the fannabinoid pathway?

Gordon: Both directions it seems. At least that is the conclusions of a new wave of emerging research in a few passienic faculties.

Mike: And in players also?

Gordon: For sure. We have to integrate football-fan hopamine signalling, fannabinoid hormone metabolism, and goalotrophin and scorekinase-1 and 2 activation, along with the new research into ghroalin release also – always keeping player physiology and psychology in the picture.

Mike: For fans' reward-seeking and emotional homeostasis, and for players' improved physiology and positive mental psychophysical sensorimotor action.

Gordon: Of course. But this work is still in the early stages.

Mike: Interesting that the work first emerged from football-fan metabolic research, as opposed to player investigations. A vast amount of work ahead, I'm sure – and always with the HPA stress axis as the major positive or negative governor over-seeing the emotional reward-seeking and homeostatic outcomes in players and fans.

Gordon: A new generation of young passienic researchers is opening new fields of investigation and avenues of possibility.

Mike: Are investigators involved?

Gordon: They are. Mainly focusing on fan aggression in football, as you may expect. However, it is an important field and we should follow it with interest.

Mike: Excellent. What's the methodology? Studies in aggression using electric shock protocols is not a fruitful avenue, I imagine?

Gordon: Indeed. Let's begin with the Hot Sauce Paradigm. Have you heard of it?

Mike: No, I haven't. What is it and how is it relevant?

Gordon: The Hot Sauce Paradigm was invented by a brilliant team of psychologists led by Joel D. Lieberman at the University of Nevada's Department of Criminal Justice, as an alternative tool for studying aggression, compared to previous methods that used electric shocks, which offended ethical principles.

Mike: Okay, but what is the relevance for football neoteny and *Homo passiens*?

Gordon: Mike, you surprise me! Football fan aggression, modulated by player aggression on the field, is a major area of study and anthropological and psychological research.

Mike: All right. So football fans can be aggressive – there's no way to deny that aspect of our culture. So can you elaborate on the Hot Sauce Paradigm?

Gordon: Let me quote the authors of a paper on the subject. They said: "*Our goal was to provide an opportunity for people to engage in behaviour that could cause direct and unambiguous physical harm to another individual, while minimising ethical concerns stemming from physical discomfort endured by participants during the procedure*". This is where the hot sauce plays an important role.

Mike: What were the ingredients in the hot sauce?

Gordon: A mixture of five parts Heinz chilli sauce and three parts Tapiato salsa picante hot sauce, produced by the Empacadora Company in Vernon, California.

Mike: Wow that's hot! I like hot food but that is incendiary, mega-hot fare! How does the paradigm work?

Gordon: In their studies, the aggressor subject sampled tasted the sauce prior to the study, and knew just how uncomfortable it would be to his intended target.

Mike: Does the target actually consume the hot sauce?

Gordon: Not usually, but the aggressor participants *think* that they do. They are only told otherwise during the debriefing, after the study is complete.

Mike: How is the Hot Sauce indexed. Is it after the Scoville Scale for hotness, named after Walter Scoville, the American pharmacist?

Gordon: No. Scoville's Organoleptic Test was considered to be too subjective, depending as it does on the subject's number of capsaicin receptors. This varies greatly among individuals, too. Furthermore, initial testing quickly results in loss of heat perception due to sensory fatigue.

Mike: Where are we going with this, Gordon?

Gordon: Many universities, including some passienic faculties, are interested in football fan aggression and behaviour, and are seeking ways both to measure and to modulate this universal practice, which can cause significant social problems, even criminal actions – personal injuries and damage to property not being unusual in football-fan confrontations. Policing can reduce it, of course, but it also sometimes exacerbates the violence.

Mike: Mostly it's the younger men, though not exclusively so.

Gordon: That's correct. Older men and female fans are much less likely to participate in the aggressive behaviour.

Mike: Racism, too.

Gordon: Yes. It's a serious concern. The problems are enhanced by unemployment and poor social conditions.

Mike: Is this also reflected in the incidence of domestic violence?

Gordon: Sadly, that's referenced by matches between the two Scottish rivals, Celtic and Rangers. Domestic violence increases significantly. In England, it happens after the loss of a World Cup game – there are reports of a 38 per cent increase. There have been suggestions of a significant increase after such losses.

Mike: Ah, well. Football reflects life, and vice versa.

Gordon: Of course.

Mike: Back to the Hot Sauce Paradigm research. Was it fruitful?

Gordon: Yes it was. Some variable was used to induce one group to aggress against another; this might be invented or real – with football fans it's easy to measure one team's fans against a rival. Leander van der Meij of VU University in Amsterdam carried out an experiment which was published recently in *PLoS One*. They carried out a laboratory study to advance a model of predictors of football-fan aggression. Fans who participated viewed a match summary in which their favoured team lost against the team's most important rival. They measured levels of aggression with the Hot Sauce Paradigm, in which the fans were given the opportunity to administer a sample of hot sauce to a rival fan to consume. I should point out that the sauce was not actually administered – the aggressor simply thought it was.

Mike: Cool. Well, actually, hot. Go on.

Gordon: They investigated whether media exposure had the ability to reduce aggression. So before watching the match summary, participants were shown a video in which fans from the rival team made comments in a neutral or positive manner about their favourite team.

Mike: Was this significant?

Gordon: No. The results showed that media exposure did not affect their level of aggression.

Mike: And the effect of the match itself?

Gordon: The participants displayed high levels of aggression and anger after watching the match.

Mike: Was it the hormones? Did they relate it to hormones?

Gordon: The aggression was greater in fans with *lower* cortisol levels, suggesting that their aggression was proactive and related to antisocial behaviour.

Mike: This seems to be paradoxical – you would expect the aggression to be linked to high levels of stress hormones.

Gordon: You would, I agree. But recent research correlates low cortisol levels in young males to highly aggressive behaviour.

Mike: Suggesting that their low levels of cortisol are indicative of low-level stress and fear, and therefore they may more easily react to confrontations with more proactive and aggressive behaviours?

Gordon: If cortisol is low, there seems to be less consideration of potential consequences.

Mike: Fascinating. And other parameters?

Gordon: As you can probably imagine, refereeism is a major modulator. Aggression is higher when the referee is blamed for a result, and lower when a fan's favourite team is blamed for the result.

Mike: Fans therefore become more aggressive when the match result is believed to be "unfair", with referee responses as the most significant influence?

Gordon: That's it, I think. Refereeism is now a growing field of study in several passienic research centres.

Mike: We have the researchers to thank for scientifically confirming what we imagined was important, and opening the field to new studies.

Gordon: We do, and of course the Hot Sauce that indexed the level of aggression was never actually given to the target participants, but so long as the participants believed that it was the measure of aggression, it provided a valid index of football fan aggression.

Mike: Is there an index of refereeism, too. Something that is modulated by player behaviour, fan hymning, chanting, activation of mirror neurones, gamma-wave signalling, the individual referee's gene expression, gene sequencing, epigenetic regulation, hormones, receptors, enzymes and peptides?

Gordon: What an extensive list. Not yet, it seems. Although two referee-exclusive hormones have recently been discovered – whistleblow-A and whistleblow-B, in the medulla oblongata area of the brain, which is involved in respiratory control. A young area in passienic research – with a long way to go.

Mike: What have they found so far about their roles in refereeism?

Gordon: That's yet to be elucidated, but initial reports suggest that whistleblow-A promotes and upgrades yellow-card and red-card signalling, via glutamate activation. Whistleblow-B, on the other hand, suppresses both – via GABA stimulation.

Mike: The homeostatic balance between the two oblongata hormones determines whether a penalty is given or rejected?

Gordon: That seems to be the outcome, if the work is repeated and confirmed.

Mike: This Hot Sauce Paradigm is a good beginning, it would seem.

Gordon: Definitely.

Mike: Okay, Gordon.

The Truth Behind This Nonsense

ON THE SCIENCE

Anthropology, game-playing and play

Anthropology of gambling
www.ongambling.org

Anthropology of human play
wwww.scholarship.rice.edu/bitstream/handle/1911/63156/
article_RIP603_part1.pdf?sequence=1

Anthropology of shamanism
www.drps.ed.ac.uk/13-14/dpt/cxscan10053.htm

Deep play and the theory of legislation
www.avorticistking.wordpress.com/2010/02/08/from-notes-on-the-
balinese-cockfight

European social anthropology
www.easaonline.org

Football play anthropology
www.free-project.eu/news/Pages/
allforPapersAnthropologyofEuropeanfootball.aspx

Game playing and the brain
www.bbc.co.uk/news/technology-34255492
www.thirteen.org/bigideas/geertz.html

Palaeo-anthropology (Stephen J. Gould's contribution)
www.isita-org.com/jass/Contents/2012vol90/Pievani/23274749.pdf

Play and the development of human adult culture
www.art.yale.edu/file_columns/0000/1474/homo_ludens_johan_
huizinga_routledge_1949_.pdf

Play as a grounding structure of reality
www.huizingainstituut.nl/call-for-papers-games-of-late-modernity-2

Playful experiences
www.academia.edu/239792/Anthropology_and_Play_The_Contours_
of_Playful_Experience

Anthropology of the performing arts
www.discoveranthropology.org.uk/about-anthropology/specialist-areas/
anthropology-of-the-performing-arts.html

Association for the Study of Play
www.tasplay.org

Archaeology and historical artefacts

Archaeology of Greek and Roman ball games
www.perseus.tufts.edu/hopper/text?doc=Perseus%253Atext%253A1999
.04.0063%253Aalphabetic+letter%253DP%253Aentry+group%253D4%
253Aentry%253Dpila-cn/

Carved stone balls (petrospheres) around the world
www.archaeologydataservice.ac.uk/archiveDS/archiveDownload?
t=arch-352-1/dissemination/pdf/vol_108/108_040_072.pdf
www.archaeologydataservice.ac.uk/

www.abdn.ac.uk/museums/exhibitions/marischal-museum.php

www.gla.ac.uk/hunterian

www.sevilla5.com/monuments/arqueologico.html

Early "football" trousers

www.chinadaily.com.cn/china/2014-06/06/content_17567124.htm

www.dailymail.co.uk/sciencetech/article-2646359/Are-worlds-oldest-

-trousers-3-000-year-old-clothing-discovered-ancient-Chinese-tomb.

html

Early "football" shoes (the Areni-1 shoe)

www.azatutyun.am/video/14313.html www.historymuseum.am/museum/

?id=0&lang=eng

Home of the oldest football in the world

www.smithartgalleryandmuseum.co.uk

Location of the Greek vase

www.ele1929.weebly.com

Sculptor of the "fitba' spheres" in Festival Square,
Edinburgh

www.remcodefouw.net/first-conundrum-2000

Venus of Willendorf carving (*Femo passiens*)

www.wikipedia.org/wiki/Venus_of_Willendorf

Biomechanics, physics and artificial intelligence

Biomechanics of football

www.brunel.ac.uk/~spstnpl/BiomechanicsFootball/

BiomechanicsFootballSoccer.htm

Biophysics research

www.biophysics.org

Intelligent machines

www.kurzweilai.net/the-age-of-intelligent-machines-can-computers-think

Negative entropy

www.wikipedia.org/wiki/Negentropy

Robot locomotion and humanoid robots

www.romela.org/dr-dennis-hong

Robots of the future

www.edinburgh-robotics.org

Dreaming, lucidity and neuroscience

Dream enactment behaviour in healthy humans

www.ncbi.nlm.nih.gov/pmc/articles/PMC2786047

Out-of-body experiences, dreams and REM sleep

www.lucidity.com/remobe.html

Neurophysiology of human behaviour (Panskepp's contribution)

www.muskingum.edu/~psych/psycweb/history/panksepp.htm

Philosophy of dreaming

www.iep.utm.edu/dreaming

Study of dreams

www.asdreams.org

Transliminality
www.archived.parapsych.org/members/m_thalbourne.html

Energy metabolism, bones and hormones

Skeletal and hormonal regulation of energy metabolism
www.cell.com/cell/abstract/S0092-8674(07)00701-5?_returnURL=
http%3A%2F%2Flinkinghub.elsevier.com%2Fretrieve%2Fpii%2FS
0092867407007015%3Fshowall%3Dtrue

Bones as endocrine organs
www.booksamillion.com/p/Translational-Endocrinology-Bone/
Gerard-Karsenty/Q675577972

Cortisol, football-fan aggression and bad referees
www.researchgate.net/publication/275221945_Football_Fan_Aggression_
The_Importance_of_Low_Basal_Cortisol_and_a_Fair_Referee

Hormonal and neural control of birdsong
www.researchgate.net/publication/279425780_Neural_and_
Hormonal_Control_of_Birdsong

Evolutionary genetics

Gene regulation and strong limb expression
www.ncbi.nlm.nih.gov/pmc/articles/PMC2658639

Genes underlying altruism
www.rsbl.royalsocietypublishing.org/content/9/6/20130395

Genes for opposable thumbs
www.sciencecodex.com/gene_enhancer_in_evolution_of_human_
opposable_thumb

Genetic polymorphism in dance

    www.academia.edu/7328247/AVPR1a_

    and_SLC6A4_Gene_Polymorphisms_

    Are_Associated_with_Creative_Dance_Performance

Human evolutionary history

    www.ynharari.com

Tripedalism (yatagarasuism)

Japanese Tradition of Yatagarasuism in soccer (three legs are better than two)

    www.tofugu.com/2014/07/23/three-legs-are-better-than-two-japanese-soccer-and-the-legend-of-yatagarasu/

Tripedalism (intermediate stage of primate locomotion and an adaptation for freeing upper limbs

    www.ncbi.nlm.nih.gov/pubmed/11735285

Social reformers

Robert Owen (social reformer and founder of progressive communities)

    www.yso.com

    www.newlanark.org/world-heritage-site/robertowen.shtml

Stephen J. Gould (paleontologist, evolutionary biologist, science historian and founder of the Great Art-Science Laboratory for art historians, scientists, artists, designers and programmers)

    www.asrlab.org/about-us/

Surrealists, philosophers and absurdists

Albert Camus (philosopher and Nobel Prize-winning author)
www.uflib.ufl.edu/spec/camus
www.camus-society.com

Andre Breton (founder of Surrealism)
www.unam.mx/index/en
www.tcf.ua.edu/Classes/Jbutler/T340/SurManifesto/
ManifestoOfSurrealism.htm

Franz Kafka (author and philosopher)
www.kafkamuseum.cz/ShowPage.aspx?tabId=-1

Frida Kahlo (artist)
www.inside-mexico.com/frida-kahlo-viva-la-vida

Jean Paul Satre (philosopher)
www.age-of-the-sage.org/philosophy/existentialism.html

Man Ray (surrealist artist and member of Dada movement)
www.manraytrust.com

Le Jeu de Marseille (card game devised by surrealists in Marseille when escaping from the Nazis in the 1940s)
www.wopc.co.uk/france/grimaud/le-jeu-de-marseille

Marcel Duchamp (conceptua; artist and member of Dada movement)
www.museum-schwerin.com/headnavi/duchamp-research-centre/
www.tate.org.uk/art/artists/marcel-duchamp-1036

Maz Ernst (surrealist artist)

www.moma.org/collection/artists/1752

www.tendreams.org/ernst.htm

Rene Magritte (surrealist artist)

www.musee-magritte-museum.be/Typo3/index.php?id=66

Salvador Dali (surrealist artist and supporter of Figueres FC)

www.uefigueres.cat

Samuel Beckett (playwright and sportsman)

www.theguardian.com/stage/2012/aug/21/samuel-beckett-sportsman

ON THE SPORT

Football fan organisations

Football Supporters Federation (represents fans in England and Wales)

www.fsf.org.uk

Inside World Football (high-quality football journalism)

www.insideworldfootball.com

Scottish Football Supporters Association (represents fans in Scotland)

www.scottishfsa.org

Supporters Direct Europe (promotes fan interests)

www.playthegame.org

Surreal Football (surreal comments on football)
http://surrealfootball.com

Gordon P. McNeil's notable football events and football heroes

Alex Ferguson

www.telegraph.co.uk/sport/football/teams/manchester-united/
10044516/Alex-Ferguson-retires-his-major-achievements-in-graphics.
html

Alf Ramsay

www.fifa.com/worldcup/archive/england1966/index.html

Andres Inesta

www.sefutbol.com/en/andres-iniesta-most-successful-spanish-player-
history

Bert Trautmann O.B.E.

www.trautmann-foundation.de

Bobby Charlton

www.fifa.com/worldcup/archive/england1966/index.html

Busby Babes (1958 air disaster for Manchester United)

www.munich58.co.uk
www.united-front.org

Christmas Truce in World War I

www.simonjoneshistorian.com/2015/01/06/understanding-the-1914-
christmas-truce

Christiano Ronaldo

www.genius.com/Cristiano-ronaldo-career-achievements-annotatedLionelMessi

www.sportskeeda.com/football/15-major-achievements-of-lionel-messi

David Beckham (Goldenballs)

www.dailymail.co.uk/tvshowbiz/article-2516514/Golden-balls-leads-way-David-Beckham-looks-dapper-premiere-The-Class-92-London.html

Diego Maradona

www.worldcat.org/identities/lccn-n90-719108

Duncan Ferguson ('Barlinnie Nine' musical dedication)

www.classicfm.com/pictures/more-pictures/football-mad-musicians-musics-obsession-beautiful/duncan-ferguson

Eric Cantona

www.soccermaniak.com/eric-cantona-biography.html

Fabrice Muamba (collapsed during a match at White Hart Lane in London)

www.standard.co.uk/news/uk/fans-praise-hero-doctor-who-rushed-on-pitch-to-save-muamba-7577708.html

First World Cup (the real one)

www.westaucklandweb.co.uk

George McLachlan (Queen of the South's 1936 tour of France and Algeria)

www.qosfc.com/content-legendsView.aspx?playerid=1056

Gordon Smith

   www.en.wikipedia.org/wiki/Gordon_Smith_(footballer,_born_December_1954)

George Best

   www.nationalfootballmuseum.com/halloffame/george-best

Hampden European Cup Final 1960 (one of the greatest games ever played)

   www.telegraph.co.uk/sport/2317064/The-greatest-matches-of-all-time.html

Hearts of Midlothian's Terrible Trio (5-0 win against Hibernian)

   www.scotsman.com/sport/football/terrible-trio-in-perfect-scoring-harmony-1-487857

Hibernian's Famous Five (5-0 win against the Busby Babes)

   www.easterroad.com/hibernian/the-famous-five/

Jack McCrae's Battalion (Hearts of Midlothian) in World War I

   www.paysducoquelicot.com/contalmaison.htm
   www.mccraesbattaliontrust.org.uk
   www.amazon.co.uk/McCraes-Battalion-Story-Royal-Scots/dp/1840189320

Jimmie Wardhaugh

   www.londonhearts.com/scores/players/wardhaughjimmy.html

Johan Cruyff

   www.worldofjohancruyff.com

John Charles (The Gentle Giant)

   www.visionofbritain.org.uk/place/23847

John Thomson (fatal collision during a match in 1931 at Ibrox Park)
wikipedia.org/wiki/John_Thomson_(footballer)

Kenneth Wolstenholme (They think it's all over –it is now)
www.telegraph.co.uk/news/obituaries/1388921/Kenneth-Wolstenholme.
html

Lisbon Lions
www.chrishunt.biz/features40.html

Luis Figo
www.zerozero.pt/equipa.php?id=28854&search=1&search_string=os+
pastilhas&searchdb=1

Magical Magyars
www.footballsgreatest.weebly.com/hungary-1950s.html

Matt Busby
www.espnfc.us/manchester-united/story/1515804/greatest-managers-
no-7-sir-matt-busby

Michael Laudrup
www.thelocal.dk/20150609/laudrup-named-best-nordic-footballer-ever

Pele
www.thefamouspeople.com/profiles/edison-arantes-do-
nascimento-2544.php

Sam English (collided with Celtic's John Thomson during match
in 1931)
www.youtube.com/watch?v=juUGNUfCpSc

Walter Tull (first black footballer and first black officer in the British Army)

www.theguardian.com/football/2010/mar/28/walter-tull-1888-1918-officer-footballer

www.bbc.co.uk/london/content/articles/2008/02/20/walter_tull_feature.shtml

CREDITS

Cover design: Anja Elsen
Interior design: Annika Naas
Layout: Amnet Services

Cover and interior illustrations: © Matt Kenyon,
www.mattkenyon.co.uk
Map of Passiens Taverns: © Ian Dewsbury

Foreword: © Irvine Welsh
Managing Editor: Elizabeth Evans

MORE GREAT READS

250 p., in color,
180 photos + illus.,
paperback, 7.7" x 10",
ISBN 9781782551348,
$19.95 US

Gino Singh

DUNGEONS & WORKOUTS

FROM WEAK AND MEEK TO BUFF AND TOUGH

Roleplaying meets fitness—
A unique combination!

Dungeons & Workouts takes everything gamers love about roleplaying—XP, level ups, side quests, and bosses—and combines it with fitness. The best part, though, is that the hero also becomes physically stronger with each level up. The various exercises in each chapter will gradually become more difficult. To move up to the next level, the boss must be defeated. Character creation is done through an initial fitness test to determine level of difficulty. Only by increasing your strength can you move up to the next level!

FROM MEYER & MEYER SPORT

Holly Zimmermann

ULTRAMARATHON MOM

FROM THE SAHARA TO THE ARCTIC

Ultramarathon Mom: From the Sahara to the Arctic tells a unique story and delivers an impactful message: Live your dreams.

A grueling 160-mile ultramarathon through the Sahara Desert is the core of the book, interspersed with heartwarming stories of friendship and camaraderie. After conquering the Sahara Desert, Holly takes on the Polar Circle Marathon in Greenland. There she experienced temperatures cold enough to cause frostbite within minutes. Training and planning for ultramarathons as well as nutritional tips for fueling the body before and during the race are also described.

200 p., b/w,
20 photos + illus.,
paperback, 5.5" x 8.5",
ISBN 9781782551393,
$14.95 US

MEYER & MEYER Sport
Von-Coels-Str. 390
52080 Aachen
Germany

Phone	+49 02 41 - 9 58 10 - 13
Fax	+49 02 41 - 9 58 10 - 10
E-Mail	sales@m-m-sports.com
Website	www.m-m-sports.com

All books available as E-books.

MEYER
& MEYER
SPORT